Aboriginal Policy Research

Setting the Agenda for Change

Volume II

Aboriginal Policy Research

Setting the Agenda for Change

Volume II

Edited by
Jerry P. White, Paul Maxim and Dan Beavon

THOMPSON EDUCATIONAL PUBLISHING, INC.

Toronto, Ontario

Information on how to obtain copies of this book may be obtained from:

Website: www.thompsonbooks.com
E-mail: publisher@thompsonbooks.com
Telephone: (416) 766-2763
Fax: (416) 766-0398

National Library of Canada Cataloguing in Publication Data

Aboriginal Policy Research Conference (1st : 2003 : Ottawa, Ont.)
    Aboriginal policy research : setting the agenda for change / edited by Jerry P. White, Paul Maxim and Dan Beavon.

Papers originally presented at the first Aboriginal Policy Research
    Conference held Nov. 2002 in Ottawa, Ont.

Includes bibliographical references.

ISBN 1-55077-142-6 (v. 1).—ISBN 1-55077-143-4 (v. 2)

1. Native peoples—Canada—Social conditions—Congresses. 2. Native peoples—Canada—Government relations—Congresses. 3. Native peoples—Canada—Congresses. I. White, Jerry Patrick, 1951- II. Maxim, Paul S., 1950- III. Beavon, Daniel J.K. IV. Title.

E78.C2A1495 2002   305.897'071   C2004-902454-X

Copy Editing: Abby Gabora
Interior Design: Danielle Baum
Cover Design: Elan Designs
Cover Illustration: Daphne Odjig, *Belonging, Grandfather Series*, 1980, 20" x 22."
                     Reproduced by permission of Daphne Odjig.
                     Courtesy of Gallery Gevik, Inc. (Toronto).

Every reasonable effort has been made to acquire permission for copyrighted materials used in this book and to acknowledge such permissions accurately. Any errors or omissions called to the publisher's attention will be corrected in future printings.

We acknowledge the support of the Government of Canada through the Book Publishing Industry Development Program for our publishing activities.

Printed in Canada.

2 3 4 5   10 09 08

Table of Contents

Acknowledgements

This book would not have been possible without the untiring and diligent work of Beverlee Moore, Erik Anderson and Eric Guimond of the Strategic Research and Analysis Directorate (SRAD), Indian and Northern Affairs Canada. These three individuals kept the book project on track, reviewed chapters, and gently managed the editors and all of the contributing authors. Lucette Dell'Oso of SRAD also contributed substantially to the books' production, and Nick Spence, a graduate student from the University of Western Ontario, contributed to the review of submissions. Abby Gabora did an outstanding job of editing all of the chapters.

We would also like to thank all of those researchers who participated in the Aboriginal Policy Research Conference (APRC). While only a small selection of your papers are published in this two-volume set, your dedication and commitment to improving the lives of Aboriginal peoples is appreciated by all. We would like to thank the University of Western Ontario and Western's Sociology Department, as well as the myriad of federal departments who financially supported the APRC. Lastly we would like to acknowledge the contribution of the national Aboriginal organizations and Aboriginal participants who helped to make the conference such a success. Who ever said that there was little horizontality across federal departments and cooperation between Universities, Aboriginal organizations and the federal government?

Introduction

Dan Beavon, Jerry White and Paul Maxim

In November 2002, the first Aboriginal Policy Research Conference was held in Ottawa. The conference was co-hosted by Indian and Northern Affairs Canada (INAC) and the University of Western Ontario (UWO),[1] with the participation of nearly twenty federal departments and agencies and four national, non-political Aboriginal organizations.[2] By promoting interaction between researchers, policy-makers and Aboriginal peoples, the conference was intended to: expand our knowledge of the social, economic and demographic determinants of Aboriginal well-being; identify and facilitate the means by which this knowledge may be translated into effective policies; and allow outstanding policy needs to shape the research agenda within government, academia and Aboriginal communities.

The 2002 Aboriginal Policy Research Conference was the largest of its kind ever held in Canada, with about seven hundred policy-makers, researchers/scientists/academics, and Aboriginal community leaders coming together to examine and discuss cutting-edge research on Aboriginal issues. The main portion of the conference spanned several days with over fifty workshops. In addition to and separate from the conference itself, several federal departments and agencies independently organized pre- and post-conference meetings and events related to Aboriginal research in order to capitalize on the confluence of participants. For example, the Social Sciences and Humanities Research Council held its first major consultation on Aboriginal research the day after the conference ended.

The Impetus

The idea for holding a national conference dedicated to Aboriginal issues grew from simple frustration. While there are many large conferences held in Canada every year, Aboriginal issues are often an afterthought or sub-theme at the best of times. More frequently, however, Aboriginal issues are as marginalized as the people themselves and are either forgotten from the planning agenda or are begrudgingly given the odd token workshop at these other national fora. While Aboriginal peoples only account for about 3 percent of the Canadian population, issues pertaining to them occupy a disproportionate amount of public discourse. In fact, in any given year, the

Aboriginal policy agenda accounts for anywhere from 10 to 30 percent of Parliament's time, and litigation cases pertaining to Aboriginal issues have no rival in terms of the dollar amount in contingent liability that is at risk to the Crown. Given these and other policy needs—such as the dire socio-economic conditions in which many Aboriginal peoples live—it seems almost bizarre that there are so few opportunities to promote evidence-based decision making and timely, high-quality research on Aboriginal issues. Hence, the 2002 Aboriginal Policy Research Conference (APRC) was born and these proceedings are one of several by-products of that event.

In order to address the shortcomings of other conferences, the APRC was designed and dedicated to cross-cutting Aboriginal policy research, and covering issues of interest to all Aboriginal peoples regardless of status, membership, or place of residence. Second, the conference was designed to be national in scope, bringing together stakeholders from across Canada in a forum for discussion on a variety of issues related to Aboriginal policy research. Finally, in designing the conference, we sought specifically to promote structured dialogue among researchers, policy-makers and Aboriginal community representatives.

Conference Goals

The specific goals of the Aboriginal Policy Research Conference were four-fold and reflect the holistic perspective that figures so prominently in Aboriginal cultures.

First, it was designed to bring together a wide body of policy research that had recently been conducted on Aboriginal issues. Although the need for Aboriginal research is widely recognized, it has not received the level of priority and co-ordination that it deserves. Bringing together a diverse array of researchers allows promising theories and methods to be shared and advanced. Moreover, by engaging policy-makers and Aboriginal peoples as active participants, rather than as passive spectators, research gaps can be more easily identified, and researchers more easily apprised of how to make their work more policy-relevant. In addition, the conference promoted the establishment of networks among the various stakeholders in Aboriginal research. It was hoped that these relationships would provide continuous feedback, ensuring that policy needs continued to direct research agendas long after the conference had ended.

Second, dissatisfaction has been voiced with respect to the "victimization" model within which Aboriginal issues are often framed; that is, in the past, researchers have overwhelmingly addressed "problems" relating to Aboriginal peoples in Canada. The APRC attempted to foster a paradigm shift away from this victimization model, affording equal attention to those studies that examine the positive aspects of Aboriginal realities.

Third, rather than addressing different research areas—such as social, economic and health—in isolation from one another, we attempted to integrate them at the conference so as to better understand and appreciate their interrelationships with respect to Aboriginal quality of life.

Finally, this conference was designed to ensure that gender-based issues were prominent. In addition to integrating gender-based issues within the many topics of the conference, specific sessions were designed to address issues of particular importance to policies affecting Aboriginal women.

Structure, Themes and Partnership

The conference was structured to reflect the emphasis on policy relevance. In order to achieve this goal, a general call for papers was not done—which is the standard practice at most academic conferences—because we did not want to encourage or showcase curiosity-driven research that might have little or no policy relevance. Instead, the various conference partners (i.e., federal departments and Aboriginal organizations) were asked to organize workshops based on research that they had initiated, or were familiar with, which had policy relevance for them. In the end, conference sessions were organized under the following themes: quality of life (with sub-themes of socioeconomic well-being, social and psychological well-being, health, justice, and education); Aboriginal culture and Indigenous knowledge; the Aboriginal population (i.e., definitions and demography); governance and community management; and economic development.

Not only was subject matter arranged into a policy-relevant framework, but workshops were organized to facilitate a dialogue between researchers, policy-makers and Aboriginal peoples themselves. Specifically, the discussants engaged for each of the fifty workshops usually included both a policy-maker and a member of an Aboriginal community or organization so that each could identify how the body of research in question did or did not serve practical policy or program needs.

Response to the APRC was tremendous, with better than anticipated attendance and numerous requests to make the APRC a regular event. Significantly, this was done without any single department or agency having to shoulder an extraordinary financial burden. The partnership model was essential to the success of the APRC, not only by making the conference financially feasible, but also by creating a community of shared interests in Aboriginal policy research. This sense of collective ownership among the partners was reflected in the effort directed by all stakeholders towards taking advantage of partnership opportunities and ensuring the highest quality of research presented.

Research, Policy and Evidence-Based Decisions: The Research-Policy Nexus

The APRC was centred on promoting evidence-based policy making. In part, the conference was designed to deal with the communication challenge that faces social scientists, both inside and outside of government, policy-makers, and the Aboriginal community. Could we bring these different communities of interest together to develop better understandings of the problems and processes that create the poor socioeconomic conditions facing Aboriginal people in Canada? Could we develop the cooperative relations that would foster evidence-based policy making, thereby making improvements in these conditions? Policy-makers and researchers, both those in and out of government, too often live and work in isolation from each other. This means that the prerequisite linkages between research and policy are not always present. This linkage is something we call the research-policy nexus.

The APRC was first and foremost a vehicle for knowledge dissemination. With a "captive" audience of many senior federal policy-makers,[3] the APRC was able to enhance dialogue between researchers and decision-makers, and, ultimately, promote evidence-based decision making. More broadly, the conference succeeded in helping to raise the profile of Aboriginal policy research issues, including research gaps, promoting horizontality and enhancing dialogue with Aboriginal peoples.

The research-policy nexus is built on the foundation of dialogue and discourse between those making policy and those discovering and interpreting the evidence that should underscore it. When superior quality research is produced and used in making policy, this structure is complete. Moreover, in order to produce superior quality research, there is much to be gained when researchers, both in and out of government, work in cooperation on problems and issues together. Beyond just disseminating the results of research, the APRC was also about the discussion and sharing of research agendas, facilitating data access and assisting in analysis through mutual critique and review.

We feel strongly that the highest quality research must be produced, and, in turn, that research must be communicated to policy-makers for consideration in formulating agendas for the future. If you wish to make policy on more than ideological and subjective grounds, then you need to help produce and use high-caliber research. It is simply not enough to delve superficially into issues, or be driven by political agendas that have little grounding in current reality. It is not entirely unfair to say that, too often, policy has roots in the anecdotal understandings of those that make it, or it is informed by the constraints that political parties, ideologies, or day-to-day exigencies dictate. This is a fact of life, and while we can recognize it, we need not be totally constrained by it.

This may seem, to some, like a call to have "objective science" rule our policy-making world. We know that it is an error to fall into the "technocratic wish" that appeals to objective measures to resolve all contentious issues. Science, and the research findings that flow from scientific work, is not entirely objective. Many scientists have argued that science cannot be value-free or thoroughly objective. Connie Ozawa (1991), in opposition to what she calls the logical positivist empiricist paradigm, argues that science can never reach its goal of objectivity, but she concedes that scientifically wise decisions are better than uninformed decisions. Research has many components and each of the components is differentially affected by, and susceptible to, ideological and political determination and conditioning. The *process* of scientific inquiry can often be more objective than the *choice of the target*. The *question* that one asks is more ideologically conditioned than the methods one employs to research an *answer* to that question.

Scientific work may often be composed of subjective choices that are debated among scientists themselves and, at times, the norms are just the brokered agreement. Objective truth is historically contingent. We are of the firm opinion that we must start with a clear view of today's reality, however flawed by the era in which we live or the level of understanding that we have. This will at least create a foundation and scientific record for future researchers to build upon.

Outlook for the Future

Aboriginal policy research is still far from reaching a renaissance in Canada, yet it has come a long way from the first major study of Aboriginal conditions that was conducted only forty years ago by a team of non-Aboriginal academics (Hawthorne 1966, 1967). We are now seeing the first generation of Aboriginal researchers and academics entering the enterprise of science, some of whom will embrace established epistemologies, while others will challenge them. The competition for ideas has begun, and non-Aboriginal scientists no longer have a monopoly on the scientific method(s). Yet just as Aboriginal peoples have entered the domain of science, so too have they entered the realm of policy. Many of the bureaucrats who now make policies affecting Aboriginal peoples are themselves Aboriginal. At the same time, new Aboriginal institutions, with their own research mandates, continue to evolve. At the time of this writing, legislation (i.e., Bill C-19) is being considered by Parliament for the creation of a First Nations Statistical Institute (FNSI). If FNSI becomes a major player with respect to creating, maintaining and disseminating community or national data, what relationship will it develop with both Aboriginal and non-Aboriginal researchers?

The dualistic fallacy of them versus us, or Aboriginal versus non-Aboriginal, is much more complicated. Many different groups have vested interests in conducting research and in the production of knowledge and its dissemination. Some battle lines have already been drawn over a wide variety of controversial issues pertaining to Aboriginal research. For example, can the research enterprise co-exist with the principles of "ownership, control, access, and possession" (OCAP)? Are different ethical standards required for doing research on Aboriginal issues (e.g., do community rights take precedence over the rights of individual consent)? Many of these issues are both emotionally and politically charged, which sometimes makes the exercise of Aboriginal research akin to walking through a landmine field. These issues, and the passion that they evoke, render Aboriginal research a fascinating and exciting field of endeavour. More importantly, these issues make a conference such as the APRC an important forum where ideas and beliefs can be openly discussed and debated.

Just as actors are important to a play, so too is the script or the content. One of the major impediments to Aboriginal research is the dearth of data. It is somewhat ironic that we often hear the sentiment expressed by Aboriginal peoples that "they are researched to death."[4] Yet, the simple reality is that there is very little relevant data pertaining to Aboriginal peoples. In order to address some of these data deficiencies, the federal government accepted one of the recommendations emanating from the Royal Commission on Aboriginal Peoples (RCAP) to conduct an Aboriginal Peoples Survey (APS) in 2001 (the first one having been conducted in 1991). While Statistics Canada only started releasing some of the initial statistical findings from the most recent APS in the fall of 2003, access to this data by researchers will be paramount to improving our understanding of Aboriginal conditions. However, gaining access to any of the data holdings maintained by Statistics Canada is always a challenge—for both researchers within and outside of government—whether one is doing research on Aboriginal issues or in any other field. Nevertheless, with the 2001 APS having been completed, there is a virtual goldmine of information that researchers may be able to capitalize on in order to move the yardstick forward. Hopefully, some of this research can be presented at the next APRC.

The Proceedings

Our set of research and policy discussions presented here are simply an attempt to bring forward some of the vast quantity of first-class research presented at the conference. These proceedings are then part of our process of building the research-policy nexus. This two-volume set is but a portion of the contributions made at the conference. Other significant research presented at the conference appears in the recent publication *Aboriginal Conditions: Research as a Foundation for Public Policy* (White, Maxim, and

Beavon 2003). All the research published in this latter book was presented for discussion at the conference, but none of these papers appear in this volume. There was also the publication of *Not Strangers in These Parts: Urban Aboriginal Peoples*, which was produced by the Policy Research Initiative (Newhouse and Peters 2003). Over half of the research articles in this latter book were presented at the conference, and again they do not appear here. It was our desire to publish only those contributions that were of good quality and did not have any, or only limited, exposure in other venues.[5]

The Contents: Volume II

The two-volume set of selected proceedings are divided into themes. Our purpose was to group research into sets of ideas where the reader might find the content complementary. In volume two we have grouped chapters under the themes of: economic development; health; gender issues; and crime, victimization, and healing.

Economic development is often contingent on the context in which it takes place. We included a paper by Curtis and Jorgensen that outlines how the United States government transfers funds to Indian tribes and the accountability structures that accompany this funding. They examine self-determination and self-government funding specifically, where significant upfront evidence of accountability capacity is required, but few post-funding reporting requirements are mandated. They argue that this gives tribes a greater flexibility in the use of funds, and ultimately supports the growth of tribal government accountability to tribal citizens. The authors conclude with some policy suggestions for Canada based on the U.S. experience.

The context of development includes the processes that are used to undertake it. Chataway looks at how high levels of social capital (trust) and social cohesion (a capacity to discuss rather than repress debate and ideas) lead to more success in development endeavours. In particular, she notes that development and maintenance of mutually acceptable cultural values, developing working relationships across groups, and the inclusion of community interest groups as part of the process enhances the success of development.

The paper by Fleury is a study of Aboriginal people residing off-reserve in comparison with other groups most at risk of experiencing social exclusion in Canada, such as lone-parent families, people with work limitations and recent immigrants. Fleury found that Aboriginal people in recent years escaped "persistent poverty" more often than other high-risk groups as a result of maintaining relatively strong participation in the labour market, despite experiencing multiple barriers. Her findings are mostly attributable to Aboriginal peoples not registered under the *Indian Act*, and her research has important policy implications for the off-reserve Aboriginal population.

The health issues facing Aboriginal peoples in Canada are of critical policy importance. Second perhaps only to education are concerns about how to approach health. Lemchuk-Favel and Jock develop an Aboriginal health systems framework for the organization of health services in Aboriginal communities. They highlight the contributions of different First Nations and Aboriginal communities in advancing the development of a model that the authors see as the beginning of a vast improvement in access to health care, with an emphasis on population wellness and general population health status improvements. Of note are the clear policy proposals for how to advance a new health model for Aboriginal communities, which includes capitation funding agreements and supports for integrating what the authors argue are other programmatic aspects of a healthy community: housing, social assistance, justice and employment.

Chandler and Lalonde review some of their work on the high rate of suicide among Aboriginal youth in British Columbia. They begin with a conundrum. Some communities have rates of suicide 800 times the national average while others have had no suicides for over fifteen years. They try to determine what may account for this puzzling difference. The authors cogently articulate the factors that seem connected to "choosing life over death" and draw some evocative conclusions. It is clear that certain factors such as being quick off the mark to achieve some form of self-government through negotiation or litigation for traditional lands seems connected to lower suicide rates, but the authors point out that the true answers, and other factors that combine to create a better world for youth, are buried in the knowledge structures of the communities themselves.

Much talk and investigation has occurred on the subject of social capital and its impact on community well-being. The World Bank, the Policy Research Initiative and university projects such as Western's First Nations Cohesion Project have looked at the complex concepts involved. All agree that the problems associated with the measurement of social capital are impeding the development of the scientific understanding of the concept. Mignone, Longclaws, O'Neil and Mustard conducted a study whose objectives included both the development of a framework of social capital for First Nations, and more refined culturally appropriate instruments to measure social capital. This rather technical piece is important because it provides some guidance to those wishing to study and understand social capital in Aboriginal communities. The authors note that there are policy implications involved, not the least of which is a warning that the study of social capital demands that the community be integral to, and supportive of, the process. Social capital and policies coming out of social capital studies are seen to impact the health of communities.

Gender issues are often overlooked in the plethora of studies done concerning Aboriginal peoples in Canada. In this volume we present five papers that cover a wide range of issues. The Cornet and Lendor article articulates the legal issues surrounding matrimonial real property issues on-reserve. While the paper is "legally oriented," it provides an interesting sociohistorical context for understanding future directions for legislation and social/economic policy. Abbott focuses less on legalities and more on the effects of legislation, or lack thereof, pertaining to socioeconomic policy. The links between domestic violence, matrimonial property rights and children are underscored in Abbott's analysis. The demographic information and other statistics gleaned from the sample provide a picture of the socioeconomic plight of women and children as a result of a lack of matrimonial real property legislation or regulations on reserve. The crux of her work, however, lies in the accounts of participants who address the issues important to them and some of the measures required to ameliorate their current social conditions.

Hull as well as Robitaille, Kouaouci and Guimond provide valuable statistical profiles and insights into Aboriginal single mothers and Registered Indian teenage mothers respectively. Hull takes a descriptive approach presenting easy-to-follow data in tables and figures that are designed to answer questions such as: What is the prevalence of single mothers and single-mother families within the Aboriginal population? What are the educational characteristics of Aboriginal single mothers? Where do Aboriginal single mothers live? Has the prevalence of single mothers been increasing? What are the employment income characteristics of Aboriginal single mothers and their families? Hull finds that Aboriginal women are much more likely to be single parents than other Canadians, and that there are differences among various Aboriginal identity groups that show that it is a mistake to consider all Aboriginal single mothers as having the same needs.

Robitaille, Kouaouci and Guimond look at the fertility of Registered Indians aged 15 to 19 years. They find that the socioeconomic characteristics and conditions of women aged 25 to 29 who had children in their teenage years are lower then those of other women, and demonstrate that Registered Indians aged 15 to 19 have a fertility rate that is five to six times that of non-Aboriginals. Together, these articles have important policy considerations for the typically underrepresented and high-needs groups of Aboriginal single mothers and Registered Indian teenage mothers. Policy and programing needs may include housing, parenting support and education.

Clatworthy's paper analyzes the serious issue of "unstated paternity," in which the Registered Indian status of a child can be affected by the father not being named in the birth registration or Indian registration processes. Prior to 1985, children born to Indian women out of wedlock, or without stated paternity, were registered under the *Indian Act* pending a band protest. Under the 1985 changes to the *Indian Act*, commonly referred to as Bill C-31, a child's Registered Indian status came to be based on that of his or her parents. Where the father's information is not known or made available, the Registered Indian status of the child is based solely on that of the mother. Clatworthy has discovered a high rate of unstated paternity that has a significant impact on national Registered Indian population projections. Clatworthy provides an analysis of contributing factors to the high rate of unstated paternity that have many practical policy implications.

The last section of the Volume II proceedings deals with crime, victimization and healing. We begin with the childhood experiences of Aboriginal offenders. Trevethan and Moore begin by noting that the disproportionate involvement of Aboriginal persons in the criminal justice system has been recognized for some time, but research has been lacking on the impact that childhood experiences have on criminal behaviour. They find that Aboriginal offenders have unstable childhood experiences, including a great deal of involvement in the child welfare system. However, it is unclear whether involvement in the child welfare system is the cause of the instability or the result of it. They draw many interesting policy conclusions, and argue for the importance of offering Aboriginal-specific programs in a correctional setting tailored to the unique developmental experiences of Aboriginal offenders. Programs, they propose, should focus more on the effects of childhood trauma and address issues associated with involvement in the child welfare system.

Corrado, Cohen and Cale look at the resources available to Aboriginal victims of crime in urban settings. High rates of victimization are reported by the team, who found that a large proportion of crimes are never reported to the authorities. They also discovered that large numbers of people who sought services from providers felt that they did not receive the services they needed. Those who did receive services, by and large, found those services to be satisfactory. Corrado et al. propose that better publicity, education (of men in particular) and improvement of screening procedures are necessary if victims are to be helped.

Concerns about high rates of sexual offending within some Aboriginal communities has been expressed for at least the past thirty years, particularly by a number of the leading national Aboriginal women's organizations. Hylton considers the available evidence about Aboriginal sexual offending, analyzes this evidence with respect to the prevalence of sexual offending in Aboriginal communities, considers gaps in available information and priorities for future research. He is quick to note that much of the available information about the prevalence of sexual offending in Aboriginal communities is anecdotal, but is able to pull together available data looking at summary statistics from police, corrections and other sources, case histories, the testimony of community leaders, grant proposals, briefs prepared by Aboriginal organizations, and community case studies. He argues that the evidence shows substantially higher rates of violence and sexual offending in Aboriginal communities than for Canada as a whole, and calls for "a significant commitment to prevention, recovery and rehabilitation efforts."

The paper by Ed Buller takes a systematic look at a holistic healing process in the Hollow Water community. He provides some useful guidelines for understanding holistic healing processes, and has undertaken a cost-benefit analysis for investments in these types of programs that deal with sexual offenders. Buller argues that the research has shown that community healing processes have the real potential to use traditional values, culture and spiritual practices to improve treatment for offenders, their victims, families and the community. Most significantly for policy implications, Buller found that the value to governments for the funds invested in community healing processes to be very high.

Preparation for 2005

The question on many conference participant's lips following the 2002 APRC was naturally—when will the next one be held? Given the success of the first one, it is clear that there is an appetite for another. Currently plans are underway to make the APRC a triennial event, with the next one planned for the fall of 2005. In doing so, we will apply lessons learned from the 2002 APRC and seek once again to maximize the involvement of stakeholders in the planning process. Information on the upcoming APRC will be posted on the website: www.ssc.uwo.ca/sociology/aprc.crmpa. We look forward to seeing you there.

Megwe'etch.

Endnotes

1. More specifically, the conference was organized by the Strategic Research and Analysis Directorate, INAC and the First Nations Cohesion Project, Department of Sociology, UWO. Dan Beavon and Jerry White acted as conference co-chairs from their respective organizations.

2. The major federal partners included: Atlantic Canada Opportunities Agency, Canada Economic Development (Quebec), Canada Mortgage and Housing Corporation, Correctional Services Canada, Human Resources Development ment Canada, Industry Canada, Justice Canada, Privy Council Office (including the Policy Research Initiative), Social Sciences and Humanities Research Council of Canada, and Status of Women Canada. Other federal sponsors included: Canadian International Development Agency, Canadian Heritage, Fisheries and Oceans Canada, Health Canada, Public Works and Government Services Canada, Statistics Canada, Transport Canada, and Veterans Affairs Canada. The four national Aboriginal organizations included: the Aboriginal Healing Foundation, the National Association of Friendship Centres, the National Aboriginal Health Organization, and the Indian Taxation Advisory Board.

3. While there are many Canadian cities with larger Aboriginal populations, in terms of both proportions and absolute numbers, Ottawa was selected as the most logical conference site because it would have otherwise been difficult to engage the participation of such a large number of senior federal policy-makers. In many ways, the conference was about educating and exposing this group to the vast array of research that has been done on Aboriginal issues.

4. Undoubtedly, one of the major roots of this sentiment is due to the manner in which Statistics Canada conducts the Census. The vast majority of Canadians fill in the Census form themselves. In fact, there are two basic types of Census forms—the 2A and the 2B. The 2A form is a relatively short questionnaire, whereas the 2B is a much longer questionnaire that is sent to one in five Canadian households. In First Nation communities, however, Aboriginal peoples do not fill in their own Census forms. Instead, a Census enumerator conducts an oral interview in order to elicit the required information. More importantly, only the longer 2B Census form is used in First Nation communities (technically, this form is known as the 2D). This cycle of obtrusive surveying is done every five years.

5. We also had many space restrictions. There were many excellent papers that did not easily fit into a specific category, some that overlapped with others, and some that were simply too long to be manageable. There is no real or implied criticism of any of the papers left out of this two-volume set.

References

Hawthorn, H. 1967. *A Survey of the Contemporary Indians of Canada: A Report on Economic, Political, Educational Needs and Policies in Two Volumes.* Ottawa: Indian Affairs and Northern Development.

Newhouse D., and Peters, E. 2003. *Not Strangers in These Parts: Urban Aboriginal Peoples.* Ottawa: Policy Research Initiative.

Ozawa, C., 1991. *Recasting Science: Consentual Procedures in Public Policy Making.* Boulder, C.O.: Westview Press.

White, J., Maxim, P., and Beavon, D., eds. 2003. *Aboriginal Conditions: Research as a Foundation for Public Policy.* Vancouver: University of British Columbia Press.

Part One:
Economic Development

1

American Indian Tribes' Financial Accountability to the United States Government: Context, Procedures and Implications

Catherine Curtis and Miriam Jorgensen

Introduction

The relationship between American Indian tribes and the U.S. government is complex and evolving. For years, it was best characterized by paternalism and hostility, but in 1975, under President Richard Nixon's leadership, Congress passed the *Indian Self-Determination and Education Assistance Act*. The policy it embodied acknowledged the failure of previous approaches and reaffirmed the government-to-government relationship between Indian nations and the U.S. government. Today, not only as a result of the Act and its "self-governance" amendments, but also because of the tribes' growing connections with departments of the U.S. government other than the Bureau of Indian Affairs (BIA), the relationship is characterized by flexibility in (or, from a tribal perspective, sovereignty over) tribal program and budget management.

This chapter, written at the request of the Research and Analysis Directorate of the Canadian federal government's Indian and Northern Affairs Canada (INAC), provides an overview of the methods used to manage the transfer of funds from the U.S. federal government to tribes.[1] Research was conducted largely through in-depth interviews with senior U.S. government staff, tribal administrators and a review of readily available background documents. Thus, this is a policy chapter more than an academic review of program effectiveness. Further, it is worth noting that at the time of the interviews, the BIA was embroiled in a court case over the mismanagement of Indian trust funds;[2] the scandal conditioned responses, since the credibility of demanding accountability from tribes is clearly affected by the agency's own financial management and accountability difficulties.

Federal Allocations

The Bureau of Indian Affairs, an agency of the Department of the Interior (DOI), is the principal federal agency responsible for the administration of federal programs for the 560 recognized tribes in the United States. The BIA, however, is far from the exclusive agent of the federal government in its relations with tribes. For example, the Indian Health Service (IHS) at the Department of Health and Human Services (DHHS) provides extensive services to tribes in its role as the primary federal health care provider and health advocate for Indian people. Within their respective areas of responsibility, most other departments and agencies administer programs specifically for tribes or, at a minimum, cite tribes as eligible applicants for services available to state and/or local governments. Federal departments with significant tribal programs include the Department of Housing and Urban Development (HUD), Department of Justice (DOJ) and the Environmental Protection Agency (EPA).

Historically, and at present, the BIA and IHS budgets provide the majority of federal funds to tribes. One commentator estimates that these agencies together account for approximately 65% of federal funding for Indian programs and services.[3] Although the amount of funds flowing to tribes from other federal departments and agencies is fairly substantial, there is a fundamental difference between the types of funding available from these sources. In a report on tribal funding, the BIA notes, "other agencies' programs provide project grants, loans, or technical assistance."[4] That is, a significant portion of BIA and IHS funding is recurring, provided on an on-going basis to tribal governments, while in contrast, most of the funds from other departments and agencies are project grants or loans provided under a specific program mandate.

Federal base funding for tribes is sourced primarily from the Tribal Priority Allocations (TPA), a specific activity within the BIA budget. In the words of the BIA, the TPA is the "principle source of funding for tribal government operations and the provision of services to tribal members."[5] The tribes' base includes funding for several programs and services provided to tribal members/citizens[6] as well as funding for local units of tribal governments and BIA agency offices on reservations.[7] There are eight TPA program categories: Tribal Government, Human Services, Education, Public Safety and Justice, Community Development, Resources Management, Trust Services, and General Administration. The task force that proposed the TPA budget system intended for most local programs to be eventually included in this funding category. However, that goal has been hampered by Congress' desire to earmark funds for specific programs. In 1998, approximately one-third of the overall BIA operating budget was base funding to tribes.[8]

TPA base funding is distinguished by the fact that tribes prioritize this BIA budget element, giving "tribal governments the power to decide how scarce federal funds should be allocated."[9] Tribes submit prioritized requests for funding to the BIA, specify the desired level of funding per category, and list categorical breakdowns for several different levels of estimated funding (such as 90%, 100% and 110% of the previous year's budget). In this way, if Congress approves an increase in TPA funding for a given year, tribes have identified their top candidate programs for additional allocations, and if TPA funding is reduced, tribes have indicated the areas in which they will make adjustments. Funding for TPA (and its precursor program) decreased in real terms from 1981 to 1990, increased in the early 1990s, decreased again in 1996 and 1997, and was restored to the early 1990s level by the late 1990s. It is widely recognized that base funding is insufficient for meeting the high level of need in Indian Country.

While tribes with a large population or land area generally receive more funds, the size of the TPA base allocation to individual tribes is not determined by consistent principles. Rather, "TPA base budgets are a result of history, geography, policies, politics and timing."[10] A tribe may have developed programs independently or been allocated special funding to meet immediate needs, and over time, some of these monies may have been absorbed into its TPA base. Conversely, some programs have been removed from the TPA budget, and tribes that had listed them as a high priority lost significant TPA funding from their bases.[11] The ad hoc way in which base funding evolved has thus led to a considerable disparity in TPA base funding between tribes. Recent increases to the TPA have exacerbated the problem, since there has been general percentage increases based on the existing distribution of funds.[12]

Although the budget estimates for base funding specify amounts allocated to individual programs, tribes and BIA agency/regional offices possess some flexibility in shifting available funds. The ability of a tribe to reallocate its base funds is determined by the nature of its program management agreement(s) with the federal government, which are described in detail in the following section.

In addition to TPA base funding, tribes receive program-specific federal funds. Many of these programs, run by the BIA, IHS or other federal departments and agencies, are ongoing programs funded yearly. With the exception of self-governance tribes discussed in the following section, these funds are not subject to prioritization by tribes and must be spent to meet specified, predetermined program objectives. Examples of recurring non-base programs within the BIA budget include contract support, welfare assistance, the housing improvement program, road maintenance, schools operation and law enforcement. In contrast to base funds, BIA resources for non-base programs are allocated to tribes using a specific method of distribution, most commonly a formula or benchmarks.

The BIA, IHS and other federal departments and agencies also fund programs and projects of limited duration. This non-recurring program funding is generally allocated through competitive grant processes. The amounts involved can be substantial for tribes that choose to actively pursue such resources.

Tribes identify funds available for yearly and special programs using a number of information sources. Chief among these is the Catalogue of Federal Domestic Assistance, a database of federal programs, projects, services and activities providing financial and non-financial assistance. The catalogue is available both in print and on-line. In addition, the Federal Register prints "Notices of Funding Availability." These information sources are used not only by tribes, but also by state governments, local governments, non-profit organizations, educational institutions and the general public.

Protocols and Conditions

In the last thirty years, the U.S. government and tribes have developed and refined new protocols and conditions to govern transfers of funds in keeping with the government-to-government relationship. The two major innovations in tribal funding arrangements—self-determination contracting and self-governance compacting—currently apply only to programs of the Department of the Interior (including the BIA) and the Indian Health Service (which, as noted above, is an agency of DHHS). This section addresses program grants first and then turns to these newer arrangements.

Program Grants

Federal departments and agencies other than the BIA and the IHS fund tribes through competitive or formula-based grants. Additionally, the non-recurring programs of the BIA and the IHS are funded as competitive grants.

Each department follows its own grant awarding procedures. Generally, a tribe will submit a "needs statement" or "general identification of need." Tribal administrators interviewed noted that the application paperwork is manageable, particularly if the tribe has a dedicated grants staff. They added, however, that the competition for certain grants can be intense.

Recognizing the fragmented nature of existing grant funding sources, attempts have begun in Congress to improve co-ordination. In introducing a Bill to improve the co-ordination of Indian development funding between federal departments, Senator Ben Nighthorse Campbell observes that

> one reason for the lack of success, despite spending billions of dollars promoting Indian economic development, is the absence of a consistent and consolidated federal mechanism that targets

development resources to the areas and projects that are most promising. Indian business, economic and community development programs span the entire federal government, and for any given project undertaken by a tribe there may be 6 to 8 or more agencies involved. This fragmentation and lack of coordination is not producing the kind of results Indian country so badly needs.[13]

While important, tribal interviewees' focus was less on consolidation than on the expansion of self-determination contracting and self-governance compacting to other federal departments and agencies. Since grants are specifically targeted and of limited duration, they are obviously not particularly well suited for the provision of ongoing tribal programs and services.

Self-Determination Contracts

The *Indian Self-Determination and Education Act of 1975* (also known as Public Law 93-638 or simply P.L. 638) recognized the limitations of direct service delivery to tribal citizens and gave tribes the option of administering programs themselves. A contract, the elements of which are described more completely below, was the vehicle chosen for the transfer of control. Under P.L. 638, tribes can elect to contract with the Department of the Interior (including the BIA) or the IHS to self-administer one or several of the existing federal programs for their tribal citizens. Approximately 525 of the 560 recognized tribes in the United States participate in at least one self-determination contract.[14]

The process of assuming management control of a BIA or IHS program, as laid out in the Act's regulations, is relatively straightforward. One of the provisions is that a tribe can find out how much the agencies are spending on any particular program for tribal citizens. Any program amount that is currently being spent can be requested for transfer.[15] Tribes submit a document identifying the program(s) that the tribal government intends to manage. The proposal specifies how many people the tribe will serve under the contract and the type of services that will be provided. Tribes can then make adjustments in the program, providing that the basic program objectives as laid out in the contract are met. Separate contracts must be negotiated for each program that the tribe intends to administer and funds cannot be transferred between contracted programs.

The underlying principle of self-determination contracting is that tribes have the right to manage their program funds. The BIA or IHS cannot refuse to work with a tribe that has chosen to contract. If a proposal is declined, the BIA or IHS must provide technical assistance to overcome the stated objections to the proposal. The regulations stipulate that a tribal proposal may only be denied, within ninety days of receipt of the proposal, for five reasons:

1.   the service rendered to the Indian beneficiaries will not be satisfactory;
2.   adequate protection of trust resources is not assured;
3.   the proposed project or function cannot be properly completed or maintained;
4.   the amount of funds proposed is in excess of the applicable funding level; or
5.   the subject of the proposal is beyond the scope of the programs, functions, services or activities covered under the Act.[16]

In practice, very few requests for contracting are denied. As one BIA representative emphasized, "It's not really a negotiation." Tribes can challenge a negative decision either by appealing to the relevant departmental Secretary or suing in a U.S. District Court.

The contracting regulations also stipulate that the tribe must meet minimal baseline standards for its organizational management systems that "permit preparation of reports required by a self-determination contract and Act and permit the tracing of contract funds to a level of expenditure adequate to establish that they have not been used in violation of any restrictions or prohibitions contained in any statute that applies." Seven system elements are specifically mentioned: financial reports, accounting records, internal controls, budget controls, allowable costs, source documentation and cash management. The regulations are very clear, however, that an Indian nation develops its financial management systems in accordance with tribal laws and procedures.

Self-Government Compacts

Self-governance compacting is the most recent development in federal-tribal relations. Pilot self-governance projects were run in the late 1980s and early 1990s, and the Tribal Self-Government Law was passed in 1994. Originally, self-governance compacts could be negotiated only for Department of Interior funds, including those of the BIA. However, eligibility for this type of funding agreement has now been extended to IHS programs.

Under self-governance, tribes are able to set their own program priorities within a global budget. Funding is transferred from the federal government for available programs chosen by the tribe using what is essentially a block grant. In late 2001, 80 tribes or tribal consortia had self-governance compacts, a figure that encompasses the participation of 221 tribes (or approximately 40% of the total number).

Tribes electing to compact must meet several criteria, which are somewhat more stringent than the criteria for self-determination contracting. The tribal government must pass a resolution in support of compacting, undertake some type of planning activity and obtain a minimum of three consecutive clean audits (conducted by an independent auditing entity) prior to becoming a self-governance tribe. The Office of Self-Governance evaluates tribal applications and negotiates compacting agreements between tribal governments and the applicable federal departments and agencies. Notably, this office is an arm's-length federal agency, separate from the BIA.

As with tribes opting to manage programs under self-determination, if the above conditions are met, the U.S. government is obligated to proceed with self-governance compacting in response to a tribal request. Once a tribe has compacted with the federal government, there are few (some say virtually no) conditions in the Act that must be upheld in order to renew funding.

Accountability

Audits and reports are the two primary tools used to ensure that U.S. government funds flowing to tribes are spent for their intended purposes. Audits provide useful post-facto accountability by exposing technical financial management problems. Non-audit reports, mostly in narrative form, are used to evaluate the extent to which program goals are being met. Generally, they are prepared at the program's completion, but they also may be requested at intervals during the program.

The *Single Audit Act* of 1984 (amended in 1996) is the primary vehicle used to monitor tribal spending of federal funds. The Act requires that state and local governments, Indian tribes and non-profit institutions receiving more than $300,000 of federal funding in a year have an audit performed. It was intended to reduce the reporting burden on non-federal entities that receive significant amounts of federal funding by setting up a uniform system of auditing. The Act attempts to replace program-specific auditing requirements by providing standardized information on the grantee's financial management and compliance system to all federal funding agencies.

An end-of-year report prepared in accordance with the *Single Audit Act* includes the following information:

- the results of a third-party audit of the grantee's financial statements;
- a description of the system of internal controls put in place by the grantee to protect assets; and
- a report on compliance with federal laws common to all federal assistance awards.[17]

Even though departments and agencies still may choose to require individual program audits, the Single Audit is widely accepted across the federal government. For example, the self-determination and self-governance legislation specifically require that an audit be carried out pursuant to the *Single Audit Act*. In fact, it is the only statutory accountability reporting required of self-determination and self-governance tribes. Federal departments and agencies also are known to use audits prepared under the Act as proof of sound management when making decisions about the provision of future monies.

The implementation of the *Single Audit Act* is clarified in Office of Management and Budget (OMB) circulars. Tribal governments follow the accounting and financial reporting standards established by the Governmental Accounting Standards Board (GASB), which sets standards for all governments in the U.S. other than the federal government.[18] Tribes, states, counties, cities and public organizations such as universities and power plants are required to follow GASB guidelines in order to obtain clean audits. Two years ago, a Native American Finance Officers Association representative was invited to join the technical advisory committee to GASB in order to provide, in addition to general advice, input and direction for tribal government financial issues. There are currently no specific GASB financial accounting and reporting standards for tribal governments.

Non-audit reporting requirements differ according to the arrangement by which the tribe receives its funds. Grants generally carry the most extensive reporting requirements. Each grant requires an annual report and some also contain provisions for quarterly or mid-year reports. There is no uniform report format, which means that each granting department or agency sets different standards for the reporting it requires. For Indian nations with significant grant monies, the burden is onerous, and for certain programs, tribal governments have been known to conclude that the administrative toll makes pursuit of a grant not worth the effort.

Tribes with self-determination contracts provide annual reports on their program operations. A BIA or IHS contracting officer monitors the tribes and is mandated to collect certain information based on the requirements of the contracted program(s).

Tribes operating under self-governance compacts are not required to provide information on their program objectives. Although they are encouraged to submit reports, unofficial estimates suggest that less than 50% of self-governance tribes do so. This creates a difficulty for federal officials, since their agencies nonetheless must report on the results of this category of funding under the federal *Government Performance and Results Act* of 1993. The BIA complies by providing Congress with reports based on information from its area and regional offices, with tribal comments attached. BIA personnel admit, however, "these reports provide no standard information about program accomplishments."

Deficits and Difficulties

According to BIA officials, it is rare for tribes to run program funding deficits. In grant and contract spending, there is a specific amount of money designated for a defined, finite task, so it is difficult for a tribe to run a deficit. Under self-governance compacts, the block grant nature of the funding means a tribe can manage specific program deficits by switching monies from one area into another.

When they arise, tribal financial difficulties most often are related to internal problems. One BIA interviewee observed that financial management difficulties are normally explained by one of two situations: inexperienced tribal officials or tribal political conflict. BIA officials pointed out that the agency's regional and area offices work closely with tribes to resolve any issues related to financial management. Tribal interviewees, however, countered that BIA help in setting up their administrative functions was negligible or that the advice, if available, was not useful.[19]

If financial management problems do occur, the granting department or agency may opt to provide funds through a monthly drawdown. This places the tribe in a "pay-as-you-go" situation. In general, the department or agency will not provide additional funding until the tribe can prove that its management and accounting procedures have been modified to rectify the problem. In drastic cases, where a funding freeze would interfere in the provision of essential programs or services, the federal funding agency may reassume direct delivery.[20] For example, the authors know of several recent situations in which the BIA has resumed administration of law enforcement services. In extreme cases, where the misappropriation of federal funds is suspected, the matter is referred to the local Federal Bureau of Investigation (FBI) office and prosecuted in a federal court.

Although tribes are not experiencing undue difficulty in maintaining their program spending within available budgets, deficits in administrative costs are a major problem. The lack of adequate financial support for contract support (including indirect costs) is a long-standing issue and one that seriously threatens the viability of the self-determination contracting and self-governance compacting programs. While the legislation and regulations for these funding programs lay out the need to properly fund contract support costs, budget appropriations from Congress have failed to meet demand.[21] In the late 1990s, courts and administrative law judges began to award tribes substantial damages against the federal funding agencies. In response, Congress imposed a temporary moratorium on any new contracting in the fiscal year 1999 and allocated an additional $10 million to contract implementation in 2000.

Both BIA and tribal interviewees pointed to this shortfall of administrative funds as a primary source of financial difficulties for tribes. In order to support the administrative costs of grants and contracts when inadequate funding is available, Indian nations are forced to cover the costs from elsewhere in the tribal budget. Obviously, this presents particular difficulties for tribes with minimal self-generated revenues, who must either use program operation dollars or shoulder an administrative deficit. The National Congress of American Indians observes that, "if tribes are not reimbursed fully for their contract support costs and they therefore experience a shortfall, they are effectively penalized for exercising their self-determination rights, since the only choice left is to actually cut into the transferred BIA and IHS programs themselves in order to cover the shortfall."[22]

There is no comprehensive or specific documentation of tribal deficits in program spending or government operations. A partial understanding of overall tribal government finances can be gained from BIA's analysis of tribal debt levels, which was conducted as a complement to the Tribal Priority Allocations review. BIA reviewed 311 tribal single audits for 1996 and found 128 tribes reporting long-term debt. The overall debt for the reporting tribes was over $1 billion U.S. While the majority of tribes had debt under $1 million U.S., 7 tribes had debts of more than $20 million. Certainly, debt per se is not a cause for concern. In fact, the ability to qualify for debt financing is an indicator of financial management strengths and the existence of relatively assured sources of tribal government income. However, debt in combination with other data is a useful indicator. For example, in the same report, the BIA noted that a third of the tribes reporting long-term debt also reported net losses from business enterprises (that is, approximately, 43 of the 311 for which single audits were reviewed). These tribes may have difficulty servicing their debts and, therefore, are more likely to carry deficits in program or government operations.

It is worth noting that tribal interviewees were emphatic that the option of running deficits and accumulating debt is their prerogative. The attitude expressed was that tribal governments should be treated no differently than any other level of government.[23] Indeed, for tribal governments with adequate income and financial controls, there is no reason for the federal government to prevent tribes from assuming long-term debt for which they are capable of taking responsibility and that may have important developmental purposes. This contrasts greatly with the responsibility of tribal governments and their federal trustees to prevent deficits that impede the delivery of critical services and core government operations.

Financial Management Incentives

In the U.S. system of tribal funding transfers, the incentive to properly manage funds is based on self-interest at the tribal level. In the words of one BIA employee, "tribes don't want to behave recklessly since they know it jeopardizes their chances of receiving additional funds." For example, unless a Native nation that has failed to manage federal funds effectively in the past can demonstrate improvement in its management systems, funding departments and agencies are unlikely to award future competitive grants.

For Department of the Interior, BIA and IHS funds, the self-determination and self-governance policies also provide an incentive to prudent management: tribes must demonstrate their abilities to take over programs. Tribes interested in administering their own programs have a strong desire to avoid direct service delivery by the federal government.[24] By 2000, over 55% of the total BIA budget and 40% of the IHS budget was being spent by tribal governments through the contracting and compacting programs. A National Congress of American Indians report notes that "the nation's self-determination policy has been a resounding success for tribal communities. Virtually every tribe in the United States is involved in the operation of at least some programs and many operate or control all available programs."[25] If a tribe has several self-determination contracts, there is a significant incentive to move to self-governance compacting in order to gain the ability to creatively design programs and redirect funds.

Certainly, there is an element of "sink or swim" in these funding relationships. Tribes are given increased responsibility to manage funds but must set up adequate financial management practices in order to take advantage of the choices offered. Tribal administrators interviewed for this chapter noted that their governments use several strategies to promote sound internal financial management. Most often mentioned is the use of quality outside consultants, particularly accountants and auditors. Interviewees also pointed out that several Indian organizations provide support, education and networking opportunities, such as the Native American Finance Officer Association (NAFOA) and the Tribal Tax Conference. Administrators agreed, however, that there is no one model, and that each Indian nation must develop its own appropriate and workable system of financial management and internal controls.

For self-governance tribes (and to a lesser degree for tribes engaged in P.L. 638 contracting), accountability has shifted away from federal procedures and requirements to oversight by tribal governments and tribal citizens. As one BIA official observed, "either you are going to trust tribes or you are not. It's a difference in attitude: you either assume they are going to fail, or you presume they want to be successful and create opportunity."

Conclusions for Canada

The U.S. experience in managing the various types of funding transfers from the federal government to tribes highlights some of the challenges inherent in balancing flexibility for tribes with the desire for the federal government to control the money it is spending. Several initial observations can be made.

First, the move to increased tribal control over programs and services being provided to tribal citizens stemmed from an essentially political decision to deal with tribes on a government-to-government basis. The resulting arrangements gave tribes more decision-making power and financial maneuvering room, and had far-reaching consequences for tribal financial management. Particularly under self-governance compacts, accountability requirements for transferred funds are kept to a minimum as federal rules mandate that tribes produce relatively little evidence of their programs' effectiveness. Further, the U.S. government has little control over which tribes get this flexibility, since under its rights-based approach tribes can choose whether or not to participate. In order to participate, tribes must prove that they can meet the established eligibility criteria.

Based on the interviews conducted for this chapter, however, it appears that the American approach has been fairly successful. Particularly under self-governance arrangements, responsibility for keeping tribal governments accountable for the way funds are handled has, in effect, been transferred to tribal citizens. Such accountability depends on the administrative mechanisms within the tribal government, their transparency and, ultimately, on voters' democratic choice to punish those who allow funds to be mismanaged. That tribal citizens actually have the resources to exercise this responsibility is not a condition for entry into compacting agreements. Whether or not they do is a question beyond the scope of this chapter, and is an important topic for future research.

Second, one of the important features of the system of accountability in the U.S. is that tribal governments are treated similarly to other levels of government that receive federal funds. Tribal interviewees' comments suggest that this gives legitimacy to the federal government's auditing and accounting procedure requirements. An additional advantage to this even treatment in evaluation is that it makes tribes eligible for a broad range of funding opportunities. In other words, they may apply for funds from many federal programs alongside state and local governments and are not restricted to applying for funds that have been set aside specifically for Indians.

Even so, it should be noted that the administrative systems required to solicit and manage U.S. federal funding are complex. Many First Nations in Canada have very small populations, which may make it difficult to find an individual within the community with the necessary financial and administrative expertise. If a small community hires expertise, it may find it difficult to oversee the relationship. Given these considerations, a third observation is that the tribal consortia model may be an interesting organizational form for Canadian First Nations to explore. In the U.S., consortia are used mainly in Alaska and California, where tribes are typically small and the settlement pattern more closely resembles that found in Canada. Since the opportunity to enter self-determination contracts and self-governance compacts is made available to both tribes and consortia, the policy ensures that small tribes with limited personnel and administrative resources may still benefit from local program control. Critical aspects of the consortia are that tribes choose membership (it is not externally dictated), that consortia action may be restricted to one or a few issues (most consortia do not deal with a smorgasbord of programs), and that they are Native-run. Together, these elements help the consortia fit within the spirit of self-governance.

A fourth issue underlined by the U.S. example is that a large number of First Nations lack access to significant non-federal revenue. South of the border, it is generally those tribes that are most reliant on federal dollars for tribal government revenue that have been most in need of adequate contract support funding (indirect cost reimbursement) and most tempted to use program funds to support purposes other than those for which they were intended. While a "pay-as-you-go" approach to program funding is one solution, it is not adequate when the real problem is an underdeveloped and insufficiently funded tribal administrative system. It is illustrative that every tribal interviewee stressed the importance of obtaining the resources to properly support the development and maintenance of tribal administrative systems. Some suggested that this could take the form of direct technical assistance from the federal government or the form of funding to hire an outside party to consult on management methods.

A final note of caution needs to be sounded on the relationship between accountability and the allocation of funds. Although the self-governance arrangement has proven to be popular with tribes, the lack of reporting of results to the federal government is somewhat problematic. While accountability to tribal citizens rather than the federal government leads to priorities more in tune with local realities, the overall budget for self-governance programs is still allocated by Congress. Without in-depth reporting, there is limited information on which Congress can base funding decisions. As one BIA employee pointed out, "it's hard to make a convincing case for extra funding for a specific need when you will not necessarily spend the money on that program." A tribal interviewee countered that lobbying at Congress takes care of this problem. In Canada, where funding allocations are determined globally by Parliament and implemented by the civil service, an approach based on lobbying is not functional. Thought must be given to finding a method or type of objective-based reporting that is not intrusive or burdensome to First Nations. To date, this goal has eluded U.S. policy-makers.

Conclusion

Financial management capacity is a crucial element of overall tribal governing capacity. As this examination has highlighted, it may also provide a critical underpinning to self-rule. As tribes and First Nations regain control over government functions and activities in their communities, other research suggests it is likely that socioeconomic development will follow.[26]

The U.S. has experienced some notable success by responding to tribes' requests for increased tribal power over the management of programs and services provided to tribal citizens. In turn, many tribes have taken over the responsibility for spending funds in their communities. Rather than producing a situation in which funds are misused or spent ineffectively, contracting and compacting have, for the most part, led to efficient programs more in tune with tribal needs. Tribes have risen to the challenge of expanding their government functions by setting up internal accountability, controls and financial management procedures. The alternatives of dissatisfied tribal citizens, a return to direct service delivery by federal departments and agencies and/or reduced grant monies, are sufficient incentives for most tribes to maintain a viable system. With attention to capacity development and adequate funding, contracting and compacting type arrangements can be considered a feasible model for moving towards an improved government-to-government relationship between First Nations and the Government of Canada. Opportunities for grant monies from a wider variety of federal departments and increased symmetry between tribal, provincial and municipal governments may be elements of an expanded model with still more incentives for good tribal government management.

Endnotes

1. While states may have a variety of contracts with tribes (informants from the State of Montana reported as many as 500 in early 2002), the U.S. federal government provides the overwhelming majority of external funds flowing to tribal governments.

2. Interviews were held between December 2001 and February 2002. During those months, there were dramatic developments in the *Cobell v. Babbitt* (now *Cobell v. Norton*), a class-action lawsuit filed in 1996. The suit's plaintiffs allege that billions of dollars in Indian trust funds are unaccounted for. The Interior Department manages over 300,000 trust accounts on behalf of individual Indians, which generate over $500 million a year in revenue from Indian-owned lands. Numerous internal and external reviews have found acute problems with missing records and poor accounting practices. In December 2001, a federal court judge ordered that all on-line operations of the Individual Indian Monies trust data system be closed down due to a severe risk of penetration by hackers and other unauthorized individuals. In response, the BIA shut down its Internet site and, for a time, all external e-mail capability. Also, in December 2001, Interior Secretary Gail Norton went on trial for contempt of court for ignoring court orders to clean up the trust and for submitting false reports on trust reform.

3. Jordan S. Dill, Indian Issues of Consequence website (www.dickshovel.com/biafnd). The percentage of funds provided to Indian Country from the BIA and IHS has been falling over time, but these agencies still provide the majority of funds to Indian Country.

4. U.S. Department of Interior, Bureau of Indian Affairs, *Report on Tribal Priority Allocations*, July 1999, 48 (hereafter, *TPA Report*).

5. Ibid.

6. The technical language of federal law in the United States refers to "tribal members." Increasingly, however, American Indians and their advocates use the phrase "tribal citizens" to reflect tribes' status as nations and their members' status as citizens of those nations.

7. The BIA area (regional) and central (national) office operations are not funded from TPA, but from separate allocations in the budget.

8. Calculation based on 1998 budget figures as reported in the *TPA Report*, 16.

9. *TPA Report*, 14.

10. *TPA Report*, 37.

11. One example is law enforcement. Congress agreed to increase spending as long as the funds were earmarked for this purpose. The program was thus removed from tribal base amounts.

12. *TPA Report*, 14.

13. U.S. Senate, *Statements on Introduced Bills and Joint Resolutions*, February 15, 2001, S1471. This Bill was introduced in the first session of the 106th Congress and referred to committee on February 15, 2001. The Senate Committee on Indian Affairs held hearings on the Bill in early May 2002, but further action was not taken before the close of the Congressional session.

14. An individual tribe or a consortium of tribes may elect to contract. Many tribes, particularly smaller ones, have elected to participate in contracting via consortia. Therefore, the estimate reflects participation in contracting and does not necessarily imply that each of the 525 has individually contracted with the BIA or IHS.

15. The program amount does not include certain administrative costs. The funding of indirect cost has been an ongoing issue for tribes and will be further discussed under the heading "Deficits and Difficulties" below.

16. *U.S. Code of Federal Regulations*, Title 25, Section 900.22.

17. *TPA Report*, 11.

18. The GASB operates under the auspices of the Financial Accounting Foundation. GASB and the Financial Accounting Standards Board (FASB), its private-sector counterpart, determine the Generally Accepted Accounting Procedures (GAAP) for audits.

19. Of course, tribal government perceptions of the BIA's capacity for giving financial management advice are coloured by the scandal surrounding the Indian trust monies. See footnote 2.

20. Federal program managers were unsure whether resumption of service delivery could be done for a self-governance tribe without a tribal request. Such a move by the BIA could perhaps lead to a court challenge.

21. Indirect cost rates are determined on a tribe-by-tribe basis by the Department of the Interior Office of the Inspector General or the Department of Health and Human Services Division of Cost Allocation. One reason for individualized administrative cost allocations is that tribal rates are generally higher than the comparable federal rate. Tribes counter, however, that the DOI and DHHS fail to take resources located at the area and central offices into account.

22. National Congress of American Indians, *National Policy Work Group on Contract Support Costs Final Report*, 22.

23. Yet it is also worth noting that some U.S. cities and states have passed "no deficit" legislation that disallows deficit program or operational spending.

24. Admittedly, some U.S. tribes choose not to administer or control federal programs on the principle that it weakens the federal government's trust responsibility.

25. *National Policy Work Group on Contract Support Costs Final Report*, op cit., 21.

26. See, for example, S. Cornell and J. P. Kalt, "Sovereignty and Nation-Building: The Development Challenge in Indian Country Today," *American Indian Culture and Research Journal*, 22, no. 3 (1998): 187–214.

References

Hinkle, J. 2001. "Chipping Away at the BIA." *American Indian Report* (December): 12.

National Congress of American Indians. 1999. *National Policy Work Group on Contract Support Costs Final Report* (July).

Native American Finance Officers Association. 2001. *New Financial Reporting Model for Tribal Governments, Implementation Guide for GASB34.*

Office of Management and Budget. 2002. *Budget of the United States Government, Fiscal Year 2003.* Appendix.

U.S. Department of Health and Human Services. Indian Health Service. 1999. *FY 1998 Accountability Report.*

———. Internal Agency Procedures Workgroup. 1999. *Internal Agency Procedures Handbook for Non-Construction Contracting Under Title I of the Indian Self-Determination and Education Assistance Act* (July).

U.S. Department of Interior. Bureau of Indian Affairs. 1999. *Report on Tribal Priority Allocations* (July).

———. Tribal Workgroup on Tribal Needs Assessments. 1999. *Empowerment of Tribal Governments: Final Workgroup Report* (May).

U.S. Government Printing Office. 2002. *U.S. Code of Federal Regulations*, Title 25. Washington, D.C.

U.S. Senate. 2001. *Statements on Introduced Bills and Joint Resolutions* (15 February).

Interviews

Note: Interviews were conducted with the promise of confidentiality. Thus, only job titles and approximate locations identify the interviewees who contributed to this report.

Program Coordinator. Tribal Government (of a Northwestern Tribe). 17 December 2001.

Programs Administrator for Social Services and Self-Government Coordinator. Tribal Government (of a Northwestern Tribe). 28 January 2002.

Chief Financial Officer. Tribal Government (of a Northern Lakes Tribe). 30 January 2002.

Financial Manager. Tribal Government (of a Northern Lakes Tribe). 30 January 2002.

Senior Executive. Office of Self-Government, U.S. Department of Interior. 20 December 2001.

Senior Manager. Office of Self-Government, U.S. Department of Interior. 20 December 2001.

Area Manager. Office of Self-Government, U.S. Department of Interior. 30 January 2002.

Senior Manager. Self-Determination Services, Bureau of Indian Affairs, U.S. Department of Interior. 30 January 2002.

Senior Manager. Trust Policy and Management (previously in Audit and Evaluation), Bureau of Indian Affairs, U.S. Department of Interior. 28 January 2002.

Analyst. Audit and Evaluation, Bureau of Indian Affairs, U.S. Department of Interior. 17 December 2001.

Attorney specializing in Indian issues. Washington, D.C. law firm. 3 January 2002.

2

Situation de faible revenu de long terme des Autochtones hors réserve au Canada: Une étude sur les groupes à risque d'exclusion sociale

Dominique Fleury

Introduction

La Direction générale de la recherche appliquée, dans le cadre de son agenda de recherche sur l'exclusion sociale, a identifié les Autochtones comme faisant partie des cinq groupes de personnes les plus à risque d'être pauvres ou exclus socialement. Les quatre autres groupes à risque étant constitués des personnes faisant partie de familles monoparentales, des personnes avec limitations au travail, des immigrants récents et des personnes âgées de 45 à 64 ans vivant seules. Le présent projet n'a pas pour objet de confirmer l'existence de ces groupes dits à risque mais plutôt de les comparer entre eux. En cherchant à savoir s'il y a des groupes qui s'en tirent mieux que d'autres au niveau économique, il s'avère que, de façon surprenante, c'est chez les Autochtones hors réserve que l'on observe la meilleure performance dans l'ensemble des groupes à risque. Cette étude vise donc plus précisément à exposer ce fait et à comprendre ce qui l'explique.

Pour ce faire, après une brève discussion au sujet du concept d'exclusion sociale, la banque de données utilisée (l'Enquête sur la dynamique du travail et du revenu) sera présentée et, la mesure de pauvreté choisie (pauvreté persistante) ainsi que les détails techniques reliés à la manipulation des données seront explicités. Ensuite, des statistiques descriptives relatives à la pauvreté persistante dans les différents groupes seront mises en évidence pour clairement illustrer la meilleure performance économique des Autochtones hors réserve. Les sections suivantes seront consacrées, dans un premier temps, à la présentation des quatre pistes d'explications les plus plausibles pour démystifier ce constat et, dans un deuxième temps, à la présentation des raisons qui expliquent effectivement leur bonne performance en ce qui a trait à la pauvreté persistante par rapport aux autres groupes à risque. Finalement, les points saillants de l'étude seront résumés dans la conclusion.

Contexte de l'étude

L'exclusion sociale

Depuis quelques années, l'exclusion sociale est un phénomène qui préoccupe de manière croissante les chercheurs, les décideurs ainsi que la population en général. Or, si le concept d'exclusion fait actuellement l'objet de nombreux débats, il n'existe toujours pas de consensus sur sa définition dans la littérature. Plusieurs définitions ont été proposées ici et là et ce, surtout en Europe d'où le concept d'exclusion sociale a émergé dans les années quatre-vingt. Par exemple, Tony Blair stipule (1999) qu'il peut y avoir exclusion sociale « lorsqu'un individu ou une communauté fait face à une combinaison de désavantages sociaux tels, le chômage, le manque de compétences, une situation de faible revenu, un environnement violent, une mauvaise santé et/ou l'éclatement familial ». De manière plus générale, l'office statistique de la commission européenne (2000) considère l'exclusion sociale comme « un phénomène multidimensionnel qui empêche les individus de participer pleinement à la société ».

Cependant, de façon théorique, on s'entend sur certains points. Premièrement, l'exclusion sociale est un phénomène plus large que celui de la pauvreté. En d'autres mots, l'exclusion n'est pas seulement causée par l'insuffisance des ressources matérielles mais aussi par des facteurs socio-démographiques et culturels. Deuxièmement, l'exclusion sociale est relative à une certaine époque et à une certaine société. La notion d'exclusion est d'ailleurs apparue dans un contexte de croissance économique où le chômage de longue durée devenait de plus en plus fréquent. En effet, cette augmentation du chômage allant de pair avec une valorisation sociale de plus en plus importante du travail, certaines personnes n'ayant pas accès à des emplois stables ont commencé à ne plus se sentir partie intégrante de la société. Toutefois, si le chômage a inspiré la prise en compte de la marginalisation possible de certains membres de nos collectivités, il n'implique pas nécessairement, tout comme la pauvreté, l'exclusion sociale. Enfin, l'exclusion sociale est un phénomène dynamique, c'est-à-dire qu'elle résulte généralement d'une situation permanente ou de long terme plutôt que d'une situation temporaire.

Comment mesurer l'exclusion sociale

Malgré les ambiguïtés qui subsistent quant à la définition du concept d'exclusion sociale, il est admis que l'exclusion existe et peut avoir des conséquences négatives sur le bien-être présent mais aussi futur des parents et enfants qui la subissent. Ainsi, l'inclusion (en réponse à l'exclusion) semble être, de façon unanime, un des objectifs sociaux les plus valorisés au Canada comme dans la plupart des pays industrialisés. Pour atteindre cet objectif, il faut pouvoir orienter les politiques de manière efficace en ciblant les groupes d'individus ou les collectivités les plus sujets à vivre de l'exclusion sociale et en cernant les caractéristiques qui aident à éviter ou qui favorisent l'exclusion de ceux-ci. Toutefois, les contraintes imposées par la disponibilité des données rendent très difficile, voir même impossible, la prise en compte de toutes les dimensions de l'exclusion sociale dans les recherches. En fait, ceux qui cherchent à mesurer l'exclusion sociale doivent considérablement simplifier sa définition. Notamment, la plupart des études visant à quantifier le phénomène de l'exclusion restreignent sa définition à la dimension économique. En effet, elles utilisent les variables disponibles de faible revenu en guise d'indicateurs de risque d'exclusion sociale.

C'est d'ailleurs ce qu'a fait la Direction générale de la recherche appliquée (DGRA) du Développement des ressources humaines Canada dans le cadre de son agenda de recherche sur l'exclusion sociale. La DGRA s'est d'abord attardée à « l'incidence » des faibles revenus après impôt[1] chez les Canadiens/ Canadiennes âgés de moins de 65 ans.[2] Cela lui a permis d'identifier certains groupes de personnes qui sont beaucoup plus enclins que d'autres à avoir de faibles revenus une année donnée et conséquemment, qui sont plus à risque de vivre de l'exclusion sociale. Ces groupes, qu'elle a nommé « les groupes à risque », sont constitués des personnes mono-parentales, des Canadiens/Canadiennes d'origine autochtone, des personnes ayant immigré au Canada dans les dix années précédent l'année de l'observation, des personnes ayant des limitations physiques ou mentales au travail et, des personnes âgées de 45 ans et plus vivant seules.

Pour se rapprocher le plus possible de l'étude du véritable phénomène de l'exclusion sociale, la DGRA a ensuite intégré dans ses recherches le caractère dynamique des situations de faible revenu. À l'aide de données longitudinales, elle s'est penchée sur la « durée » passée dans une situation de faible revenu. Notamment, Ross Finnie a démontré (1999), pour le compte de la DGRA, en considérant la nature dynamique de la pauvreté, qu'il existe deux groupes distincts de pauvres[3] soient, ceux qui le sont de façon temporaire et ceux qui restent pauvres pour de longues périodes. Il s'avère d'ailleurs, que les membres de nos groupes à risque sont également ceux qui sont les plus susceptibles de connaître de longs épisodes de faible revenu dans la population canadienne, et ainsi, de faire partie du second groupe.

Objet de la présente étude

Dans le présent document, les groupes à risque sont toujours étudiés dans une perspective longitudinale. Or, ce n'est plus pour confirmer leur existence en les comparant au reste de la population canadienne mais plutôt pour les comparer entre eux. En effet, les personnes faisant partie des groupes à risque sont, selon les indicateurs économiques de court et de long terme, définitivement plus sujettes que le reste des Canadiens/Canadiennes à remplir les critères économiques de risque d'exclusion sociale. Néanmoins, cela ne permet pas de déduire qu'elles ont toutes de faibles revenus, qu'elles font toutes face aux mêmes problèmes et qu'il s'agit de les traiter de la même façon pour favoriser leur inclusion sociale. Les personnes faisant partie de ces groupes ont leurs particularités, et les raisons qui font que certaines d'entre elles échappent à la pauvreté alors que d'autres connaissent des épisodes longs de pauvreté peuvent possiblement différer entre les groupes. Ainsi, il est intéressant de vérifier dans un premier temps si les membres de certains de ces groupes s'en tirent plus ou moins bien que d'autres, d'un point de vue économique, et d'expliquer ces différentes performances si elles existent.

Méthodologie

Une mesure de pauvreté persistante, telle que proposée par Morissette et Zhang (2001) dans *À faible revenu pendant plusieurs années,* sera principalement utilisée. Plutôt que de calculer le nombre d'années consécutives que chaque personne passe dans une situation de faible revenu, cette mesure permet de savoir quelles personnes ont eu un revenu après impôt cumulé entre 1993 et 1998 inférieur au cumul des seuils de faible revenu après impôt qui leur étaient associés[4] entre ces mêmes années. En effet, vérifier le nombre d'années passées sous le seuil de faible revenu pour chaque personne offre un portrait de la durée passée dans la pauvreté. Toutefois, cela n'informe pas sur la sévérité de la situation de pauvreté à laquelle elle fait face. Il est tout à fait possible qu'une personne faisant partie d'une famille sous le seuil de faible revenu une année donnée mais n'en faisant plus partie l'année suivante ait connu une situation globale de faible revenu pire que celle d'une personne ayant vécu ces deux années sous le seuil de faible revenu. Prendre en compte la pauvreté persistante offre non seulement un portrait de la « durée » mais aussi de la « sévérité » de la situation de faible revenu. En effet, c'est une mesure sensible non seulement au fait qu'une personne ait vécu de la pauvreté au moins une fois durant une période et au temps passé dans la pauvreté, mais aussi, à l'écart moyen entre le revenu et le seuil de faible revenu durant la période de pauvreté.

Ainsi, dans la présente étude, on considère qu'une personne a vécu une période de pauvreté persistante entre 1993 et 1998 si et seulement si:

$$\sum_{t=\gamma} RAI_t \prec \sum_{t=\gamma} SAI_t$$

où,

RAI = Revenu *familkial après transferts et impôts*[5]

SAI = *Seuil de faible revenu familial après transferts et impôts*

γ = 1993,1994,1995,1996,1997,1998

Qui plus est, comme l'intérêt des chercheurs se situe au niveau de groupes de personnes plutôt qu'au niveau des personnes uniquement, l'attention sera portée sur les taux de pauvreté persistante, à savoir, sur la proportion d'individus faisant partie d'un groupe particulier en 1993 ayant vécu de la pauvreté persistante entre 1993 et 1998. Évidemment, le calcul de ces taux nécessite l'utilisation d'une banque de données longitudinale soit, dans ce cas-ci, l'Enquête sur la dynamique du travail et du revenu.

Données

L'Enquête sur la dynamique du travail et du revenu

L'Enquête sur la dynamique du travail et du revenu (EDTR) est une banque de données longitudinales qui a été conçue pour réussir à cerner les changements qui affectent le bien-être économique des personnes au fil du temps ainsi que les facteurs ayant une influence sur ce bien-être. Les personnes choisies au départ font partie d'un panel et un nouveau panel débute tous les trois ans. Chaque répondant faisant partie d'un panel est interrogé une ou deux fois par année durant six ans et répond à des questions concernant son expérience de travail, son revenu et sa situation familiale. Pour obtenir un portrait exhaustif des familles ainsi que des données valides en coupe transversale, des informations sont aussi recueillies sur les personnes qui vivent à un moment ou à un autre avec les répondants originaux.

Dans le présent document, les données du 1er panel sont utilisées, soit celui qui a débuté en 1993 et s'est terminé en 1998. Il est constitué d'un échantillon national représentatif[6] d'environ 15 000 ménages ou 31 000 personnes sélectionnées à la fin de 1992 à partir de l'Enquête sur la population active.

Critères de sous-échantillonnage et détails techniques

Si l'utilisation d'une banque de données longitudinales permet de considérer le caractère dynamique de l'exclusion sociale et d'enrichir ainsi les analyses sur ce thème, plusieurs contraintes surviennent lorsque ce type de données est utilisé. D'ailleurs, ces contraintes obligent ceux qui les traitent à faire des choix, parfois subjectifs, selon ce qu'ils jugent le plus adéquat. Premièrement, ils doivent faire face à un important problème d'attrition entre la première et la dernière année de l'enquête. En effet, un grand nombre de personnes sélectionnées au départ ne se soumettent plus à l'enquête au cours des années subséquentes. Dans ce cas-ci, comme les chercheurs s'intéressent à ce qu'il advient des répondants initiaux jusqu'à la fin de la période à l'étude, ils n'ont conservé que les personnes qui ont été interrogées à toutes les années entre 1993 et 1998. Deuxièmement, interroger les mêmes personnes durant plusieurs années consécutives rehausse le risque qu'il y ait des valeurs manquantes associées aux variables d'intérêt. Notamment, il est possible qu'une personne accepte de déclarer son revenu une année donnée mais qu'elle le refuse l'année suivante et, dans ce cas, à moins d'imputer un revenu pour l'année où elle a refusé de le dévoiler, l'analyse longitudinale des variables de revenus de cette personne est largement complexifiée puisqu'il y a des années pour lesquelles il n'existe pas d'information relative à son revenu. Toutefois, comme l'EDTR est une enquête qui vise l'étude dynamique du travail et du revenu, Statistique Canada a, sauf pour quelques exceptions qui ont été exclues du sous-échantillon, imputé des valeurs de revenu aux valeurs manquantes.[7] Enfin, cela complexifie la pondération,[8] le traitement et l'analyse des données. Par exemple, l'analyse des performances économiques de long terme des groupes à risque a forcé les chercheurs à faire des choix, quoique éclairés, quelque peu arbitraires. En effet, pour pouvoir observer ce qu'il advient des groupes à risque en terme de pauvreté persistante entre 1993 et 1998, il faut d'abord définir ces groupes. En analyse longitudinale, l'identification des groupes est plus ardue qu'en analyse transversale puisque chaque personne ne fait pas nécessairement partie du même groupe durant toute la période à l'étude. En raison du nombre d'observations et du fait que la situation familiale peut avoir une influence sur la dynamique de faible revenu des personnes, les groupes ont été définis selon les caractéristiques des personnes au début de la période considérée soit, en 1993.[9] Conséquemment, pour qu'aucune personne ne dépasse l'âge de 64 ans durant la période étudiée toutes les personnes âgées de plus de 59 ans en 1993 ont été exclues. Enfin, lorsque les critères de sélection relatifs à l'attrition, aux valeurs manquantes et à l'âge sont imposés, il ne reste que 25 519 personnes faisant partie du sous-échantillon et pondérées, ces 25 519 personnes en représentent 21 757 394.

Il faut aussi préciser que l'étude porte sur la situation des personnes et non sur celle des familles En effet, une analyse longitudinale de la famille est pratiquement impossible étant donné que sa composition évolue avec le temps. Toutefois, comme la situation économique d'une personne repose fortement sur celle de sa famille, on attribue à chaque personne la situation économique de sa famille.[10] Dans la même optique, pour savoir si les personnes font partie ou non d'un groupe à risque, les caractéristiques du principal soutien économique[11] ont été associées aux autres membres de sa famille. Pour justifier ce dernier choix les auteurs ont, à titre d'exemple, jugé que les membres d'une famille où la personne gagnant le plus haut revenu est limitée au travail sont eux aussi, d'un point de vue financier, susceptibles de subir les répercussions de cette limitation. Il en est évidemment de même pour les individus faisant partie de familles dont le principal soutien économique est un immigrant récent, une personne monoparentale ou un Autochtone.

Par conséquent, une personne est:

- Monoparentale: si elle fait partie d'une famille monoparentale en 1993.
- Seule 45+: si elle vit seule et a 45 ans et plus en 1993.
- Immigrant récent: si elle fait partie d'une famille dans laquelle le principal soutien économique a immigré au Canada depuis 10 ans ou moins en 1993.
- Limitée au travail: si elle fait partie d'une famille dans laquelle le principal soutien économique a une limitation au travail en 1993.
- Autochtone hors réserve[12]: si elle fait partie d'une famille dans laquelle le principal soutien économique est un Autochtone vivant hors réserve en 1993.

De manière plus générale, une personne est dans le groupe:

- À risque: si elle fait partie de l'un ou l'autre des cinq groupes à risque d'exclusion sociale soient, des Monoparentale et/ou des Seule 45+ et/ou des Immigrant récent et/ou des Limitée au travail et/ou des Autochtone hors réserve.
- Non à risque: si elle ne fait partie d'aucun des cinq groupes à risque d'exclusion sociale.
- Résiduel: s'il n'est pas clair qu'elle fasse partie d'au moins un des cinq groupes à risque d'exclusion sociale.[13]

La figure 1 démontre de quelle façon les membres du sous-échantillon sont répartis à l'intérieur des différents groupes décrits précédemment.

Figure 1:   Répartition des personnes dans les différents groupes en 1993

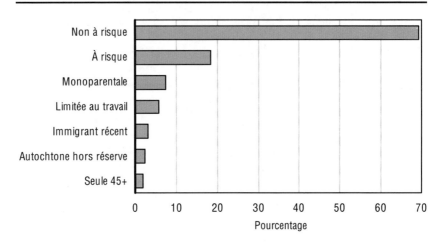

En 1993, la plus grande proportion de personnes se retrouve dans le groupe Non à risque (69,2 %) mais, il y a tout de même 18,4 % des personnes qui font partie d'au moins un des cinq groupes à risque.[14] Les groupes Seule 45+ et Autochtone hors réserve sont les groupes à risque à l'intérieur desquels il y a le moins grand nombre de personnes soit, 2,2 % et 2,3 % des personnes du sous-échantillon.[15] C'est toutefois ce dernier groupe qui attirera particulièrement l'attention des chercheurs dans les prochaines sections de l'étude.

Les Autochtones hors réserve et leur situation économique

Selon le recensement canadien de 1996, près de 800 000 personnes, soit moins de 3 % de la population totale, se sont déclarées Autochtones. De celles-là, seulement 30 % environ vivaient dans les réserves.[16] Tandis que les autres vivaient en grande majorité dans les régions urbaines, puisque seulement 20 % des Autochtones hors réserve demeuraient en région rurale. Par ailleurs, sur l'ensemble des Autochtones, plus de 60 % étaient inscrits en vertu de la *loi sur les Indiens du Canada*. Mais, cette proportion chute considérablement lorsque l'on ne considère que les Autochtones vivant hors réserve. En effet, les Autochtones inscrits ne représentaient en 1996 que 46 % de la population autochtone vivant hors réserve comparativement à 98 % de la population autochtone vivant dans les réserves.

Ces divergences, quant aux lieux où ils habitent et à leur statut, portent à croire que les Autochtones ne font pas tous face à la même réalité et qu'il est possible que certains d'entre eux soient davantage à risque d'exclusion sociale que d'autres. Voyons d'abord comment les Autochtones hors réserve s'en sortent d'un point de vue économique par rapport aux autres groupes dits à risque.

Figure 2: Taux de pauvreté persistante entre 1993 et 1998, selon le groupe

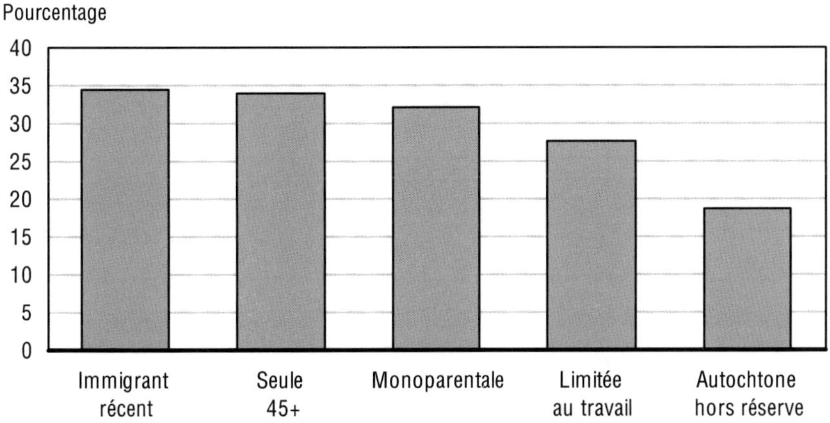

La figure précédente nous indique clairement que, parmi tous les groupes à risque, ce sont les membres du groupe Autochtone hors réserve qui sont les moins susceptibles d'avoir connu une période de pauvreté persistante dans les dernières années. En effet, la proportion d'entre eux qui ont vécu une période de pauvreté persistante entre 1993 et 1998 (18,6 %), quoique supérieure à celle des non à risque (4,8 %), est entre 1,5 fois et 2 fois plus faible que celle observée dans chacun des autres groupes à risque (varient entre 27,6 % et 34,5 %).

Tel que brièvement mentionné dans la section méthodologie, trois facteurs peuvent influencer le taux de pauvreté persistante dans chacun des groupes soient, la proportion de personnes qui connaissent la pauvreté durant la période à l'étude, l'écart moyen entre le revenu familial et le seuil de faible revenu et la durée moyenne passée dans la pauvreté chez celles qui l'ont connue. Il est donc intéressant d'observer lesquels de ces facteurs expliquent le mieux le fait que les membres du groupe Autochtone hors réserve aient connu moins souvent la pauvreté persistante entre 1993 et 1998 par rapport aux membres des autres groupes à risque.

Tableau 1: Statistiques concernant les trois facteurs influençant les taux de pauvreté persistante, selon le groupe

Facteurs		Monopa-rentale	Seule 45+	Immigrant récent	Limitée au travail	Autochtone hors réserve	Non à risque
						Groupes	
Pourcentage pauvres au moins une fois entre 1993 et 1998	%	57,9	51,4	50,8	50,4	38,1	18,5
Durée moyenne de la pauvreté pour ceux qui ont été pauvres	Ans	3,5	4,3	4,1	3,7	3,3	2,4
Écart moyen entre le revenu familial et le seuil de faible revenu pour ceux qui ont été pauvres	$	5 679	5 518	7 820	5 266	5 832	8 143

Selon le tableau 1, le fait que les individus faisant partie du groupe Autochtone hors réserve aient évité plus souvent la pauvreté persistante s'explique en partie parce qu'ils ont moins de chance d'avoir connu la pauvreté à un moment donné entre 1993 et 1998, mais aussi, parce que lorsqu'ils sont pauvres, ils le sont généralement moins longtemps que les membres des autres groupes à risque. Le troisième facteur, c'est-à-dire l'écart moyen entre le revenu familial et le seuil de faible revenu, ne contribue pas à restreindre leur risque de pauvreté persistante puisque le groupe Autochtone hors réserve est le second groupe à risque, après celui des Immigrants récents, pour lequel l'écart moyen est le plus élevé durant cette période. Il est cependant intéressant de noter que c'est chez les personnes non à risque pauvres que l'on observe l'écart moyen le plus prononcé entre le revenu familial et le seuil de faible revenu. Cela suggère que, même s'ils sont plus rarement et moins longtemps pauvres que les membres des groupes à risque, lorsqu'ils le sont, les membres du groupe Non à risque sont, en général, dans un état de pauvreté plus sévère que les membres du groupe À risque.

Nonobstant lequel des trois facteurs en est le plus responsable, il ne demeure pas moins que les Autochtones hors réserve ont, de façon étonnante, échappé beaucoup plus souvent à la pauvreté persistante durant les dernières années que les membres des autres groupes à risque. Ainsi, cette mesure offre un portrait moins pessimiste, du moins en comparaison avec les autres groupes à risque, de la situation économique de long terme de ce groupe particulier d'Autochtones. Or, elle amène également à s'interroger sur ce qui explique cette meilleure performance économique relative.

Les caractéristiques propres aux individus qui influencent leur situation économique de long terme

Lorsque les individus font partie de la population en général

Plusieurs caractéristiques peuvent contribuer à rendre un individu plus vulnérable qu'un autre à la pauvreté persistante. Les deux plus probables s'appliquent à l'ensemble de la population. C'est le niveau d'éducation et l'appartenance au marché du travail. En effet, plusieurs études sur le rendement de l'éducation ont déjà démontré que le revenu est positivement lié au niveau de scolarité atteint. Autrement dit, plus une personne est scolarisée, plus son intégration au marché du travail sera facilitée, son salaire potentiellement élevé, et par conséquent, plus ses revenus risquent d'être importants. Inversement, moins elle est instruite, moins ses chances d'obtenir un emploi bien rémunéré sont grandes, et, plus elle est susceptible d'avoir un faible revenu. De surcroît, le salaire des personnes avec un haut niveau de scolarité a tendance à croître plus rapidement dans le temps que celui des personnes moins scolarisées ce qui implique qu'elles ont la possibilité de sortir plus rapidement de la pauvreté lorsqu'elles y sont.[17]

L'influence positive du niveau d'éducation sur le revenu est vraie autant pour les personnes à risque que pour celles qui ne sont pas à risque. En effet, la figure 3 de la page suivante montre que, même si les personnes non à risque sont nettement moins enclines à connaître la pauvreté persistante que les personnes à risque et ce, quel que soit leur niveau de scolarité, le fait que le principal soutien économique de la famille n'ait pas de diplôme d'études secondaires (< DES) fait presque que doubler les chances de pauvreté persistante des personnes à risque et des personnes non à risque.

Toutefois, selon des récentes conclusions de la Direction générale de la recherche appliquée, même si investir dans des études postsecondaires constitue, en moyenne, un investissement rentable au niveau monétaire, la rentabilité de cet investissement varie aussi en fonction d'autres facteurs tels que le type de diplôme obtenu, certaines caractéristiques individuelles, etc.[18] En fait, si le niveau d'éducation est significativement et positivement lié au revenu, c'est d'abord et avant tout parce qu'il permet une meilleure intégration au marché du travail. En effet, un niveau de scolarité élevé facilite l'accès aux emplois bien rémunérés et stables, soit deux conditions permettant presque systématiquement d'échapper à la pauvreté persistante.

Figure 3: **Taux de pauvreté persistante entre 1993 et 1998, selon le groupe et le niveau d'éducation du principal soutien économique en 1993**

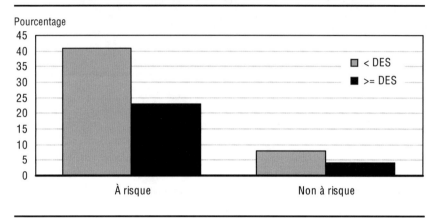

Néanmoins, éducation et intégration au marché du travail ne sont pas parfaitement corrélés. Il est fort possible qu'une personne détenant un diplôme universitaire ne réussisse pas à intégrer le marché du travail alors qu'une autre l'intègre aisément avec moins d'un diplôme d'études secondaires et, dans ce type de cas, l'emploi occupé constitue un moyen plus efficace d'éviter la pauvreté que le diplôme détenu. D'ailleurs, selon la figure 3, une personne à risque faisant partie d'une famille dont le principal soutien économique avait moins d'un diplôme d'études secondaires en 1993 était environ deux fois plus susceptible de connaître la pauvreté persistante dans les années subséquentes qu'une autre dont le principal soutien économique était plus scolarisé. Tandis que, la figure 4 indique que le risque de pauvreté persistante est aux alentours de quatre fois plus important chez les personnes à risque appartenant à une famille où le principal soutien économique ne travaillait pas en 1993 par rapport à une famille où il occupait un emploi.[19] Ainsi, la comparaison des figures 3 et 4 permet d'affirmer que le statut d'activité sur le marché du travail à un moment donné est un meilleur indice du risque qu'une personne subisse éventuellement une période de pauvreté persistante que le niveau de scolarité atteint et, s'il s'avère que cette observation est vraie chez les personnes à risque, elle l'est particulièrement chez les personnes non à risque.

Figure 4: **Taux de pauvreté persistante entre 1993 et 1998, selon le groupe et le statut d'activité sur le marché du travail du principal soutien économique en 1993**

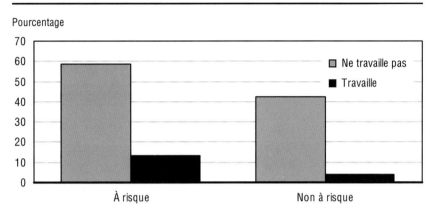

Évidemment, encore une fois, avoir un emploi n'est pas la seule condition requise pour se soustraire à la pauvreté persistante et à l'exclusion puisque 13,2 % des personnes à risque ainsi que 3,7 % des non à risque appartenant à des familles dont le principal soutien économique travaillait en 1993 ont tout de même connu la pauvreté persistante entre 1993 et 1998. En effet, un bon nombre d'emplois existants sont instables et peu rémunérés ce qui rend ceux qui les détiennent ainsi que ceux qui dépendent d'eux, vulnérables à la pauvreté. Cependant, selon le tableau 2 ci-dessous, pour les personnes à risque qui étaient dans des familles où le principal soutien économique était en âge de travailler et n'était pas à l'école en 1993, le fait que ce dernier ait eu un emploi stable, peu importe son salaire, a constitué un moyen efficace pour les membres de sa famille d'échapper à la pauvreté persistante. Dans ces conditions les personnes à risque ont évité quasiment aussi souvent la pauvreté persistante que les personnes non à risque (5,5 % vs 4,2 %). Cette observation vient d'ailleurs confirmer les dires de Ross Finnie (2000) qui a affirmé que l'incapacité de conserver un emploi est le facteur le plus important pour expliquer les épisodes de pauvreté des groupes à risque.[20] Il faut néanmoins ajouter qu'une proportion considérablement plus importante de personnes non à risque ont vécu dans une famille où le principal soutien économique n'a connu aucune période de chômage entre 1993 et 1998 en comparaison avec les personnes à risque (50,5 % vs 33,5 %).

Tableau 2: Taux de pauvreté persistante selon le groupe et la situation d'emploi du principal soutien économique en 1993 lorsque ce dernier n'étudiait pas

Groupes	À risque	À risque sans période de chômage (1993–98) %	Non à risque
Pourcentage de personnes ayant connu la pauvreté persistante (1993–98)	25,3	5,5	4,2

Lorsque les individus font partie d'un groupe à risque

Selon les données, deux autres moyens sont efficaces afin d'éviter la pauvreté persistante pour les personnes à risque. Le premier, c'est de sortir du groupe à risque auquel elles appartiennent et le second, c'est de posséder le moins de facteurs de risque possible.

En effet, les individus ont été répartis, tel que mentionné précédemment, dans les différents groupes à l'étude selon les caractéristiques de la famille économique à laquelle chacun d'entre eux appartenait en 1993. Or, parmi ces groupes, il est possible de distinguer deux catégories de personnes. La première est constituée des personnes qui sont toujours demeurées dans des familles avec les même caractéristiques que celles qui prévalaient en 1993, c'est-à-dire dans le même groupe jusqu'en 1998. La deuxième regroupe les personnes qui ont transité au moins une fois vers un autre type de famille entre 1994 et 1998 soit, vers le groupe Non à risque pour les personnes à risque.[21] En comparant les performances économiques des personnes à risque selon qu'elles font partie de la première (47,2 % des personnes à risque)[22] ou de la deuxième catégorie (43,5 % des personnes à risque), cela permet de se faire une idée de l'impact de la sortie du groupe à risque auquel une personne appartient sur sa situation économique.

La figure 5 illustre que, pour les personnes à risque en 1993, la chance qu'elles soient pauvres de façon persistante est tributaire du fait qu'elles changeront de groupe ou non dans les années suivantes. En effet, pour les personnes à risque, demeurer dans le même groupe à risque jusqu'en 1998 fait en sorte de plus que doubler leurs chances de pauvreté persistante par rapport aux personnes qui deviennent non à risque à un moment donné (37,8 % vs 15,8 % respectivement).

Figure 5: **Taux de pauvreté persistante entre 1993 et 1998 des personnes à risque, selon qu'elles sont restées à risque toutes les années durant cette période ou non**

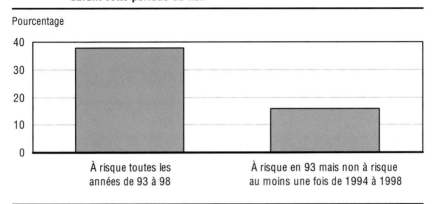

Enfin, le dernier moyen efficace mentionné pour que les personnes à risque échappent à la pauvreté persistante, c'est qu'elles possèdent le moins de facteurs de risque d'exclusion sociale possible ou, en d'autres mots, qu'elles ne fassent pas partie de plus d'un groupe à risque à la fois. En effet, dans la présente analyse, appartenir à un groupe à risque n'exclut pas la possibilité de faire partie des autres groupes à risque. Ainsi, il est assez aisé de figurer que généralement une personne qui fait partie, par exemple, d'une famille monoparentale dont le principal soutien économique est un Autochtone hors réserve et a des limitations au travail, est plus susceptible de vivre de la pauvreté persistante qu'une personne qui vit dans une famille monoparentale mais dont le principal soutien économique n'a aucun autre facteur de risque d'exclusion. La figure 6 à l'appui, il s'avère en fait qu'un peu plus d'une personne sur deux a connu la pauvreté persistante entre 1993 et 1998 chez celles qui faisaient partie de plus d'un groupe à risque en 1993 tandis que cette proportion chute à un peu plus d'une personne sur cinq chez celles ne faisant partie que d'un seul groupe à risque cette même année.

Figure 6: Taux de pauvreté persistante entre 1993 et 1998, selon que le principal soutien économique fait partie de plus d'un groupe à risque à la fois ou non en 1993

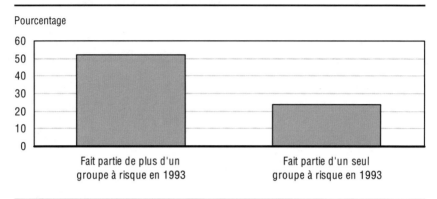

Pourcentage

Fait partie de plus d'un groupe à risque en 1993   Fait partie d'un seul groupe à risque en 1993

Ce qui explique la meilleure performance économique de long terme des Autochtones hors réserve parmi les groupes à risque

Dans la section précédente, il a été démontré que quatre principales « caractéristiques » permettent aux personnes à risque d'éviter plus souvent la pauvreté persistante.[23] Il s'agit d'un niveau de scolarité élevé, de la participation au marché du travail, de la sortie du groupe À risque vers le groupe Non à risque et d'avoir le moins de facteurs de risque d'exclusion sociale possible. Comme les membres du groupe Autochtone hors réserve sont ceux qui évitent le plus fréquemment la pauvreté persistante dans l'ensemble des membres des groupes à risque, on s'attend à ce qu'ils possèdent, du moins en partie, ces caractéristiques. Or, il semble que ces caractéristiques n'expliquent pas de façon évidente la meilleure performance économique des Autochtones hors réserve.

En effet, de toutes les personnes à risque, celles faisant partie du groupe Autochtone hors réserve sont celles qui ont le plus de chances de faire partie de plus d'un groupe à risque à la fois (voir figure 7). Pour être plus précis, près d'une personne Autochtone hors réserve sur trois possédait au moins un autre facteur de risque d'exclusion sociale en 1993. Tandis que dans les autres groupes, cette proportion variait entre moins de un sur dix chez les immigrants récents à un peu plus de un sur quatre chez les personnes limitées au travail.[24] Notamment, la monoparentalité est beaucoup plus fréquente dans le groupe Autochtone hors réserve que dans le reste de la population à l'étude. En effet, une personne sur cinq faisant partie d'une famille dans laquelle le principal soutien économique est Autochtone fait également partie d'une famille monoparentale alors que dans l'ensemble de l'échantillon à l'étude, on trouve plutôt une proportion de moins d'une personne sur 10 (soit 7,5 %, revoir figure 1). En outre, plus de 10 % des Autochtone hors réserve sont associés à un principal soutien économique qui a des limitations au travail, cette proportion n'étant surpassée que par le groupe Seule 45+.

Figure 7: **Proportion d'individus qui étaient dans plus d'un groupe à risque en 1993, selon le groupe**

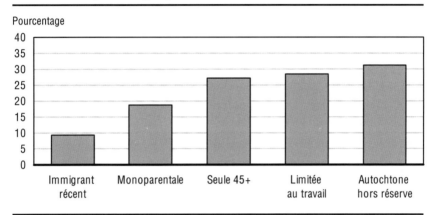

De plus, la figure 8 indique que peu de personnes faisant partie du groupe Autochtone hors réserve sont sorties de ce groupe dans les années suivant 1993 (18,6 %). Cette mobilité entre les groupes est d'ailleurs beaucoup plus fréquente chez les personnes limitées au travail (58,6 %), les personnes monoparentales (44,6 %) ainsi que chez les immigrants récents (33,2 %). Elle ne peut donc pas clairement expliquer la propension moindre des Autochtone hors réserve à connaître la pauvreté persistante parmi les différents groupes à risque.

Figure 8: **Proportion d'individus qui sont devenus non à risque au moins une année entre 1994 et 1998, selon le groupe**

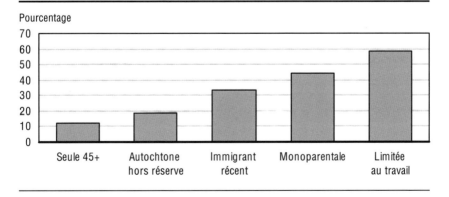

Enfin, il s'avère que le niveau d'éducation moyen des Autochtones hors réserve n'a pas non plus un rôle important à jouer dans l'explication du fait qu'ils échappent plus souvent à la pauvreté persistante puisque leur niveau d'éducation se situe plutôt dans la moyenne de ceux de l'ensemble des groupes à risque (voir figure 9). En fait, la proportion des personnes Autochtones hors réserve faisant partie de familles où le principal soutien économique détenait au moins un diplôme d'études secondaires en 1993 se situe environ à mi-chemin (69 %) entre celle des personnes faisant partie du groupe dans lequel le principal soutien économique détenait le moins fréquemment un DES, soit les personnes limitées au travail (59 %), et celle dans lequel il était le plus probable qu'il en détenait un, soit les immigrants récents (80 %).

Figure 9: **Proportion de personnes à risque dont le principal soutien économique avait au moins un diplôme d'études secondaires en 1993, selon le groupe**

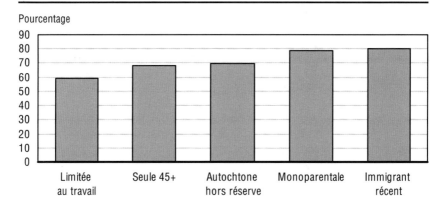

Note: N'inclut que les personnes dont on connaît la situation sur le marché du travail de leur principal souties économique.

Cependant, en dépit du fait que les principaux soutiens économiques Autochtones hors réserve ne sont pas particulièrement scolarisés, une plus grande proportion d'entre eux avait un emploi par rapport aux principaux soutiens économiques des autres groupes à risque.

Figure 10: Proportion de personnes à risque dont le principal soutien économique travaillait à temps plein, partiel ou de façon autonome en 1993, selon le groupe

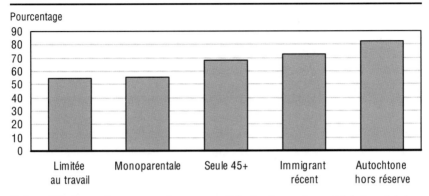

Pourcentage

Note: N'inclut que les personnes dont on connaît la situation sur le marché du travail de leur principal souties économique.

En effet, la figure 10 indique que les personnes faisant partie du groupe Autochtone hors réserve sont celles qui avaient le plus de chance de faire également partie d'une famille dans laquelle le principal soutien économique travaillait à temps plein, partiel ou de façon autonome en 1993 (83 %) parmi les groupes à risque. Qui plus est, selon la figure 11 qui suit, de toutes les personnes appartenant à une famille où le principal soutien économique travaillait en 1993, les Autochtones hors réserve occupaient le deuxième rang quant à celles qui étaient les plus susceptibles d'avoir fait partie d'une famille dont le principal soutien économique travaillait à temps plein toute l'année (68 %); tout de suite après les personnes seules 45 + (71 %).

Figure 11: Proportion de personnes à risque dont le principal soutien économique travaillait à temps plein toute l'année en 1993 sur l'ensemble de ceux qui travaillaient cette même année, selon le groupe

Pourcentage

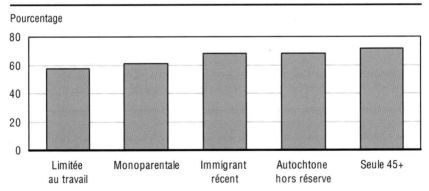

Note: N'inclut que les personnes dont on connaît la situation sur le marché du travail de leur principal souties économique.

Le principal soutien économique est donc, en général, plus enclin à travailler une année donnée s'il est Autochtone et vit hors réserve que s'il est monoparental, immigrant récent, limité au travail ou est seul et a 45 ans et plus. Mais de surcroît, selon les figures 12 et 13 subséquentes, il est aussi plus sujet à connaître une situation stable sur le marché du travail et à ne jamais dépendre des transferts gouvernementaux. En effet, une personne faisant partie du groupe Autochtone hors réserve en 1993 a plus de 50 % de chance que le principal soutien économique de sa famille ait tiré la majeure partie de son revenu d'un salaire ou d'un revenu d'emploi autonome jusqu'à la fin de la période étudiée soit, 1998. Et, bien que les personnes faisant partie du groupe Immigrant récent soient près de connaître cette même chance (49 %), celle-ci tombe à moins de 35 % dans les trois autres groupes à risque. Enfin, moins de 40 % des personnes Autochtones hors réserve sont associées à un principal soutien économique en 1993 dont le revenu familial dépendait à un moment ou à un autre des transferts gouvernementaux entre 1993 et 1998. Tandis que cette proportion varie entre environ 50 % et 70 % chez les autres groupes à risque.

Figure 12: **Proportion de personnes à risque dont le principal soutien économique de 1993 a eu comme principale source de revenu un salaire ou un revenu d'emploi autonome à toutes les années de 1993 à 1998, selon le groupe**

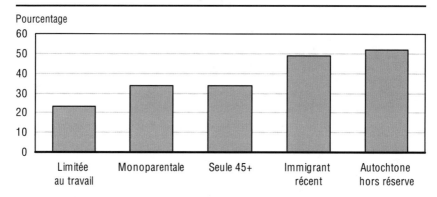

Note: N'inclut que les personnes dont on connaît la situation sur le marché du travail de leur principal souties économique.

Figure 13: Proportion de personnes à risque dont le principal soutien économique de 1993 n'a jamais eu comme principale source de revenu des transferts entre 1993 à 1998, selon le groupe

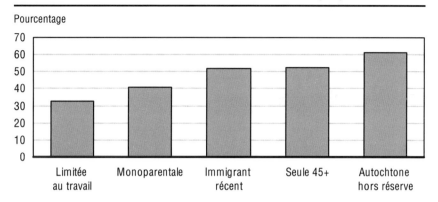

Pourcentage

Note: N'inclut que les personnes dont on connaît la situation sur le marché du travail de leur principal souties économique.

Ce qui explique la meilleure performance économique de certains Autochtones dans l'ensemble des Autochtones hors réserve

Dans les sections précédentes les chercheurs ont observé que les Autochtone hors réserve s'en tirent généralement mieux d'un point de vue économique que les membres des autres groupes à risque. De plus, il a été démontré que leur intégration plus importante et plus stable au marché du travail constitue la seule explication évidente de leur meilleure performance économique globale dans l'ensemble des groupes à risque. Toutefois, à l'intérieur même du groupe Autochtone hors réserve certaines caractéristiques propres à ce groupe font en sorte que les personnes qui les possèdent échappent de façon plus probante à la pauvreté persistante.

En effet, dans la plupart des groupes à risque, il est possible d'identifier certains de leurs membres qui sont plus sujets à connaître la pauvreté de long terme. Par exemple, dans le groupe Immigrant récent, des études ont démontré que les minorités visibles sont plus susceptibles de connaître des difficultés financières. Dans le cas des Autochtone hors réserve, il s'avère que ce sont les personnes qui vivent dans des familles où le principal soutien économique est inscrit en vertu de *la loi sur les Indiens du Canada* qui sont les plus enclines à faire face à ce genre de situation.

Figure 14: Taux de pauvreté persistante des Autochtones hors réserve entre 1993 et 1998, selon que leur principal soutien économique est inscrit ou non en 1993

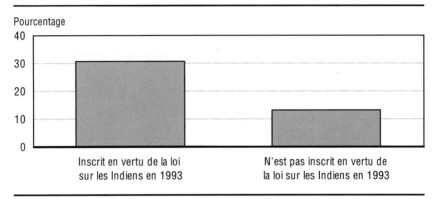

En effet, lorsque l'on considérait l'ensemble des Autochtone hors réserve, le risque qu'ils aient vécu de la pauvreté persistante entre 1993 et 1998 était de 18,6 % (revoir figure 2). Cette proportion amenait à conclure que leur risque de pauvreté persistante, quoique élevé par rapport aux personnes non à risque, était considérablement inférieur à celui des autres groupes à risque. Néanmoins, la figure 14 indique de façon claire que lorsque l'on se penche uniquement sur l'expérience en terme de pauvreté persistante des personnes Autochtone hors réserve mais dont le principal soutien économique de la famille était inscrit en vertu de la *loi sur les Indiens* en 1993, ce risque s'élève à 30,7 %. Contrairement à la précédente, cette dernière proportion ne permet pas de conclure que les Autochtones hors réserve s'en tire mieux économiquement que les autres groupes à risque puisqu'elle se situe à un niveau similaire aux proportions associées à ces derniers groupes (tel que vu à la figure 2 de la page 12, le taux de pauvreté persistante varie entre 27,6 % et 34,5 % dans chacun des quatre autres groupes à risque). Par conséquent, il semble que la bonne performance économique de long terme des Autochtone hors réserve par rapport aux autres groupes à risque soit en majeure partie attribuable à ceux qui ne sont pas inscrits.

Conclusion et prochaines étapes de recherche sur les Autochtones

Les Autochtones font partie des cinq groupes qui ont été identifiés comme particulièrement à risque de connaître l'exclusion sociale dans la population canadienne. Si ces groupes ont été identifiés comme tels, c'est que ceux-ci (les monoparentaux, les personnes seules de 45 ans et plus, les personnes avec limitations au travail, les immigrants récents et les Autochtones) sont plus sujets à être pauvres à un moment donné et à connaître des épisodes longs de pauvreté. Toutefois, ce constat effectué, le présent document s'attarde non plus à la comparaison de la performance économique de ces groupes dits à risque par rapport au reste de la population canadienne, mais à la comparaison des groupes entre eux. Ce faisant, les chercheurs veulent vérifier si la vulnérabilité à la pauvreté est similaire dans tous les groupes à risque et sinon, ils veulent savoir quelles sont les particularités de chacun d'entre eux.

Pour ce faire, les données longitudinales de l'Enquête sur la dynamique du travail et du revenu (EDTR) sont utilisées, ainsi qu'une mesure de pauvreté persistante permettant de prendre en compte trois différentes facettes influençant la situation de pauvreté de long terme des individus: le fait qu'ils aient connu la pauvreté à un moment donné, l'écart moyen entre le revenu familial et le seuil de faible revenu lorsqu'ils sont pauvres et la durée passée dans la pauvreté. Ces outils techniques ont permis de faire des constatations intéressantes concernant un groupe particulier d'Autochtones soit, les Autochtones vivant hors réserve. En effet, c'est le groupe, parmi les groupes à risque, pour lequel la meilleure performance économique a été observée entre 1993 et 1998.

En se fiant à l'expérience globale de l'ensemble de la population puis à celle de l'ensemble des groupes à risque, quatre pistes d'explications plausibles de cette meilleure performance relative sont proposées. La première a trait au niveau de scolarité atteint; la seconde est en rapport avec l'intégration au marché du travail; la troisième est relative à la mobilité entre le groupe à risque et non à risque, puisqu'on a observé que les personnes mobiles sont plus enclines à éviter la pauvreté persistante; et enfin, la dernière est liée au nombre de facteurs de risque d'exclusion sociale d'un individu car il s'avère que, plus un individu a de facteurs de risque, plus il a de chance d'être pauvre. Puisque ces relations sont en général véridiques, on s'attendait à ce que ces quatre raisons expliquent la meilleure performance relative des Autochtone hors réserve. Or, il semble qu'une seule d'entre elles l'explique clairement soit, l'intégration au marché du travail. En effet, les principaux soutiens économiques appartenant au groupe Autochtone hors réserve sont mieux intégrés au marché du travail canadien que ceux des autres groupes à risque. En d'autres mots, une personne a plus de chance de faire partie d'une famille dans laquelle la personne gagnant le revenu le plus élevé travaille une année donnée si cette dernière est Autochtone hors réserve que si elle fait partie de tout autre groupe à risque. Par ailleurs, le principal soutien économique autochtone hors réserve est plus susceptible d'avoir une situation stable sur le marché du travail et de ne jamais dépendre des transferts gouvernementaux. En effet, il y a une probabilité plus importante par rapport aux autres groupes à risque qu'une personne fasse partie d'une famille dont le principal soutien économique travaille durant toute la période à l'étude et dont la principale source de revenu ne provienne jamais des transferts. De façon étonnante, cette participation plus forte au marché du travail des Autochtones hors réserve par rapport aux autres groupes à risque est vraie en dépit du fait que leur niveau de scolarité n'est pas le plus élevé, que leur mobilité entre les groupes est rare comparée à celle de la majorité des autres groupes à risque et, qu'ils possèdent généralement plus de facteurs de risque que ces derniers.

Il faut cependant noter que les Autochtones vivant hors réserve qui ne sont pas inscrits en vertu de la *Loi sur les Indiens* du Canada s'en tirent économiquement beaucoup mieux que les autres. Or, les Autochtones hors réserve qui ne sont pas inscrits sont souvent des personnes dont un seul parent est Autochtone et/ou qui ont très peu ou pas du tout habité en réserve ce qui implique qu'ils s'apparentent davantage au reste de la population canadienne. Cela amène donc à se demander si, pour les Autochtones, sortir des réserves et se détacher de leur communauté d'origine constitue un bon moyen d'éviter les difficultés financières. Mais, si nous savons que les Autochtones hors réserve inscrits font face à un risque de pauvreté persistante plus important que ceux qui ne le sont pas, les présents résultats ne fournissent aucune information concernant la situation des Autochtones vivant dans les réserves. Ainsi, ils ne permettent pas de tirer des conclusions quant à la situation économique des Autochtones hors réserve inscrits par rapport à celle des Autochtones inscrits dans les réserves soit, deux populations davantage comparables pour permettre de tirer ce genre de conclusion. Il serait toutefois pertinent d'effectuer ce type de vérifications dans des travaux futurs mais pour ce faire, il faudra avoir recours à une autre source de données.

Notes de fin de chapitre

Les opinions exprimées dans les documents publiés par la Direction générale de la recherche appliquée sont celles des auteurs et ne reflètent pas nécessairement le point de vue de Développement des ressources humaines Canada ou du gouvernement fédéral. La série des documents de travail comprend des études analytiques et des travaux de recherche réalisés sous l'égide de la Direction générale de la recherche appliquée, Politique stratégique. Il s'agit notamment de recherches primaires, soit empiriques ou originales et parfois conceptuelles, généralement menées dans le cadre d'un programme de recherche plus vaste ou de plus longue durée. Les lecteurs de cette série sont encouragés à faire part de leurs observations et de leurs suggestions à l'auteure.

1. Utiliser le revenu après impôt plutôt que celui avant impôt permet de prendre en compte les effets de redistribution liés au régime fiscal en vigueur. Pour en savoir plus sur les pours et les contres de l'utilisation d'une mesure de faible revenu après impôt, voir: C. Cotton, et M. Webber (sept 2000).

2. La DGRA s'est intéressée à cette population cible puisque les personnes âgées de plus de 65 ans sont moins susceptibles que le reste de la population de connaître des périodes de faible revenu vu le régime de pensions auquel elles ont droit.

3. La mesure de la pauvreté fait aussi l'objet de débats dans la littérature. Dans le présent document, on considère alternativement comme « pauvre » ou « à faible revenu », une personne dont le revenu familial net est inférieur au seuil de faible revenu (SFR) après transferts et impôts qui lui est associé (base de 1992). Les seuils de faible revenu étant définis par Statistique Canada.

4. Le seuil de faible revenu associé à chaque personne une année donnée dépend de la taille du ménage auquel elle appartient ainsi que de la taille de la région où elle habite.

5. Tous les revenus ainsi que les seuils de faible revenu considérés dans ce document sont en dollars constants de 1993. En effet, il a déjà été observé que certaines personnes ayant un revenu familial très près du seuil de faible revenu entrent et sortent de la pauvreté avec de minimes variations de revenu. L'utilisation des dollars constants constitue une façon de réduire ce nombre d'entrées et de sorties puisque cela réduit le « bruit » dans les données.

6. L'échantillon exclut les habitants des territoires, les gens résidant en institution, *les personnes vivant dans les réserves* ainsi que les membres des Forces armées canadiennes vivant dans les casernes.

7. Pour en savoir plus sur les techniques d'imputation de Statistique Canada, voir L'EDTR, Guide de l'utilisateur, catalogue 75M0001GPF, 66.

8. Le poids longitudinal de l'EDTR proposé par Statistique Canada et qui contrôle entre autre pour l'attrition, a été utilisé.

9. Les chercheurs ont vérifié l'impact de ce choix antérieurement et, quoiqu'il amoindrisse les écarts observés entre la situation économique des groupes à risque par rapport aux groupes non à risque, il a peu d'impact sur les tendances globales observées.

10. Le concept de famille utilisé est celui de la famille économique, soit toutes les personnes habitant le même logement et étant apparentées par le sang, l'alliance ou l'adoption à un moment donné.

11. Le principal soutien économique de la famille est la personne qui a le revenu personnel (de toutes sources) le plus élevé.

12. Premièrement, l'échantillon initial de l'EDTR n'inclut pas les personnes vivant dans les réserves. C'est pourquoi, seuls les Autochtones hors réserve sont considérés. Deuxièmement, pour identifier les Autochtones vivant hors réserve, le critère « d'équité en matière d'emploi » a été choisi, c'est-à-dire que les Autochtones hors réserve ont été définis comme suit: toute personne qui a déclaré être Autochtone selon son origine ou selon qu'elle est inscrite aux termes de la loi sur les Indiens du Canada.

13. Il existe des valeurs manquantes aux variables relatives à l'immigration, aux limitations et au statut d'Autochtone. Cela implique que certaines personnes ne peuvent être associées à coup sûr au groupe À risque ou Non À risque.

14. Une personne peut se retrouver dans plus d'un groupe à risque à la fois. C'est pourquoi la somme des proportions associées à chacun des groupes Monoparentale, Seule 45+, Immigrant récent, Limitée au travail et Autochtone hors réserve n'équivaut pas à celle associée au groupe À risque.

15. Non pondéré, le nombre de personnes faisant partie de chacun des groupes à risque varie entre 395 chez le groupe Immigrants récents à 1754 chez le groupe Monoparentales. Avec les données du 1er panel de l'EDTR, pour que les résultats pondérés soient fiables et répondent aux standards de publication, il faut qu'ils soient calculés à partir de 25 observations ou plus et que pondérés, ils soient supérieurs ou égaux à 22 500 observations. C'est donc des conditions auxquelles les chercheurs se sont restreints tout au long de la présente étude.

16. Ce chiffre exclut les habitants de 77 réserves qui n'ont pas pris part au recensement, soit environ 44 000 individus.

17. Voir R. Morissette, et X. Zhang, 10.

18. Bulletin de la recherche appliquée, Développement des ressources humaines, Hiver/Printemps 6 (1): 21.

19. Dans la figure 4, aucune distinction n'a été faite quant au statut d'activité du principal soutien économique sur le marché du travail (travail à temps plein, partiel ou travail autonome).

20. Bulletin de la recherche appliquée, 3.

21. Dans ce type d'analyse, il existe plusieurs raisons qui font qu'une personne sort d'un groupe à risque particulier et devient non à risque. Par exemple, il est possible que les caractéristiques de la famille à laquelle elle appartient changent, que les caractéristiques du principal soutien économique changent, qu'elle change de famille ou que le principal soutien économique de la famille change. Mais, plus précisément, selon les travaux des auteurs, les principales raisons qui expliquent que les membres de chacun des groupes à risque sortent de leur groupe sont les suivantes:

    • Une grande proportion des immigrants récents cessent de l'être puisque cela fait plus de dix ans que le principal soutien économique a immigré.

    • Plusieurs personnes monoparentales cessent de l'être puisque le parent seul forme une union ou que le plus jeune enfant de la famille dépasse l'âge de 18 ans.

    • La grande majorité des personnes limitées au travail cessent de l'être puisque la limitation du principal soutien économique n'est que temporaire.

    • Les quelques personnes seules 45+ qui sortent de ce groupe le font en majorité parce qu'elles entrent en union.

    • Comme les Autochtones ne peuvent, en théorie, devenir non Autochtones, lorsque les Autochtone hors réserve sortent de ce groupe à risque c'est majoritairement parce que le principal soutien économique de la famille change ou qu'il change de famille.

22. Il existe aussi des personnes pour lesquelles la trajectoire entre les différents groupes de 1993 à 1998 est inconnue à cause des valeurs manquantes aux variables d'intérêt.

23. D'autres caractéristiques qui n'ont pas été exposées dans la section précédente sont susceptibles d'influencer les performances économiques des membres des groupes à risque comme l'âge moyen du principal soutien économique, le nombre moyen de personnes qui contribuent au revenu familial, etc. Or, des travaux préliminaires ont amené les chercheurs à limiter l'analyse en choisissant les quatre caractéristiques les plus pertinentes à l'étude ou en d'autres mots, à celles qui fournissaient les résultats les plus significatifs.

24. La présence des personnes seules de 45 ans et plus parmi les groupes à risque ne s'explique pas de façon aussi intuitive que celle des autres groupes à risque. Ainsi, certains travaux ont été effectués par des chercheurs de Développement des ressources humaines Canada pour comprendre la ou les raisons de leur présence dans le groupe à risque. Ces travaux ont principalement permis de trouver qu'une importante partie d'entre elles avait d'autres facteurs de risque d'exclusion sociale dont, le plus souvent, des limitations au travail (selon leurs observations, environ 25 % des personnes seules de 45 ans et plus avaient aussi des limitations au travail en 1993).

Bibliographie

Cotton, C., et Webber, M. 2000. *Devraient-on revoir les seuils de faible revenu?* Un résumé des commentaires formulés à l'égard du document de travail de Statistique Canada.

Développement des Ressources Humaines Canada. 2000. « Est-il toujours rentable d'investir dans un diplôme d'études postsecondaires? ». *Bulletin de la recherche appliquée*. Hiver/Printemps 6 (1): 21–25.

Développement des Ressources Humaines Canada. 2000. « Facteurs à risque élevé associés à la pauvreté et à l'exclusion ». *Bulletin de la recherche appliquée*. Hiver/Printemps 6 (1): 1–4.

Hatfield, M. 1997. *Concentration de la pauvreté et de la détresse dans les quartiers urbains du Canada*. Document de travail de la Direction générale de la recherche appliquée, Développement des ressources humaines Canada.

Le Soleil. 2001. *La politique autochtone fédérale*. Québec (29 octobre).

Affaires Indiennes et du Nord Canada. 2001. *Caractéristiques de la population active autochtone d'après le recensement de 1996*.

Morissette, R., et Zhang, X. 2001. « À faible revenu pendant plusieurs années ». *L'emploi et le revenu en perspective*. Statistique Canada 2 (3).

Paquet, B., et Schecter, S. 2000. « Inclusion et exclusion à l'aune de la sociologie luhmannienne: l'exemple de la pauvreté au Canada ». *Sociologie et Société* 32 (2).

Sliver, H. 1995. *Social Exclusion, Social Inclusion*. http:/www.democraticdialogue.org/report2/report2a.htm

Statistique Canada - EDTR. *Guide de l'utilisateur*. Cat. #75M0001GPF, 179.

Statistique Canada. 1998. « Le recensement de 1996: données sur les Autochtones ». *Le Quotidien* (13 janvier).

Statistique Canada. 2001. *Les Autochtones au Canada*. Série de profils du Centre canadien de la statistique juridique, N°85F0033MIF (juin).

Statistique Canada. 2001. *Les Canadiens à faible revenu*. Série de profils du Centre canadien de la statistique juridique, N°85F0033MIF.

Vera-Toscano, E., Phimister, E., et Weersink, A. 2001. *La dynamique du revenu et de l'emploi dans le Canada rural: le risque de la pauvreté et de l'exclusion*. Statistique Canada, Division de l'Agriculture, Document de travail 43 (février).

Adresses électroniques:

http://www.rural-europe.aeidl.be/rural-fr/biblio/exclusion/intro.htm

http://www.europarl.eu.int/igc1996/fiches/fiche40-fr.htm

3

Aboriginal Development: The Process Is Critical to Success

Cynthia Chataway

Introduction

With the resolution of outstanding claims and growing Aboriginal authority over their lands and resources, the potential for Aboriginal communities to grow economically is greater now than ever before. Anderson[1] notes that corporate-Aboriginal partnerships have increased enormously over the last ten years, primarily because business people believe that partnering with Aboriginal people will improve their long-term profitability. Concurrently, Aboriginal nations in Canada seem to be adopting an approach to economic development that includes business alliances among Aboriginal and non-Aboriginal people, and capacity building through education, institution building, and the acquisition of land and resources.[2] Within the Department of Indian Affairs, policy and practice increasingly emphasizes economic development and good governance—structural changes that can make important differences in the lives of Aboriginal people.

The process by which these structural changes are brought about can either undermine or develop the cohesiveness of the social systems they impact. Cohesiveness, or the ability of a community to deal effectively with collective problems, can make the difference in dealing with problems that inevitably arise in the course of development. The research reviewed in this chapter strongly suggests that the cohesiveness of the social system is essential to successful development.

Unfortunately, social cohesion is low in many Aboriginal communities. While factionalism is present in all political systems, the factionalism and distrust that exist in Aboriginal communities may be deeper given more than a century of colonization. In many communities, the introduction of Band Council elections by the Canadian government took power away from subgroups within the communities (e.g., women/men, youth/elders, different families) that, under traditional systems, had often had some form of built-in representation.[3] The Band Councils were not initially designed for self-governance, but rather to administer the laws of the Canadian state. Greater authority and control has been acquired by Band Councils over time, but in a way that has sometimes created deep internal power struggles and a sense of ambivalence toward the Band Council system, which is neither well-designed nor culturally appropriate.[4]

Societies with similar resource endowments, labour capacity, capital, governance structures and governance procedures can have very different levels of economic performance. The process by which development takes place, and the impact this has on the cohesiveness of the social system, sets the foundation on which training and infusions of capital (the focus of much development literature)[5] make a lasting difference or not. Sustainable ends and means are inseparable.[6]

After reviewing some of the recent research on social capital and social cohesion, this chapter outlines the kind of process that is most likely to support long-term development, at least in part because of its ability to increase social cohesion. This process begins with a collective definition of cultural values that creates the possibility for building social cohesion in the context of personal, social and institutional empowerment, which provides the necessary base for economic and institutional development. Key principles of this process are that it be, (1) consistent with cultural values, (2) focussed initially on building working relationships across groups, and (3) actively inclusive.

Social Capital and Successful Development

A growing body of research suggests that the difference between successful and unsuccessful economic and political development is attributable to the "social capital" of that system. Social capital refers to the generalized trust embedded in informal networks and associations through which decision making and policy formation occur.[7] The term currently used to describe successful political development is "good governance." Good governance refers to characteristics such as democratic elections, stable laws, constitutional legitimacy, transparency, tolerance, public participation, absence of corruption, freedom of information, accountability regimes, administrative competence and independence of government from the judiciary and the media.[8] Good governance and social networks of trust and cooperation are thought to be so mutually reinforcing that the terms Government Social Capital and Civil Social Capital have emerged to refer to each.[9]

In general, the more people who are engaged together in a variety of civic associations—from singing groups to informal loan cooperatives—the higher the level of generalized trust and cooperative problem solving in the system[10] and the greater the strength and productivity of that community.[11]

Social networks of trust, in combination with accountable government and stable laws, are thought to contribute to economic development because they allow a more free-flowing exchange of information, reduce the uncertainty and inefficiency of transactions, and increase the incentives for producing wealth and creating jobs (rather than diverting wealth from others). Considerable research indicates that economic development, a well-developed governance infrastructure and greater levels of social capital tend to co-occur.[12] Engagement in civic associations also seems to lead to greater self-respect and facility in the skills necessary for democratic participation.[13]

A questionnaire study of eight northern Aboriginal communities explored the interconnections between social vitality, economic viability, and political efficacy.[14] Similar to social capital, social vitality refers to informal reciprocal relations through which community members share information and resolve problems. Similar to good governance, political efficacy refers to the extent to which the community has a commonly acceptable process for mobilizing power and distributing resources so that decisions can be made and initiatives collectively launched. Economic viability refers to the ability of a community to sustain the material needs of its members over the long term.

This study[15] found that social vitality was more important to supporting economic viability and political efficacy than vice versa. Economic viability decreased wherever development was initiated in a community that had low social vitality and/or low political efficacy. They also found that social vitality was the hardiest community characteristic of the three, as it could compensate for low economic viability and low political efficacy to some extent; however, economic and political strength could not compensate for low social vitality. Economic viability was found to be most fragile— once it was lost both social vitality and political efficacy were required to regain it.

Case studies in Aboriginal contexts concur that the ability of the community to solve collective problems through formal and informal networks and associations seems to be crucial to economic and political success. If community members are not effectively connected for decision making and collective problem solving, structural changes tend to "come apart behind them"[16] through lack of commitment or even because community members actively undermine initiatives. The Royal Commission on Aboriginal Peoples reflected these concerns in concluding that rebuilding a sense of trust and connectedness is necessary for the successful growth of civil, economic and political institutions.[17]

The current governance system within Aboriginal communities puts considerable power and resources into the hands of the elected Grand Chief with few checks and balances. Within the "first past the post" electoral system, the candidate from the largest family can be consistently elected, giving that family the power to control resources and make decisions over time. This creates the conditions within which social vitality is frequently reduced. "A significant proportion of band members, then, feel shut out from political processes and reliant on this elite for any improvement in their social and economic well-being."[18] "Now that five, six, and perhaps seven generations have been subjected to the powers of extra-community exploitation, domination, and alienation, similar powers have taken root within their communities. Outsiders are no longer required for negative, demeaning, and dehumanizing treatment to occur."[19]

Outsiders can unknowingly exacerbate this disempowering situation by working *exclusively* with the "existing authority structure" as represented by the Band Council. Erasmus and Ensign[20] recommend that entry into a community *must be* through the Band Council, but this directive can be over-applied to mean that outsiders must work *only* with the Band Council. Of course, it can be just as destructive to successful development to be perceived as going around the Band Council—or to undermine that authority—as it is to marginalize other voices. What is required is a delicate process of respecting Band Council authority to make decisions on behalf of the community on the one hand, and of listening to and integrating diverse interests on the other hand. If outsiders do not take the opportunity to create and strengthen constructive social relations and networks, as detailed later in this chapter, "development can destroy social capital, setting off a vicious circle of social and economic decline."[21]

However, it is important to realize that not all forms of social capital support economic development. Social capital that extends beyond the immediate group, and exists in multiple overlapping social groupings with crosscutting ties, is more likely to support economic growth. When trust is restricted to a particular social group, the obligations to that group can limit participation in broader networks outside the group, which is important to continued economic growth. In addition, groups can place highly particularistic demands on group members: restricting innovation, individual expression and the belief in the possibility of advancement through individual effort.[22] Particularly when trust is restricted to immediate family or ethnic attachments, members can be discouraged from advancing economically, moving geographically and engaging in amicable dispute resolution with others outside the group.[23] Thus, any initiatives that contribute to the development of multiple overlapping networks of trust are also contributing to the potential long-term prosperity and success of these communities.

The Importance of Process

Social capital, which has also been called generalized or "working" trust, is clearly important. The process by which generalized trust is developed is less clear, but is likely central to whether social capital results in negative or positive effects. A broader concept, social cohesion, seems to encompass the means by which the positive forms of social capital are developed. Social cohesion describes the state of a community in which there is a sense of collective identity, equality of opportunity and inclusion, broad-based participation in decision making and a capacity to mediate rather than suppress conflict.[24] So in addition to identification and trust, social cohesion includes broad participation in finding solutions to conflict. Research finds that participating with others in a process of collective problem solving results in greater commitment and implementation of solutions developed than other forms of problem solving (e.g., in which an outside party makes the decision).[25]

The importance of process, in addition to good structures, is often overlooked. However, a brief reflection on one's own experiences with decision making indicates that the same outcome—depending upon how it is arrived at—can alienate, divide and anger us, or can connect, empower and reassure us.[26] This sense of procedural justice, the sense that one has had a voice and been treated respectfully, is so important that it has been found to predict our level of trust in our political representatives—independent of whether decisions are made in our favour or not.[27] For instance, the almost universally opposed White Paper (proposed in 1969 to terminate the *Indian Act*) may have been largely acceptable to Aboriginal people if it had been developed through a broad-based decision-making process with Aboriginal people.[28]

Procedural fairness is most important to maintaining support for leadership when new organizations are being created, or when there is strong dissatisfaction with the distribution of resources,[29] as is the case in Aboriginal communities today. In research on governments in transition around the world, Reilly and Reynolds[30] found that the uncertainty of the transition period is best countered by maximizing inclusiveness in decision making. Dukes[31] found that participating in community decision making results in an increased sense of connection with leadership and the practices of governance, a greater sense of meaning and community, and optimism about solving social problems. Without broad-based participation in decision making, communities can fragment and consume resources in contentious debate, or opposition goes underground only to resurface later in destructive ways.

Processes to Build Social Cohesion

Processes that involve people in a meaningful way in collective decision making increase social cohesion. To do this well may take considerable time depending on how well the issues are defined, prior experience of the parties with collaboration and the need to equalize power differences.[32] Investment in a good process within which people feel it is safe and desirable to participate is an investment in the social infrastructure of a system, and in developing the web of mutual obligation and interconnection that is integral to successful economic development.

The characteristics of a good process can vary considerably across contexts and cultures. The principles of a good process are more consistent when (1) grounded in cultural values; (2) working relationships are prioritized before making structural decisions; and (3) when actively inclusive through attention to all aspects of empowerment.

Consistent with Cultural Values

Aboriginal people in Canada are in a period of restoration, which involves relearning of historical Aboriginal traditions, animated by a set of foundational ideas. These ideas include: holism or the interconnectedness of things, sharing and collectivity, respect, life as a learning journey, and guidance from elders.[33]

Research indicates that institutions and initiatives in Aboriginal communities are more likely to succeed if Aboriginal people can identify with them. They are then perceived to be grounded in culturally relevant values. For instance, in my own questionnaire research, I found that the degree to which people perceived the elected Band Council to be culturally appropriate was a much stronger predictor of whether people supported the Council than the extent to which Band Council decision making was perceived as fair. People across this community said things like: "I agree with everything they [the Band Council] are doing, but don't do it in an illegitimate way" or "It's not an acceptable system, it's a combination and bastardization of the traditional system and elective system."[34]

In economic research on Native American reservations,[35] researchers coded communities for whether the structure, scope, source and location of authority in traditional government matched these characteristics in the current governmental system. They determined that there was a "cultural match" if they judged these four characteristics to be the same in both traditional and current government. Across sixty-seven American Indian reserves, holding constant variables such as human capital endowments, natural resource endowments, and marketplace opportunities, a "cultural match" was related to higher levels of employment and income.[36]

In an in-depth interview study, Aboriginal administrators indicated that they are often faced with an almost impossible task of balancing internal social and cultural needs with political demands.[37] For instance, if they acquire formal education (one of the most frequent suggestions for good governance) they are perceived to distance themselves from the cultural and local needs of their community, which delegitimizes them as local leaders. This kind of dilemma cannot be resolved by an individual leader alone. To resolve this and myriad other dilemmas faced by Aboriginal leaders requires collective decisions by community members. These collective decisions provide direction for leaders struggling to meet the demands of working effectively with outsiders while remaining legitimate in the eyes of their constituency.

In some communities, leadership initiatives can be effectively blocked by calling into question the Aboriginal identity of the initiators.[38] Given centuries of pressure to assimilate and considerable intermarriage, there are few "pure blood" Aboriginal people left. Hence, many Aboriginal people can become delegitimized by questioning whether their heritage is truly Aboriginal. Such attacks on their cultural identity can be quite painful. It is understandable that outsiders want to keep some distance from these internal issues. However, it is because of the central importance of unresolved identity conflicts and their ability to block successful change that outside partners would do well to offer support for resolving them. Outsiders, who do not have the same vulnerability, can make unique contributions to resolving these conflicts through initiating and supporting the development of working relationships within which collective decisions can be made.

In a study comparing two Aboriginal organizations, one that was successful and one that was unsuccessful at adopting Aboriginal traditions, Newhouse and Chapman[39] found that in the successful organization change began with a collective commitment to culturally appropriate principles (rather than structural change). This traditional code of principles was put on display, and in dialogue with each other, organization members proceeded to discover how to bring their behaviour into consonance with the code. Structural change never took place as the goal of becoming more traditional was met to the satisfaction of the members through this culturally grounded process.

Becoming culturally grounded does not necessarily require radical change. Slight cultural nuances can mean the difference between people's willingness to accept leadership[40] and their willingness to participate in a process.[41] Grounding in a set of values with which all can identify, and to which all have committed, provides clarity and safety within limits acceptable to all. The collective process of developing these limits together can be an important contribution to social cohesion, and, ultimately, successful development.

Prioritize Working Relationships

> You can have the most beautifully worded constitution, with the clearest recognition of the inherent right of self government, but if communities can't deal with themselves it's all for naught.[42]

Considerable research recommends a sequenced approach to structural change in divided societies—first, relationship building, followed by structural change. If relations between people and groups are hostile, communication has broken down and trust is low. A process to improve relationships is initially recommended before attempting to reach agreement on concrete issues.[43] It is very difficult for people in such a situation to alter their perspectives and behaviour patterns without the assistance of an outside party.

Experimental research has contrasted two types of intervention: (1) an outside party facilitates dialogue designed to improve communication and understanding between disputants; and (2) an outside party focuses interaction between disputants on reaching an agreement. When the outsider facilitates dialogue to improve understanding, the disputant's perceptions of both the chances for ultimate agreement and an improvement in the relationship (e.g., increased trust) are significantly higher than when the outsider focuses upon reaching agreement.[44] A process designed to arrive at substantive agreements ideally takes place after, or at least concurrent with, a facilitated process to develop working relationships—particularly if relations between the parties are hostile.[45]

Aboriginal people often speak about the need to rebuild good working relationships in their communities, to provide an appropriate climate to rebuild the human foundations of self-government and negotiating or mediating structural arrangements and constitutional change.[46] Ethical guidelines for the Royal Commission on Aboriginal Peoples (RCAP) prescribed that whenever possible conflict between interests within the community should be identified and resolved in advance of commencing a project.[47] How this was to be done was left unspecified. Summarizing Aboriginal testimony to the RCAP, John O'Neil[48] noted that, although theoretical models identify structural change as a necessary precondition to change in people's lives, roundtable participants said that change occurs through communicative action and a dialogic process among individuals, communities and social institutions.

Susskind, McKearnan, and Thomas-Larmer have specified four preconditions to consensus building. First, there must be a good third party who can explain the process clearly to participants and then effectively manage the process from beginning to end. Second, participants must commit to consensus-building ground rules, preferably in writing. Third, sufficient time is required to allow participants to shift from an adversarial mindset to considering how to meet the needs of all parties. Finally, one needs a clear map of how to build consensus. Their map is detailed in the *Consensus Building Handbook.*[49]

Active Inclusivity

> We have always done consensus building. We call a community meeting for people to put in their two cents. If they don't speak up, that's their problem.[50]

The above quote from an elected Band Councillor illustrates a form of token consultation with community members rather than real sharing of decision-making power. The quote also illustrates a passive form of participation in which those with a stake in the decision are not assisted in effectively participating. This approach to development is fairly common— community members are simply invited to express their opinions.[51] Unfortunately, this approach does little to alter existing power relations, and thus development initiatives tend to reinforce the status quo. What is needed is real empowerment rather than token gestures and invitations to participate.[52] The ideal situation is one in which all stakeholders are committed to reaching consensus within a situation, and all have equal, respectful and complete opportunities to participate.[53]

People who have been shut out of decision making—who have experienced numerous broken promises, have been told for generations that they do not have the capability to understand or contribute, or feel very vulnerable to their leadership—require considerable support and reassurance before they will enter into dialogue. Formal processes and institutions, individual characteristics and social conditions are all crucial to the experience of real empowerment.[54] Formal empowerment, in which institutions provide mechanisms for real public influence, must combine with relevant individual skills and social norms that support participation. An empowering process engages people as co-participants and designers of their own change, particularly orchestrating the experience of empowerment among the "silent majority."[55]

Formal Empowerment

Formal institutional empowerment means that institutions and professionals are committed to sharing power; to entering into a decision-making process of mutual vulnerability in which no party has the ability to make unilateral decisions. This is very different from simply giving people a voice or access to speak to the decision-makers.[56] Giving people a voice has often been used by powerful groups as a way of manipulating, co-opting, or placating lower power groups.[57] In many Aboriginal communities, open community meetings are generally considered a waste of time since most people do not attend and meetings may be dominated by an angry few. Authorities need to actively seek out those who do not attend meetings to understand their perspectives, create small decision-making groups of people who have not been involved before and ensure that the range of perspectives are integrated into decisions. Elected chiefs and corporate representatives who make a commitment to balanced representation on all committees from the various stakeholder groups (e.g., each clan) and set a high criterion for finalizing decisions (i.e., greater than majority rule), can make an enormous difference in the lives of underrepresented people.

Personal Empowerment

Even when people are formally empowered through inclusion on decision-making committees, they need a sense of personal competence and possibility, and the actual capacity to participate (e.g., knowledge, material resources, persuasive ability) before participation can result.[58] Material changes and capacity building are frequently required to change power dynamics within the community.[59] This might involve training in literacy, basic accounting, public speaking, or covering the expenses for people to both prepare for and attend meetings. The specific kind of capacity building that would support active participation by the "silent majority" is best determined in early private consultation with the individuals themselves, or perhaps through a community survey.[60]

Social Empowerment

Finally, social conditions of mutual respect and honesty are important for an experience of true empowerment and ability to participate. While many Aboriginal people hold values of consensus building, respect and honesty, a self-protective atmosphere of distrust and cynicism frequently pre-dominates. Facilitating social norms that make it safe to express different opinions and to develop consensus on actions to be taken is crucial. Developing a sense of collective identification, shared vision, ownership and responsibility (as suggested above) may help to overcome the disrespect and distrust that prevent a sense of social empowerment.[61]

Putting It Together

The interdependence of cultural values, social cohesion, empowerment, economic development and self-government is illustrated in Figure 1.[62] The sixteen elements included in this model by the First Nations Development Institute (FNDI) have consistently been identified as important indicators of successful development for more than a decade of "working with tribes and Native people to change the economic environment of reservations to one that builds on local resources, recognizes Native knowledge and culture, and supports development from within."[63] Concentric circles indicate levels of development with the individual at the centre, followed by the group, then the community and finally the nation on the outside. While attention to these elements seems to occur spontaneously, the FNDI now uses this figure to assist community leaders and external parties in identifying and enhancing the elements that are less strong.

Figure 2 is adapted from the FNDI model. The labels for the quadrants of the wheel are renamed to correspond with the terminology used in this chapter: cultural values, social cohesion, empowerment, self-government and economic development. The research reviewed above suggests that these elements are mutually supporting, and, for any particular initiative, may best be pursued in sequential order starting from a collective definition of cultural values. The following example illustrates how an initial commitment to active inclusivity and consensus decision making clarified collective values and enhanced social cohesion and empowerment, which supported structural change.

Figure 1: The elements of development

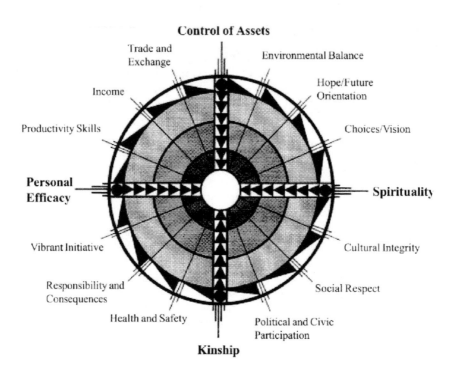

© First Nations Development Institute, reprinted with permission.

Figure 2:   The process to successful development

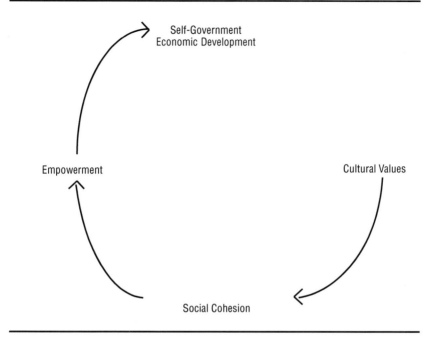

A Mohawk Example[64]

This community was very divided. Only 10 to 15 percent of eligible voters participated in Band Council elections, and there was no constructive involvement by the three traditional Longhouses in community decision making. Band Council initiatives were consistently criticized and delegitimized by the Longhouses because the Band Council was "not a Mohawk system." Divisions between the Longhouses were deeply antagonistic and personalized.

Because the various factions in the community initially refused to meet together, I actively sought out input from as many individuals within each group as possible. After several weeks of discussion on possible focuses for our work, members of all groups agreed to work on the question: "What are the barriers to designing and adopting a new structure of government in this community?"

Each faction contributed questions to be asked in interviews. These questions tended to ask for people's opinion about the technical design of a new system of government. Responses to these questions in interviews, however, frequently focused on the values that should underlie community decision making: the need to embody Mohawk culture, to protect Mohawk culture and land, to treat everyone respectfully and for all relevant information to be openly communicated. Focus groups within each interest group also endorsed these values and emphasized the need for more trust, a greater sense of community and clarity about their cultural identity. To meet these needs, focus groups recommended that representatives of each group meet together for facilitated dialogue.

This intergroup dialogue most directly reflected the interdependence between developing better working relationships within the community and bringing about structural change. In the first few meetings the group focused on constructing a structural model for community self-government. However, when we arrived at a model with which all felt comfortable, group members immediately raised concerns about trust, cultural legitimacy and security. For instance, any cooperation with the traditional leaders raised fears of betrayal and a sense that, given their own internal divisions, the Longhouses could not really be trusted to act consistently with the traditional ideals. Any cooperation with the elected leaders raised fears that foreign processes would be introduced and that their cultural future would be jeopardized. So we focussed the dialogue on how the Longhouse and Band Council members of this group could model respectful interaction and constructive discussion of conflictual issues for the community. In the course of this discussion, people began to raise questions about their own abilities to engage constructively in the community and to consider the need for personal capacity building. By the last meeting several members had launched new projects for developing greater social vitality (e.g., pairing elders with youth, family conferencing).

At subsequent public meetings members of the group modelled respectful problem solving where insults and attacks had predominated before. For example, when community members responded aggressively to the speech of a member of a Longhouse that is considered to be "extremist," a member of our dialogue group (from a different faction) stood up and explained the valuable ideas that were embedded in the somewhat "extreme" speech.

Community members went on to organize many subsequent collaborative initiatives, such that now several acceptable models of government are before the community, most of which combine the elected Band Council and the Longhouse systems. In addition, the Band Council regularly undertakes extensive consultations with traditional people regarding negotiations with the federal government and other major decisions.[65] As one elected councillor said:

> We're trying to perfect the consultative process in the council, in that we take a personal interest in going to select individuals who are representative in the community and speaking to them and having sort of what you would call focus group sessions where

individuals are invited to come and review policies. . . . soliciting opinions on paper doesn't always work either. I think you just have to get there, sort of the same way you're doing with your research. I mean you have to get there and talk to people. . . . Everyone should have input, everyone who is affected by it.[66]

In this deeply divided Aboriginal community, participants welcomed the opportunity to develop a "working relationship" before beginning to discuss changes to the structure of government. They remarked: "We've never done it before. We always jump right into the nitty gritty, without clearing the air first. It may be lengthy but we have to address these issues" of distrust and destructive communication patterns. "That's just what we need. I was thinking about that. We always just jump right into a task, and get hung up on name calling, pointing fingers."[67]

A consultation service has emerged in the community and is frequently hired by the elected council to collect broad-based community input through focus groups, open community meetings, questionnaires, interviews, workshops and other methods. This private company takes care to educate people about the details of a policy before asking their opinion, actively reaching out to inform and involve people in decision making.

In 2000, the elected council made a formal declaration to return to traditional government and asked for volunteers to form a committee to identify the steps to this goal. This group includes traditional people, elected people and other community members.

Implications for Partnerships with Aboriginal Communities

Corporate or governmental partnerships with Aboriginal communities have similar opportunities to support a balanced approach to structural change. Corporate and governmental partners of Aboriginal communities can provide crucial support to Aboriginal leaders who want to ground structural change in mutually acceptable cultural values and actively inclusive processes that enhance personal, social and institutional empowerment. It can be very difficult for existing leaderships within Aboriginal communities to initiate this kind of process on their own when there are entrenched negative patterns of interaction. A professional facilitator helps to manage this delicate process, which allows all stakeholders to fully participate and to maintain a constructive atmosphere as they adjust to a new way of relating to each other.[68] External facilitation and support in time and resources can also generate the confidence necessary to enter this kind of process[69] and make it possible for a broad range of people to actively participate. In addition, if trusting, working relationships with external parties are formed the base broadens within which social capital is developed, mitigating its potential negative effects. Over time, inclusive decision-making processes can be established in more permanent organizations, creating a vibrant civil sector to balance and support the economic and governmental sectors in Aboriginal communities.

Numerous sources document the success of broad-based collaborative decision-making in private industry,[70] national environmental efforts,[71] community disputes[72] and organizational settings.[73] In these examples, all parties that have a stake in the outcome of a decision can safely express their perspectives because there is an agreed-upon process for working with disagreements. When this kind of social cohesion is not present in Aboriginal communities, spending time up front to develop constructive working relationships is recommended before undertaking self-government or land claims negotiations and before making concrete decisions about economic development.

Conclusion

Development efforts in Aboriginal communities tend to focus on structural control and responding to technical needs. Clearly these are necessary considerations for economic success and self-government. However, an exclusive focus on structure and technical details neglects the importance of informal social relations, the quality of working relationships and the contributions these make to long-term development and self-determination. When outside parties partner with a community they have the opportunity to contribute to strengthening the social infrastructure, which in turn strengthens any structural initiatives. This does not mean a delay in structural changes, but a balanced investment of time and resources to create greater social cohesiveness, ideally before formal negotiations begin.

Endnotes

A version of this paper was previously published as: C.J. Chataway, "Successful Development in Aboriginal Communities: Does it Depend upon a Particular Process?" *Journal of Aboriginal Economic Development* 3 (1): 76–88.

1. R.B. Anderson, "Corporate/Indigenous Partnerships in Economic Development: The First Nations in Canada," *World Development* 25 (9): 1483–1503.

2. R.B. Anderson and R.M. Bone, "First Nations Economic Development," *Journal of Aboriginal Economic Development* 1 (1): 13–34.

3. T. Alfred, *Peace Power and Righteousness* (Toronto: Oxford University Press, 1999).

4. F. Cassidy and R. Bish, *Indian Self-Government: Its Meaning in Practice* (Lantzville, B.C.: Oolichan Books, 1989); C.J. Chataway, "Imposed Democracy: Political Alienation and Perceptions of Justice in an Aboriginal Community" (Ph.D. diss., Harvard University, 1994). However, there have been many gains in the last twenty years, in both structural control and social vitality, which should be recognized and celebrated. That is the focus of a research program on *Understanding the Strengths of Indigenous Communities* that can be found at: www.usic.ca.

5. R.B. Anderson, "Corporate/Indigenous Partnerships in Economic Development," 1483–1503; S.E. Cornell and J.P. Kalt, "Successful Economic Development and Heterogeneity of Governmental Form on American Indian Reservations" in *Getting Good Government: Capacity Building in the Public Sectors of Developing Countries*, ed. M. Grindle (Cambridge, M.A.: Harvard University Press, 1998), 257–298; Institute on Governance, *Exploring the Relationship between Aboriginal Peoples and the Canadian Forest Industry* (Study Report completed for the Canadian Forest Service, Natural Resources Canada, 1998); P. Sloan and R. Hill, *Corporate Aboriginal Relations: Best Practice Case Studies* (Altona, M.N.: Friesen Printers, 1995); United Nations Development Programme, *Governance for Sustainable Human Development* (New York, N.Y.: UNDP, 1997), also available at http://magnet.undp.org/policy/default.htm.

6. M. Wackernagel, *Framing the Sustainability Crisis: Getting from Concern to Action* (Sustainable Development Research Institute, University of British Columbia, 1997). Http://www.sdri.ubc.ca/publications/Wackerna.html.

7. C. Grootaert, "Social Capital: The Missing Link?" (World Bank, Social Capital Initiative, Working Paper No. 3, 1998).

8. See Institute on Governance, *Exploring the Relationship between Aboriginal Peoples*; United Nations Development Programme, *Governance for Sustainable Human Development*.

9. S. Knack, "Social Capital, Growth and Poverty: A Survey of Cross-Country Evidence" (World Bank, Social Capital Initiative, Working Paper No. 7, 1999).

10. J. Helliwell and R. Putnam, "Economic Growth and Social Capital in Italy," *Eastern Economic Journal* 21 (1995): 295–307; D. Stolle, "Bowling Together, Bowling Alone: The Development of Generalized Trust in Voluntary Associations," *Political Psychology* 19 (3): 497–526; L. Young, "Civic Engagement, Trust and Democracy: Evidence from Alberta" (Trends seminar on Value Change and Governance, Toronto, 1999).

11. J. J. Mondak, "Special Issue: Psychological Approaches to Social Capital," *Political Psychology* 19 (3).

12. S. Knack and P. Keefer, "Does Social Capital Have an Economic Payoff? A Cross-Country Investigation," *Quarterly Journal of Economics* 112 (4): 1251–1288; E. Pantoja, "Exploring the Concept of Social Capital and its Relevance for Community-Based Development" (World Bank, Social Capital Initiative, Working Paper No. 18, 1999).

13. P. Dekker, R. Koopmans, and A. vanden Broek, "Voluntary Associations, Social Movements and Individual Political Behavior in Western Europe" in *Private Groups and Public Life: Social Participation, Voluntary Associations and Political Involvement in Representative Democracies*, ed. J. van Deth (London: Routledge, 1997), 220–240; S. Verba, K. Schlozman, and H. Brady, *Voice and Equality: Civic Voluntarism in American Politics* (Cambridge, M.A.: Harvard University Press, 1995).

14. B. Blishen and A. Lockhart, *Socio-Economic Impact Model for Northern Development* (Ottawa: Department of Indian Affairs, 1979).

15. Blishen and Lockhart, *Socio-Economic Impact Model for Northern Development*.

16. C. Wesley-Esquimaux, I. Johnson, and C.J. Chataway, *The Relationship between Systemic Change, Cultural Renaissance, and Personal Healing in Aboriginal Communities* (CASCA, Canadian Anthropological Meetings, Toronto, 1998).

17. Royal Commission on Aboriginal Peoples, *Report of the Royal Commission on Aboriginal Peoples* (Ottawa: Canada Communications Group, 1996).

18. W. McKay, *Instruments of Governance: Restoring First Nations Governments* (Prepared for CESO, Aboriginal Services, 1999), 230.

19. W.J. Mussell, "Deficits, Foundations and Aspirations Signal Need for Restructuring" in *A Path to Healing: Report of the National Round Table on Aboriginal Health and Social Issues* (Royal Commission on Aboriginal Peoples, 1993), 114.

20. P. Erasmus and G. Ensign, *A Practical Framework for Community Liaison Work in Native Communities* (Brandon, Manitoba: Justin Publishing, 1991).

21. Grootaert, "Social Capital," 17.

22. M. Woolcock, "Social Capital and Economic Development: Towards a Theoretical Synthesis and Policy Framework," *Theory and Society* 27 (1998): 151–208.

23. E. Banfield, *The Moral Basis of a Backward Society* (N.Y.: Free Press, 1958).

24. J. Jensen, "Mapping Social Cohesion: The State of Canadian Research" (Canadian Policy Research Network Study No. F/03, Ottawa: Renouf Publishing, 1998).

25. R. Petty, J. Priester, and D. Wegener, "Cognitive Processes in Attitude Change" in *Handbook of Social Cognition*, vol. 2, ed. R. Wyer and T. Srull (New Jersey: Lawrence Erlbaum Associates, 1994), 69–142; B. Stephenson and R. Wicklund, "Self-Directed Attention and Taking the Other's Perspective," *Journal of Experimental and Social Psychology* 19 (1983): 58–77.

26. T. R. Tyler, R.J. Smith, and Y.J. Huo, *Social Justice in a Diverse Society* (Colorado: Westview Press, 1997); T. Tyler and A. Lind, "A Relational Model of Authority in Groups," *Advances in Experimental Social Psychology* 25 (1992): 115–191.

27. T. Tyler, K. Rasinski, and K. McGraw, "The Influence of Perceived Injustice on Support for Authorities," *Journal of Applied Social Psychology* 15 (1985): 700–725.

28. S. M. Weaver, *Making Canadian Indian Policy: The Hidden Agenda 1968–70* (Toronto: University of Toronto Press, 1981), xii.

29. G. Leventhal, J. Karuza, and W. Fry, "Beyond Fairness: A Theory of Allocation Preferences" in *Justice and Social Interaction*, ed. G. Mikula (Vienna: Hans Huber Publishers, 1980), 167–213.

30. B. Reilly and A. Reynolds, *Electoral Systems and Conflict in Divided Societies* (Washington, D.C.: National Academy Press, 1999).

31. F. Dukes, *Resolving Public Conflict: Transforming Community and Governance* (New York: Manchester University Press, 1996).

32. S. Carpenter and W. Kennedy, *Managing Public Disputes* (San Franscisco, C.A.: Jossey-Bass Inc., 1988); F. Dukes, *Resolving Public Conflict*; W. Potapchuk and C. Polk, *Building the Collaborative Community* (Washington, D.C.: National Institute for Dispute Resolution, 1993).

33. D. Newhouse, *The Emerging Aboriginal Social Contract* (Edmonton, A.B.: Canadian Indigenous/Native Studies Conference, 2000).

34. Chataway, "Imposed Democracy," 157.

35. S. Cornell and J. Kalt, *Reloading the Dice: Improving the Chances for Economic Development on American Indian Reservations* (Harvard Project on American Indian Development, Kennedy School of Government, Harvard University, 1992).

36. Cornell and Kalt, *Reloading the Dice*, 8; Cornell and Kalt, "Successful Economic Development," 257–298.

37. L. Brown, *Community and the Administration of Aboriginal Governments* (Ottawa, O.N.: Royal Commission on Aboriginal Peoples, 1994).

38. C.J. Chataway, *Cultural Identity: An Obstacle to Self-Government?* (Portland: National Conference on Peacemaking and Conflict Resolution, 1993); C.J. Chataway, *Justice in Aboriginal Governance: Contrasting Representative with Procedural Justice* (Glasgow, Scotland: Law and Society Conference, 1996).

39. D. Newhouse and I. Chapman, "Organizational Transformation: A Case Study of Two Aboriginal Organizations," *Human Relations* 49 (7): 995–1011

40. L. Pye and M. Pye, *Asian Power and Politics*: *The Cultural Dimension of Authority* (Cambridge, M.A.: Belknap Press, 1985).

41. Chataway, "Imposed Democracy."

42. Phil Fontaine cited in L. Brown, *Community and the Administration of Aboriginal Governments* (Ottawa, O.N.: Royal Commission on Aboriginal Peoples, 1994).

43. S. Cross and R. Rosenthal, "Three Models of Conflict Resolution: Effects on Intergroup Expectancies and Attitudes," *Journal of Social Issues* 55 (3): 561–580; C.J. Chataway, "An Examination of the Constraints on Mutual Inquiry in a Participatory Action Research Project," *Journal of Social Issues* 53 (4): 749–767; R. Fisher and L. Keashly, "The Potential Complementarity of Mediation and Consultation Within a Contingency Model of Third Party Intervention," *Journal of Peace Research* 28 (1991): 29–42; P. Carnevale, R. Lim, and M. McLaughlin, "Contingent Mediator Behavior and Effectiveness" in *Mediation Research: The Process and Effectiveness of Third Party Intervention*, ed. K. Kressel, D. Pruitt and Associates (San Francisco: Jossey-Bass Inc., 1989), 213–240.

44. S. Cross and R. Rosenthal, "Three Models of Conflict Resolution: Effects on Intergroup Expectancies and Attitudes," *Journal of Social Issues* 55 (3): 561–580; Carnevale, Lim, and McLaughlin, "Contingent Mediator Behavior and Effectiveness," 213–240.

45. Dukes, *Resolving Public Conflict*.

46. W. Warry, *Unfinished Dreams: Community Healing and the Reality of Aboriginal Self-Government* (Toronto: University of Toronto Press, 1998).

47. B. Kavanagh, *Aboriginal Governments in Canada: The Methodological Foundations of Collaborative Research* (Paper prepared for the Royal Commission on Aboriginal Peoples, 1992).

48. J.D. O'Neil, "Report from the Round Table Rapporteur" in *The Path to Healing*, ed. J. O'Neil (Ottawa: Royal Commission on Aboriginal Peoples, 1993), 13–24.

49. L. Susskind, S. McKearnan, and J. Thomas-Larmer, *The Consensus-Building Handbook: A Comprehensive Guide to Reaching Agreement* (London: Sage, 1999).

50. Chataway, "Imposed Democracy."

51. Pantoja, "Exploring the Concept of Social Capital."

52. S.R. Arnstein, "The Ladder of Citizen Participation," *Journal of the American Institute of Planners* 35 (4): 216–224.

53. J. Habermas, *The Theory of Communicative Action* (Boston, M.A.: Beacon Press, 1987).

54. R. Rich et al., "Citizen Participation and Empowerment: The Case of Local Environmental Hazards," *American Journal of Community Psychology* 23 (5): 657–676.

55. D. Perkins and M. Zimmerman, "Empowerment Theory, Research, and Application," *American Journal of Community Psychology* 23 (5): 569–581.

56. B. Troyna, "Blind Faith? Empowerment and Educational Research," *International Studies in Sociology of Education* (1994): 3–23; M. Mac an Ghaill, "Beyond the White Norm: The Use of Qualitative Methods in the Study of Black Youths' Schooling in England," *International Journal of Qualitative Studies in Education* 2 (1989): 175–189.

57. S.R. Arnstein, "The Ladder of Citizen Participation," *Journal of the American Institute of Planners* 35 (4): 216–224.

58. S.B. Fawcett et al., "Using Empowerment Theory in Collaborative Partnership for Community Health and Development," *American Journal of Community Psychology* 23 (5): 677–698.

59. S. Welch, *A Feminist Critique of Risk* (Minneapolis, M.N.: Fortress Press, 1990).

60. S. Ameyaw, *Presenting a Contingency Model for CED Decision-Making: Selecting CED Capacity Assessment Methods* (Simon Fraser University, Community Economic Development Centre, 2000), www.sfu.ca/cedc/forestcomm/assessment.

61. C. Hardy and S. Leiba-O'Sullivan, "The Power Behind Empowerment: Implications for Research and Practice," *Human Relations* 51 (4): 451–483.

62. S. Black, *Redefining Success in Community Development* (Washington D.C.: Lincoln Filene Ctr., 1994).

63. S. Black, *Redefining Success in Community Development* (Washington D.C.: Lincoln Filene Ctr., 1994), 2.

64. Chataway, "Imposed Democracy"; Chataway, "An Examination of the Constraints," 749–767.

65. For example; Mohawk Council of Kahnawake, "A Letter to the People: Movement on the Traditional Government File," *Kwatokent: Newsletter of the Mohawk Council of Kahnawake* (18 January 2002): 1.

66. Chataway, "Imposed Democracy," 153.

67. Chataway, "Imposed Democracy," 228.

68. W. Potapchuk and C. Polk, *Building the Collaborative Community* (Washington, D.C.: National Institute for Dispute Resolution, 1993); N. Uphoff, "A Field Methodology for Participatory Self-Evaluation," *Community Development Journal* 26 (4): 271–285.

69. S. Benhabib, "The Utopian Dimension in Communicative Ethics" in *Critical Theory: The Essential Readings*, ed. D. Ingram and J. Simon-Ingram (New York: Paragon House, 1991), 388–399.

70. C. Constantino and C. Merchant, *Designing Conflict Management Systems: A Guide to Creating Productive and Healthy Organizations* (San Francisco: Jossey-Bass Inc., 1996); Human Resources Development Canada, *Labour-Management Innovation in Canada* (Ottawa: Ministry and Supply Services, 1994).

71. G. Cormick et al., *Building Consensus for a Sustainable Future: Putting Principles into Practice* (Ottawa: National Round Table on the Environment and the Economy, 1996); Susskind, McKearnan, and Thomas-Larmer, *The Consensus-Building Handbook*.

72. S. Carpenter and W. Kennedy, *Managing Public Disputes* (San Franscisco, C.A.: Jossey-Bass Inc., 1988); F. Dukes, *Resolving Public Conflict*.

73. B. Bunker and B. Alban, "The Large Group Intervention: A New Social Innovation?" *Journal of Applied Behavioral Science* 28 (4): 473–479.

Part Two: Health

4

A Framework for Aboriginal Health Systems

Laurel Lemchuk-Favel and Richard Jock

This chapter presents an Aboriginal health systems framework for the organization of health services to Aboriginal communities. The term "Aboriginal health systems" is not commonly used in the Canadian health services literature. This is not surprising in that there are numerous reasons to query whether or not Aboriginal health systems actually exist. Firstly, there are multiple jurisdictions involved in health services to Aboriginal communities, a situation which is a classic impediment to the co-ordination, linkages and integration one would generally expect from a "system." Secondly, Aboriginal communities have only in the past ten to fifteen years achieved any meaningful control over even a part of the health services within their territories or populations. Thirdly, Aboriginal health systems imply that the services delivered would be alternative or traditional rather than those that the mainstream system provides. Fourthly, Aboriginal suggests a homogenous milieu of First Nations, Inuit, Métis and other Aboriginal populations, a perception that is rejected out of hand by all Aboriginal groups.

Despite the challenges inherent in the statements above, Aboriginal health systems, be they First Nations, Inuit, Métis or a collaboration of all groups, do exist in many different forms across Canada. This chapter will highlight the contributions of different Aboriginal nations and communities in advancing a model of health service delivery that improves access to health care, contains costs, responds to local needs, uses resources effectively, emphasizes population wellness over individual health, and ultimately improves the health status of the population. These systems have been strengthened by self-empowerment realized through Aboriginal ownership and control of health services. They are founded on a holistic approach to health and wellness, much like the broad health determinants model strived for in other health systems. Traditional and Western health philosophies are synergistically combined to result in uniquely Aboriginal approaches to health services, and within the constraints imposed by multiple jurisdictions, the system is organized around multidisciplinary primary care. Integrated health service delivery in an Aboriginal context has many expressions, from multi-community partnerships to the ability to pool funds from various sources into a single health envelope.

The Aboriginal health systems framework presented in this chapter is based on currently available knowledge obtained from the documented experiences of Aboriginal and non-Aboriginal health systems, and the outcomes of a series of meetings held to discuss First Nations, Metis, Inuit and urban health systems convened by the National Aboriginal Health Organization (NAHO). These discussions were followed by a synthesis discussion as part of a forum "Dialogue on Aboriginal Health: Sharing our Challenges and Successes" jointly sponsored by NAHO and the Commission on the Future of Health Care in Canada in June 2002. The authors recognize that there are Aboriginal health systems other than those summarized here. The framework is being presented to stimulate a needed debate on how other models or frameworks for Aboriginal health systems may continue to evolve.

The needs of Aboriginal populations with respect to health are vast, and will not be addressed by a single simplistic solution. There are many as yet unmet challenges in addressing the myriad of poor health issues in Aboriginal communities, whether they be rural, reserve or urban. These include health provider recruitment and training issues; ensuring access and restructuring services to focus on holistic population health; providing supportive technology, infrastructure and capacity development; and adapting existing health programs and services to meet the cultural, social, economic and political realities of different Aboriginal groups.

This chapter addresses in detail only one facet in the response to this complex array of health needs and concerns: the governance, funding and broad structure of the health system. It is our premise—supported by successful Aboriginal health systems across Canada—that only when meaningful control is vested in Aboriginal people themselves will effective, sustainable solutions to health issues become possible. Furthermore, the present, multi-jurisdictional patchwork quilt of health services, unless remedied, will limit the success of any system-wide health reform.

The definition of an Aboriginal health system used in this discussion is:

All organizations, institutions and resources that are devoted to producing health actions in an Aboriginal community, where the health action is defined as any effort, whether in personal care, public health services or through intersectoral or interjurisdictional initiatives, whose primary purpose is to improve health.[1]

This is a broad definition—how to interpret it and realize Aboriginal health systems in terms of governance, system design and financing form the core of this chapter. The model advanced is one of integration, or as it was originally coined by Shortell and others in 1993, an organized delivery system (ODS). They described ODS as "networks of organizations that provide or arrange to provide a coordinated continuum of services to a defined population and who are willing to be held clinically and fiscally accountable for the outcomes and health status of the population being served."[2] From this initial broad description, the concept of integrated health systems has emerged that are inclusive of all levels of care, from primary through tertiary, rehabilitative and continuing care, and focus specifically on the co-ordination of health services and collaboration among providers and provider organizations in service delivery.[3]

At this point in time, health reform in Canada has not achieved a fully integrated delivery system, as provinces have geographically co-ordinated and integrated facets of health services into regional models with local governance. Commonly, either similar activities such as hospital services have been consolidated (horizontal integration) or a portion of various activities across the continuum of care have been brought under a common umbrella (vertical integration).

To preface this discussion of an Aboriginal health systems framework, an overview of major drivers in the Canadian environment that are supportive of devoluted, integrated health delivery models is provided, as is an overview of the benefits of integration and the barriers and challenges to its implementation.

Drivers for Health Service Integration

The drivers for integration in an Aboriginal context are economic—the need to find cost-efficiencies in a financially constrained system that can then be applied to priority health concerns. They are social, in that a system is required that will provide better health care and result in improved population health outcomes. They are also political in the sense that Aboriginal communities are seeking self-determination through self-government. In terms of health, this means control of all resources that are directed to health services for residents in their communities. The Royal Commission on Aboriginal Peoples (RCAP) recognized the need for a holistic approach to health services, which are Aboriginally controlled and based on a population health model. In their 1996 report, the commissioners proposed an integrated service delivery model that would bridge jurisdictions and individual ministries and be responsible for pooled resources from all sources, including federal, provincial, territorial, municipal and Aboriginal. This model would operate through a system of healing centres and lodges under Aboriginal control and situated in urban, rural and reserve settings.[4]

A unified Aboriginal health policy focus was missing in the early years after RCAP that could sustain the momentum towards a reformed Aboriginal health system. In 2000, the National Aboriginal Health Organization (NAHO) was created as an Aboriginally run, non-profit corporation encompassing the health-related interests of all Aboriginal groups in Canada. Similarly to RCAP, NAHO has advanced an integrated system as a key element for health service change. In 2001, NAHO made submissions to the two national health care studies/commissions that were conducting consultations: the Standing Senate Committee on Social Affairs, Science and Technology, which was investigating the federal role in the health of Canadians (Kirby Report); and the Commission on the Future of Health Care in Canada (Romanow Report).

In both, NAHO stressed the need for permissive policy development at federal and provincial levels that would allow for the creation of integrated health system models, where communities, tribal councils or other groupings of Aboriginal people would control health funds from all jurisdictions and deliver health services based on the needs of the population.[5, 6]

This vision of an integrated health system supported by block funding was a common theme in community presentations at an Aboriginal Forum sponsored by NAHO and the Commission on the Future of Health Care in Canada in 2002. Its commissioner, Roy Romanow, provided his interpretation of this vision when he recommended in his final report that Aboriginal health funding be consolidated from all sources and be pooled into Aboriginal health partnerships that would manage and promote health services for Aboriginal peoples. These partnerships recommended by Romanow would have a broad mandate, encompassing all levels of health services, and recruitment and training strategies. Key elements of the Romanow partnership model include

- per capita funding based on the number of persons who sign up to be served by the partnership (capitation), where the funds are obtained from the consolidated budgets in each region, province or territory;
- operation through a fund-holder model where the partnership would have responsibility for organizing, purchasing and delivering health care services that are defined based on the scope of the partnership. This could vary from large regional health authorities to community or urban partnerships; and
- a not-for-profit community governance structure with a board comprising representatives of the funders (all Aboriginal and non-Aboriginal governments) and other individuals involved in establishing the partnership (key organizers, users and health care providers).[7]

The other major health study in this time period—that of the Senate Standing Committee led by Senator Michael Kirby—did not advance an Aboriginal-specific integration model but strongly supported the concept in the broader provincial and territorial health systems. In volume six of *Recommendations for Reform*, through its intensive examination of the federal role in the health of Canadians, strong support is given to regional health service delivery seen in many provinces. The regional health authority (RHA) model was praised by the Senate Committee as doing a "commendable job of integrating and organizing health services for people in their regions in the last decade in Canada."[8] The RHA model varies greatly throughout nine provinces (all except Ontario) and one territory (Northwest Territories) in terms of population served and services administered by the authorities. Not surprisingly, the consensus definition of an RHA is broad, and speaks of autonomous health organizations, defined geographic regions, mandate for administration of health services and governance that is generally appointed and has the responsibility for funding and delivering community and institutional services.

The Senate Committee observed that greater integration of health services is found through increased responsibility for decision making over the full range of health services, enhanced responsibility for planning and better control over the allocation of resources. These were all seen as appropriate roles for RHAs in the publicly funded health system of today and in the future. More specifically, the committee recommended that RHAs' control over health services be extended to include physician services and prescription drug spending, and that RHAs should have the ability to choose between providers on the basis of quality and costs.[9]

The integration of Aboriginal health systems was not specifically considered by the Senate Committee. Their major contribution in this area was to recommend that the federal government undertake, in collaboration with the provinces, territories and Aboriginal representatives of all groups, the development of a National Action Plan on Aboriginal Health to improve interjurisdictional co-ordination of health service delivery.[10]

Aboriginal Models of Health and Social Service Integration

In Aboriginal health systems, integration has many expressions, spanning functional (financial and/or administrative) and clinical models. For example, some communities have financially and clinically integrated continuing care services where funding may be received from Health Canada, Indian and Northern Affairs Canada (INAC) and, in some cases, the provincial government. In five Health Transition Fund home care pilot projects in First Nations and Inuit communities, home care (Health Canada) and adult care

(INAC) were functionally and clinically integrated. Positive developments, which were linked to integration, included the increased professionalism and/ or self-esteem of staff, improvements to the overall quality of care and appreciation by clients for this improved quality and accountability and a decreased number of complaints regarding services due to improved program management.[11]

The Aboriginal Healing and Wellness Strategy (AHWS) in Ontario— which funds ten health access centres in rural and urban locations—features a primary care model that integrates Western and traditional medicine, is community-based and includes a multidisciplinary team comprising salaried physicians, different levels of nursing expertise (nurse practitioners, registered nurses and/or licensed practical nurses), a nutritionist, psychologist, traditional coordinator, diabetes educator and others. In the first phase of a longitudinal evaluation of the health access centres, components were identified that form the core of the centres' effective, distinctive service delivery. These include a supportive environment where staff are role models, mentors and friends, and a marrying of traditional and Western approaches to care. Clinical interventions encompass cultural teachings and spiritual development in a holistic balance of the physical, mental, spiritual and emotional aspects of a person. Furthermore, the evaluation found that communities were empowered through the use of centres as community resources.[12]

Administrative efficiencies can be an important outcome of financially integrating Health Canada and INAC health and health-related programs. In one tribal council (anonymous), the efficiencies realized from the dismantling of program stovepipes have been invested into ongoing, community-driven continuing education for all health and social employees. The common governance ensures that a system-wide focus is maintained and adjustments can be made quickly in response to new programming or health system needs.[13]

Weeneebayko Health Authority in northern Ontario is in the process of developing an integrated health system. Hospital, physician, dental and some community health services are now being administered by the authority. It was created out of a vision that all provincial and federal health services and programs could be united under one board, which had fair and balanced representation from the communities. The authority receives funds from both the provincial (including funds for physicians who are then contracted from an academic centre) and federal governments. Both levels of government contribute to the hospital budget.

The Nisga'a Valley Health Board provides another model of a federal-provincial health resource integration. The remoteness and small size of its four member communities has meant that the system focuses on community health, nursing stations and a diagnostic and treatment centre—the latter two provide 24/7 care. The board provides health services to all residents within its territory, including the non-Aboriginal population. All communities are capable of first response treatment. The system relies on a strong budgetary system, which clearly defines the scope of services funded and value for money on a program-specific basis. Benchmarks and goals are set and regularly evaluated.[14]

The Labrador Inuit Health Commission (LIHC) delivers Inuit-specific health programming to the seven Inuit communities of Labrador via a $13 million dollar health system that employs 120 people. It has responsibility for Health Canada's community health programs and the non-insured health benefits (NIHB) program,[15] as well as the province's community and public health services. This scope is expected to expand when the Labrador Inuit land claim agreement-in-principle is successfully concluded. This agreement will include a provision for self-government that will facilitate the transfer of responsibility for provincial treatment centres and nurses to the LIHC. At this time, hospital and physician services are not being considered for transfer to the LIHC.[16]

Perhaps the most comprehensive examples of an integrated Aboriginal health system are the two regional health and social service boards established as a result of the James Bay and Northern Quebec Agreement (JBNQA). Both the James Bay Cree and the Inuit of Nunavik operate health systems under a provincially legislated authority. Under the terms of the JBNQA, federal funds for health flow to the Quebec government, which then funds the two regional boards in a manner similar to other regional boards in the province. In both the Crees' and Inuits' cases, the health authority has responsibility for hospitals (establishments), community-based nursing stations and health clinics in their respective territories.

One observation of integrated health systems, particularly the provincial approach, is that there have been few evaluations that substantiate claims of improved access, more efficient use of resources and better health outcomes.[17] In the AHWS evaluation of four health access centres, 87% of urban respondents and 64% of rural respondents reported that their centre had improved access to health care "a lot or a great deal." A high level of satisfaction with the full range of services was reported, including emotional and mental health services, health promotion activities and spiritual guidance. This was attributed, in part, to the way the services are provided, the non-judgemental attitude of staff and their respect for cultural and spiritual beliefs.[18]

The experiences of Aboriginal health systems with integrating health services have provided some general lessons:

- integration requires flexibility in designing Aboriginal/federal/ provincial/ territorial relationships and approaches;
- clinical integration is a priority in communities, particularly better communication mechanisms such as case management that bridges provincial and Aboriginal health care providers, or health and social service agencies that use a multidisciplinary team approach to holistically meet the needs of their clients;
- a primary objective of integration is to facilitate the organization of the community health system around primary care;
- the health governance structure is segregated from the administration of health services. Accountability to communities is achieved through a community-appointed board, dialogue between communities and the executive director, performance measures and/or annual community-based consultations;
- in northern areas of provinces, where Aboriginal people share primary care services with other residents, the most practical health systems are those that administer both federal and provincial services to *all* residents;
- devolving second- and third-level federal health services (such as nursing supervision or medical officer of health) to First Nations communities require multi-community partnerships in order to achieve the necessary economies of scale;
- alternative physician reimbursement mechanisms, such as salaries, facilitate integrated multidisciplinary care focussed on holistic, population-based health programs;
- administration of basic health services by individual communities will promote capacity development and should be a moderating force in the move towards centralization that often accompanies an integrated health system;
- innovative models are required for Aboriginal communities that are very small and that cannot find workable partnership arrangements; and
- the presence of multiple federal departments, each with their own multiple program funding arrangements presents real opportunities for administrative cost efficiencies when integrated financial agreements are struck. Health systems gain flexibility in designing programs and allocating resources based on existing and emerging needs.[19, 20]

Despite the stated advantages to Aboriginal health systems, which have integrated health and social services or are moving in this direction, this approach has been spotty across the country. In the absence of any formal federal or provincial policy that would support integration, change has often required a unique set of circumstances where officials from all jurisdictions have a good working relationship, and Aboriginal leadership have the vision and commitment to tackle system change. Altering long-established policies and practices of providers and gathering community support for change takes time. Particularly in larger communities, integration of services can lead to fears of job loss. Officials in government departments can also be entrenched in their beliefs, making it difficult to obtain buy-in from all government levels required. The federal government has not integrated its programs internally, which causes additional barriers to seamlessly combining programs and services at the delivery level. Auditor General Sheila Fraser, in her 2002 review of federal reporting and audit requirements in selected First Nations communities, found that a First Nation without multi-year funding arrangements may have to submit as many as 200 reports annually.[21] She added her voice to the many First Nations and Inuit who have called for more co-ordinated and streamlined federal programming.

Existing provincial policies can hinder or create disincentives to integration. Through a federal, provincial and academic collaboration, Eskasoni First Nation embarked upon integrated primary care that sought to improve access and co-ordination of local health services. It has realized significant health system improvements over a three-year period, with reductions in physician, outpatient and emergency room visits, concurrent with the establishment of an interdisciplinary health team. However, the province will only provide primary care funding for physicians, with a small amount of overhead in the physician contracts that can be applied to nurse clinician or nurse practitioner positions. This has resulted in a ratio of three funded physician positions to one nurse clinician, and a heavy medical bias to the model. In additions, savings from the provincial hospital system, estimated to be $250,000 annually, from reduced outpatient and emergency room utilization are not recoverable by the community and cannot be reinvested into extending the integration model to further areas such as substance abuse and mental health.[22, 23]

Challenges to health service integration, which have been summarized by Howard et al., include medical model dominance and focus on the diagnosis of disease, role ambiguity and lack of trust among providers, lack of readiness to change, lack of education and training in multidisciplinary care and inadequate information systems.[24] Although these issues have been summarized from many different health systems, they are universal to integration and often more acute in Aboriginal systems.

System redesign will take a high amount of management time and resources, and change cannot be implemented at the expense of existing service delivery. This means that, although savings may be created in the long term, resources will initially be required for community consultation, needs assessments and community health plans, capital improvements, training, and project management. Furthermore, the financial health of the community may affect its ability to institute an integrated system. For example, if one program has a significant deficit, then financially merging programs may mean that existing funds from a second program are used to cover this deficit.

Lessons from Other Health Systems

In 1996, a World Health Organization study group identified the following positive impacts of integrated health services:

- cost-effective health services, including improved efficiency and productivity (such as better use of staff time and less duplication);
- cost-savings related to reduced training (i.e., one multi-purpose health professional versus many);
- improved health status that was credited to a holistic, client-empowered approach to care;
- improved satisfaction by users; and
- improved equity as responsibilities for health care are redistributed among the public, non-governmental and private providers as appropriate.[25]

Integrated health service delivery in Canada is somewhat paradoxical, in that it is championed by many provinces as a key feature in their RHA models. However, some contend that in reality there is little integration occurring. Leatt et al., in a review of Canadian integrated health care, flatly stated that a RHA without responsibility for physicians and pharmaceuticals cannot provide integrated health care. Other hallmarks of integrated systems seen internationally are also missing in the Canadian context, for example, capitation for all practitioners with money following the consumer, membership defined by consumer choice through rostering, financial incentives to providers for good performance, system-wide and provider-specific information systems and a primary care focus.[26]

In 2001, the B.C. Select Standing Committee on Health reported that regionalization based on boundaries has promoted a fragmented system with redundancies and duplications, poor co-ordination, competition among service providers for control of resources and little or no incentives for collaboration. Providers may place their own concerns over retaining autonomy and existing practices ahead of change directed at improving patient health.[27]

Despite this, testimony to the Senate Standing Committee and related literature suggest that integration and co-ordination of institutions and organizations under a RHA model can provide greater efficiencies and higher quality of service, allow for the use of least costly providers commensurate with accessibility and individual health goals, and enhance a RHA's ability to respond to service demands through integrated responses such as home care, continuing care and acute care.[28]

Using geographic boundaries to define a system's catchment population, such as regions, may impede natural population flows within the health system. Population in one region may seek both primary and secondary care across the boundaries if it is more convenient. In the Netherlands, geographic monopolies were replaced by roster-based systems of related, competitive, integrated organizations.[29] This has direct relevance to Aboriginal health where secondary and tertiary care is often provided from institutions at distances far from the patient's community.

Integrated systems can exist through networking of organizations without financial pooling of resources. These virtual networks have been proposed as a good intermediary step towards an ultimate governance model. In this approach, organizations that provide full continuum care can partner around common visions and goals as well as more practical issues of client flow, care protocols and information systems.[30] In many respects, this has already happened out of necessity in Aboriginal health systems, when communities develop protocols with neighbouring communities, RHAs, hospitals and private providers for certain programs and services.

New Zealand has implemented a system of budget holding where purchasers and providers of services are separate. Maori organizations are involved in budget holding as health service purchasers to enrolled members. For example, in an urban environment where Maori are dispersed throughout the city, a Maori organization may have capitation contracts with physicians to provide primary care to people enrolled in the organization. Other organizations may hold funds for secondary care, which allow Maori to contract with specialists and hospitals on a performance contract basis. Other examples of budget holding include pharmacies, pathology services, disability services, community nursing services and traditional healers.[31]

There are significant dissimilarities between Maori and Canadian Aboriginal peoples in terms of relationship with the federal government, number of treaties, presence of Aboriginal governments and the recognition of the inherent right to self-government. As well, there is only one New Zealand health system under federal control. The success of Maori organizations with budget holding is likely due, in large part, to their guaranteed political representation in Parliament, as well as legislation that imparts a statutory obligation of district health boards to foster Maori capacity to participate in the health and disability sector, and to provide for their own needs. This includes exploring new health provider models if Maori communities have identified these as appropriate. Maori providers include Maori development organizations, Maori co-funding organizations and collectivities of Maori providers. Between 1993 and 2000, the number of independent Maori providers increased from approximately 20 to more than 2,000. These providers are seen as key players in reducing access barriers and improving the effectiveness and appropriateness of services to Maori.[32]

Lessons from Australia's experience with integrated delivery systems suggest that not everyone requires integrated primary health care—the most effective systems are those that service individuals and families that do. Nine co-ordinated care trials with over 16,000 participants were initiated in different parts of Australia in 1997. The interim evaluation results were inconclusive on many system outcomes, such as client health and well-being, service cost and use, and hospitalization.[33] However, the trials did show that the most successful ones were those that were targeted to a specifically defined population. The Aboriginal trials were directed at reforming local health care systems and delivering locally based and managed comprehensive primary care services in a culturally appropriate manner. Significant progress was noted in improving health service access, health care planning and population health programs that address priority community needs—all of which was linked to the many partnerships among government, communities, health services and organizations.[34]

A Framework for Aboriginal Health Systems

Organize the health system around multi-disciplinary primary care health service delivery and administration, featuring a single entry point and case management.

Often integration has focussed on the higher levels of service delivery, bringing together hospitals, long-term care services, public health, rehabilitation and emergency services under common governance. This level of integration, while important, does not automatically ensure that a multidisciplinary approach exists that is complementary to board level partnerships and can facilitate a seamless continuum of care at the patient level.

Many Aboriginal communities have a strong foundation in community health services from which to build a comprehensive integrated system. Generally speaking, this is less the circumstance in Métis communities. A criticism of international initiatives has been that little consideration has been given to co-ordinating services at the community and individual levels, providing consumers with information, or understanding their needs and preferences.[35] This is one area where many Aboriginal communities are well prepared. First Nations involved in Health Transfer, a financial mechanism to transfer control of federal health programs, have completed community health plans as part of the implementation process. The community health focus of urban Aboriginal health centres has also meant that extensive consultations were undertaken on grassroots health needs and service design of the centres.

Establish a health authority that is accountable to the member Aboriginal communities.

The characteristics of the legal entity that will serve as the service organization for the respective community will vary depending on the province, territory and other political-legal circumstances relevant to the population being serviced. A key element of success is the selection of a governing board based on the communities and groups that are members of the authority. In the Romanow model, seats are designated for major funders (federal, provincial/territorial), as well as key organizers, users and health care providers. While this may be considered, depending on the design of the system and perceived contributions of the partners and scope of services covered, there is equal consideration that such a model would not be consistent with Aboriginal interest in self-government and self-determination. An alternative may be to have ex-officio participation of major funders at the planning stages. In any case, Aboriginal directors must form the majority of voting members on the board. Governance design is a separate topic in itself; even so, it is fair to state that total membership, generally, should not exceed twenty as an absolute upper limit, which has been associated with effective board operation.

Establishment of a health authority board provides a distance between communities' political systems and the health service delivery system. A "neutral" governing body can act as a buffer so that health care does not become a political commodity, as well as provide the context for a non-political approach to decision making. The health authority board can ensure accountability through an appointment process of its directors—by member communities and/or community elections—and annual performance and financial reporting requirements. A performance orientation to governance should include the ongoing review of health status, service access, user/stakeholder satisfaction, cost-effectiveness of services, evaluation of partnership initiatives, collaboration and communication.

Involve practitioners in the system planning and governance in order to instill a sense of ownership in the system.

To facilitate staff retention and promote better system outcomes, various practitioners, viewpoints, and needs should be recognized in the administrative and organizational structure of the health system. Traditionally, physicians have provided a gate-keeper role in the health system; for example, they are fund holders in Britain and are often the administrative choices for program managers in Canadian hospitals. The exclusion of other health professional groups from administrative decisions that affect them has been criticized as contradictory to the notion of professional autonomy and independence of practice and thought to be a contributing factor to staff turnover and burnout.[36] Aboriginal custom, which stresses consensus and consultation, provides the opportunity for a system management strategy that is broadly inclusive of all health professionals.

Define the population to be served by the health authority.

Both Aboriginal and non-Aboriginal individuals should be eligible to join the health authority. In rural and remote areas, the catchment population will initially be based on geography (e.g., partnerships of communities that share existing or potential client flows). Individuals would register with the health authority's roster in order to receive services. This would ensure all persons are accounted for in the health authority's budget. Rostering implies that individuals have a choice whether or not to join the health services. However, in rural and remote First Nations and Inuit communities, such a choice generally would not exist. The population base could not support two parallel systems—the status quo and the health authority. Rostering is more critical in urban populations, as the Aboriginal health authority would be a relatively small component of the provincial system, and persons interested in registering would be dispersed throughout the city and environs.

The entire continuum of services—from health clinics to diagnostic laboratories, outpatient care and hospital services—should be accessible by the covered population. The population size should provide sufficient economies of scale for extra human resource capacity to deal with unanticipated demand in areas such as palliative care, where the additional resources required to care intensively for one terminally ill person in the home can often overwhelm a small community health clinic.

Structure the health authority to promote collaboration of the various service partners within the system and without.

A number of health authorities may network or partner for certain health services, such as administration of the NIHB program, or for common goods and supplies purchased in bulk. The NIHB program client base should be a sufficient size (5,000 or higher) in order to provide a reserve pool of funds for catastrophic or unplanned events, such as epidemics. The philosophy of the health system should be to maximize networks, strategic alliances and other partnership arrangements in order to optimize patient care. Whereas integration based on ownership can produce economies of scale and ensure that a common information system and clinical practice guidelines be adopted, integration based on networks and contractual arrangements can provide flexibility, a quicker response to needs, build trust between organizations, and allow organizations to identify services they provide well and obtain others from partners.[37]

Encompass a broad health and health-related spectrum in the health authority's services.

The scope of the system will include all federally and provincially/territorially funded health services as well as social programs that are closely linked to the health system. In a First Nations context, this would include the adult care, child care and family violence programs funded by INAC, and in other Aboriginal systems, comparable provincial or territorial programming. Clinical patterns of care are beyond the scope of this framework, except for the observations that the system would be inclusive of both Western and traditional approaches to care depending on the needs and expectations of the rostered population. For example, care models such as the Aboriginal Medicine Wheel Life Promotion provide a holistic way for practitioners to look at the entire person and his or her environment when providing care, and are complementary to an integrated service delivery model.[38]

Develop sound community health plans through extensive consultation.

Integrated systems should incorporate needs-based planning, utilize an evidence-based decision-making process, and be designed from the bottom up, not imposed as a standard template where community needs are squeezed into a generic model. This has been a perennial complaint of First Nations and Inuit communities who object to the imposition of standard national program criteria and elements on very diverse populations. One of the strengths of the health service reforms in New Zealand was the enabling of communities to plan their system, for example, the primary care model being implemented is flexible to accommodate a variety of approaches with no preconditions detailing ownership, population served, or location of primary care organization.[39]

Visible expressions of the health system should be an integral part of the community fabric, such as the use of health clinic buildings for community events during off hours. In the AHWS, this is regarded as an important component of improving accessibility of health services and promoting the community's capacity development and self-empowerment.

A critical support element will be the approach to organizational capacity building, including sufficient resources for personnel, information systems and capital requirements. Often a limitation in Aboriginal health systems today is the lack of availability of capital projects. In an integrated approach—such as was undertaken by Akwesasne in their health and social system development—all jurisdictions (Health Canada, INAC and the Ontario and Quebec governments) put a notional capital budget into a general capital fund that was used to build a single facility. This facility then provided an infrastructure that facilitated the integration of the various program areas under a common governance and administration.

The system should feature a common clinical information system or connected information infrastructure.

Development of health information systems and technological supports for distance care (telehealth) are ongoing in Canada, in both a general health context and specific to Aboriginal systems. Common patient records, either paper or electronic, facilitate the seamless provision of a continuum of care, reduce duplication of clinical efforts, improve diagnosis and improve the overall quality of care provided to patients.[40] An integrated Aboriginal health system will provide the governance and administrative framework necessary for implementation of a system that is compatible with all service settings and protects patient confidentiality.

Provide practitioners with the skills for multidisciplinary care.

The community health plan should encompass health provider education to ensure that providers have the necessary training and tools to make the change to multidisciplinary service delivery. A review of the literature on implementation of multidisciplinary teams found a positive correlation between success measures (i.e., high levels of staff morale, better diagnosis and efficient, co-ordinated care), joint training and team building exercises.[41]

Provide funds based on capitation and a rostered population.

Capitation financing, which provides a set amount of money per enrollee, should use a formula that adjusts for the age and sex of the rostered population, and geographic variability in the cost of health goods and services. Other adjusters are population-specific, and for the Aboriginal population could include utilization and/or prevalence rates of diabetes and arthritis, functional disabilities, mental disorders/suicides, or other community-relevant health and social indicators. In practical terms, this may mean a number of capitation formulae comprising different funding authorities that are consolidated into the health authority's budget. Although these funds are identified with different authorities, the health authority should have the flexibility to allocate resources in response to new or emerging health priorities.

The health authority's budget should encompass the continuum of care for either the delivery or purchase of services. The capitation amount will include community health and health-related services in all disciplines, long-term care, public health, environmental health, physician services, hospital services (community, secondary and tertiary), the NIHB program for First Nations, and provincial/territorial health benefits for other Aboriginal groups. With respect to purchased hospital services, in the vast majority of cases where there is only one hospital that serves a primarily non-Aboriginal population, this hospital's services will be purchased back. The inclusion of an Aboriginal element in the hospital budget process will provide opportunities for a long-term partnership, and the establishment of performance goals and measures by both parties. In a truly market-driven scenario, where there are multiple hospital choices (such as in urban areas), hospitals would compete for the Aboriginal health system's business, thereby providing the means for an ultimate performance measure. This element of competition could be a long-term goal of the system depending on provincial willingness to consider movement of resources among hospitals, particularly if the majority of their catchment populations are not members of enrolled systems. In northern environments where Aboriginal people form the majority of residents, the hospital would likely become part of the health authority and would serve both the Aboriginal and non-Aboriginal population.

Financial incentives are often cited as a positive feature in integrated delivery systems. In Canada—under its publicly funded system—consumers cannot purchase improved services (a classic incentive), and the population mass in most Aboriginal systems will not support competition among providers. Therefore providers will not have to provide a better service to attract clients, another market-based incentive. On the other hand, in a capitation system, practitioners would no longer operate through fee for service, thus removing incentives to provide unneeded services or referrals. A guaranteed per-person health budget through capitation financing will provide incentives for an Aboriginal health authority to find efficiencies that can be used to fund more and better health programs, and support practitioner incentives to recruit and retain qualified health providers.

Conclusion

The health systems framework advanced in this paper is founded on holistic, multidisciplinary primary care as the central component in a network of services spanning the care continuum and uninterrupted by jurisdictional boundaries or individual funding authorities. An integrated system takes time to vision, plan and implement, and experience suggests that it should be built gradually, starting with community-based health services. A holistic model of care encompasses an individual's physical, spiritual, social, mental and emotional well-being at personal, family, community and nation levels. An integrated health system in Aboriginal communities should not simply be a larger version of the program silos that it seeks to remedy. This will require linkages of the health system with all facets of community services, including education and training, housing, social assistance, justice and employment programs.

Endnotes

1. This definition of an Aboriginal health system has been adapted from a general definition of health systems developed by the World Health Organization.

2. S.M. Shortell et al., "Creating Organized Delivery Systems: The Barriers and the Facilitators," *Hospital and Health Services Administration* 38 (Winter 1993): 4.

3. P. Leatt, G.H. Pink, and M. Guerriere, "Towards a Canadian Model of Integrated Health Care," *Healthcare Papers* 1, 2 (2000): 13–35.

4. Royal Commission on Aboriginal Peoples, *Report of the Royal Commission on Aboriginal Peoples*, vol. 3 of *Gathering Strength* (Ottawa: Minister of Supply and Services Canada, 1996).

5. National Aboriginal Health Organization, "An Examination of Aboriginal Health Service Issues and Federal Aboriginal Health Policy." Presentation to the Standing Senate Committee on Social Affairs, Science and Technology, May 31, 2001.

6. National Aboriginal Health Organization, *Roadmap for Change: NAHO Submission to the Commission on the Future of Health Care in Canada* (Ottawa, 2001).

7. Commission on the Future of Health Care in Canada, *Building on Values: The Future of Health Care in Canada* (Ottawa, 2002).

8. Standing Senate Committee on Social Affairs, Science and Technology, *The Health of Canadians: The Federal Role,* vol. 6 of *Recommendations for Reform* (Ottawa, 2002), 63.

9. Standing Senate Committee on Social Affairs, *Health of Canadians*, 6: 69.

10. Standing Senate Committee on Social Affairs, Science and Technology, *The Health of Canadians: The Federal Role,* vol. 4 of *Issues and Options* (Ottawa, 2001), 132.

11. J. Wentworth and A. Gibbons, *Health Transition Fund Project NA108: First Nations and Inuit Home Care* (Ottawa: Minister of Public Works and Government Services Canada, 2000).

12. Aboriginal Healing and Wellness Strategy, *Annual Report* (Toronto: Aboriginal Healing and Wellness Strategy, 2000/2001).

13. L. Lemchuk-Favel, "Financing a First Nations and Inuit Integrated Health System," in pt. 3 of *British Columbia, New Brunswick and Nova Scotia* (Ottawa: First Nations and Inuit Health Branch, 2000).

14. L. Lemchuk-Favel and R. Jock, *Aboriginal Health Systems in Canada* (Ottawa: National Aboriginal Health Organization, 2002).

15. The NIHB program provides prescription drugs, optometry services, dental services, medical aids, and medical transportation to First Nations (Registered Indians) and Inuit.

16. Lemchuk-Favel and Jock, *Aboriginal Health Systems in Canada*, 30.

17. Standing Senate Committee on Social Affairs, *Health of Canadians*, 6: 66–67.

18. The Centre for Applied Social Research in conjunction with the Longitudinal Working Group, Aboriginal Healing and Wellness Strategy, *Aboriginal Healing and Wellness Strategy: Longitudinal Study, Phase 1* (Toronto: Centre for Applied Social Research, Faculty of Social Work, April 2000).

19. L. Lemchuk-Favel, *First Nations and Inuit Health System Renewal: A Situational Analysis* (Ottawa: First Nations and Inuit Health Branch, Health Canada, 2000).

20. Lemchuk-Favel and Jock, *Aboriginal Health Systems in Canada*, 17–34.

21. Office of the Auditor General of Canada, "Streamlining First Nations Reporting to Federal Organizations." Report of the Auditor General of Canada, December 2002.

22. M.J. Hampton, "The Eskasoni Story." Final report of the Eskasoni Primary Care Project, 2001.

23. M.J. Hampton, "Help Wanted: Successful Model Seeks Policy Framework." Presentation for Primary Care and First Nations Health, Ottawa, April 25, 2002.

24. D.C. Howard et al., *Primary Health Care: Six Dimensions of Inquiry* (Howard Research and Instructional Systems Inc., 2000).

25. World Health Organization, *Integration of Health Services Delivery*. Report of the WHO, Study Group No. 861, 1996.

26. Leatt, Pink, and Guerriere, *Towards a Canadian Model*, 18–19.

27. Select Standing Committee on Health, *Patients First: Renewal and Reform of British Columbia's Health Care System* (Legislative Assembly of British Columbia, 2001), 13.

29. J. Marriott and A.L. Mabel, "Integrated Health Organizations in Canada: Developing the Ideal Model," *Healthcare Papers* 1, 2 (2000): 77.

30. Leatt, Pink, and Guerriere, *Towards a Canadian Model*, 29.

31. D. Scrimgeour, "Funding for Community Control of Indigenous Health Services," *Australia and New Zealand Journal of Public Health* 20, 1 (1996): 17–18.

32. Ministry of Health, *He Korowai Oranga: Maori Health Strategy Discussion Document* (Wellington: Government of New Zealand, 2001).

34. Dr. M. Wooldridge, "Coordinated Care Trials in Aboriginal Communities: Evaluation Finds Great Benefits." Media release, Government of Australia, Minister for Health and Aged Care, Australia, April 12, 2001.

35. Leatt, Pink, and Guerriere, *Towards a Canadian Model*, 25.

36. J. Shamian and S.J. LeClair, "Integrated Delivery Systems, Now or . . . ??" *Healthcare Papers* 1, 2 (2000): 66–75.

37. S.M. Shortell et al., *Remaking Health Care in America: Building Organized Delivery Systems* (San Fransisco: Jossey-Bass Inc., 1996).

38. This model has been developed by Judith Bartlett and is currently in use at the Aboriginal Healing and Wellness Centre in Winnipeg, Manitoba.

39 B. Gribbon and G. Coster, "A Future for Primary Health Care in New Zealand," *Australian Health Review* 22, 4 (1999): 118–31. Cited in S. Legatt and M. Walsh, 2000.

40. Howard et al., *Primary Health Care*, 26.

41. Howard et al., *Primary Health Care*, 23.

5

Transferring Whose Knowledge? Exchanging Whose Best Practices? On Knowing about Indigenous Knowledge and Aboriginal Suicide

Michael J. Chandler and Christopher E. Lalonde

Over the better part of a decade we have been hard at work refashioning a still earlier decade's worth of work on identity development and youth suicide in order to better fit these efforts to the special circumstances of Canadian Aboriginal youth—an ongoing effort aimed at explaining two deeply puzzling matters. One of these concerns the heart-breakingly high rate of suicide widely known to mark and often stigmatize Aboriginal youth; an overall suicide rate that is reported to be higher than that of any culturally identifiable group in the world (Kirmayer 1994). The second of these known facts of the matter (owed largely to our own research) is that the rate of Aboriginal youth suicide varies dramatically from one community to another. As our research in British Columbia clearly demonstrates, more than 90% of Aboriginal youth suicides occur in only 10% of the bands, with some communities suffering rates as much as 800 times the national average, while more than half of the province's 200 First Nations bands have not experienced a single youth suicide in the almost fifteen years for which such figures are available. What obviously needs explaining in the face of such disparities—what inquiring minds most want to know—is what is different about those communities without such suicides, and those in which youth suicide occurs in epidemic proportion?

Since 1998 we have provided more than a half dozen journal articles and book chapters (Chandler 2000; Chandler 2001; Chandler and Lalonde 1998; Chandler and Lalonde 2000a, 2000b; Chandler, Lalonde, and Sokol 2000; Chandler and Sokol in press; Lalonde 2003), as well as a book-length monograph (Chandler et al. in press)—a total of more than 300 published pages—all detailing what we take to be our best interim answers to these two troubling questions. In particular, we have shown not only where in the province Aboriginal suicides occur and re-occur, and where they are absent, but also what community-level risk and protective factors especially distinguish such have- and have-not bands. More significantly, we have also demonstrated that bands that are well on their way towards preserving or rehabilitating their threatened cultures, and that have met with measurable success in recovering community control over their civic lives (i.e., that, in addition to having taken concrete steps to preserve their cultural past, have achieved a measure of self-government, have effectively militated for Aboriginal title to traditional lands, and have gained a measure of control over their own health, education, child protection and jural systems) suffer *no* youth suicides, while those who fail to meet all or most of these standards of self-determination have youth suicide rates more than 150 times the national average. In addition, we have individually interviewed and assessed more than 200 Aboriginal youth and their culturally mainstream peers, all in an effort to understand individual counterparts of cultural-level continuity, and to determine the different ways in which developing youth from both of these cultures struggle to understand their own personal persistence in the face of inevitable change. Here our findings make it plain that, in contrast to their more "essentialist" majority culture counterparts (who root their beliefs about self-continuity in the persistence of particular self-attributes), First Nations youth overwhelmingly elect to warrant their own diachronic sense of temporal connectedness by running a narrative thread through the distinctive time-slices of their own and others' lives.

While it did not take all of our several hundred published pages to say only this much (e.g., we have chosen to leave out of this current account a mountain of detail about what does and does not especially distinguish suicide-prone and suicide-free individuals and whole communities), all of what has previously been said elsewhere hardly needs repeating here. Rather, the few short pages of this chapter are given over in an attempt to highlight what we take to be some of the potential action or policy implications of our work. To do this, of course, is to move out on very thin ice. If we are to take our own subsequent message about community control seriously, it is hardly our place, as uninvited guests, to attempt to instruct Aboriginal communities about how they ought to behave. If anything, we are even less expert still about the world of government policy practices. Still, with a certain appropriate dose of fear and trembling, we are persuaded, and so emboldened, to make and elaborate upon two strong points that, given the evidence in hand, would be irresponsible not to emphasize.

One of these talking points arises as a consequence of the extreme variability we have documented in the rates of youth suicide as they differentially occur in Aboriginal bands across the province of British Columbia. Something important—maybe several important things—we believe, turn on this new evidence, both for the communities described, and for those agencies of provincial and federal government charged with addressing the special health concerns of these Aboriginal youth.

Second, we believe our findings say something of actionable importance about what can, and should, be done to better address the problem of Aboriginal youth suicide. At least to date, our own findings themselves remain, of course, much too superficial to be taken as a concrete guide for solving anyone's problems, least of all the dense and layered problems surrounding the task of persuading Aboriginal youth that we have allowed them a life worth living. What is not in serious doubt, however, is that our research makes plain a large and poorly appreciated source of real cultural knowledge about how such problems not only might be, but already have been, solved to some important degree of satisfaction. Clearly contained in the finding that more than half of British Columbia's Aboriginal communities have not suffered a single youth suicide in the last fifteen years (a suicide rate remarkably lower than that of the general population) is, for example, the evident fact that real knowledge about how to address this problem is already well sedimented within these Aboriginal communities themselves. What is less clear, and what we mean to introduce as a topic for discussion in the second and final part of this chapter, is how this especially encouraging fact can be preserved and shared more widely among Aboriginal communities, and how governments can best nurture and conserve this overlooked and underdeveloped resource of indigenous knowledge.

What we will undertake to argue is that our new evidence in hand speaks strongly in favour of a different vision of the much heralded notions of "knowledge transfer," and the "exchange of best practices"—a vision that sees relevant knowledge and practices as also moving "laterally" from community to community, rather than only *from* Ottawa or some provincial capital *down* to the level of Aboriginal communities.

Part One: The Myth of the Monolithic Indigene

No one, of course, is in serious doubt about the economies and pragmatics of scale responsible for the existence of governmental policies and practices aimed at the whole of Canada's Aboriginal population. What is perhaps surprising is that, all too often, social scientists and health professionals, who are at least potentially free of such bureaucratic necessities, also appear to endorse a similar "monolithic" view (Duran and Duran 1995, 107) by mistakenly imagining that it is possible to capture the diversity of a whole province's or country's Aboriginal life in a single (often statistical) gaze. Such attempts at bulk processing are, as it turns out, as common as clay. Consequently, no one is any longer shocked, for example, when told on "good authority" that Aboriginal people at large have an elevated suicide rate, experience problems with alcohol or too commonly drop out of school. Why shock (and, if not, anger or outrage) is the more appropriate response to such generic claims is, of course, because such totalizing commentary obscures the evident fact that to talk of "the" Aboriginal is to reinscribe what Berkhoffer (1978) calls an arbitrary category, a European invention, that exists only as a kind of recoiling from the "other" (Said 1978)—a construction that serves primarily to justify and reinforce a dangerous cultural stereotype.

Rather, the real truth is that the Aboriginal population of Canada and the United States is remarkably diverse, accounting for what Hodgkenson (1990) reports to be upwards of 50% of the actual cultural diversity of the whole continent. In British Columbia, where our own research was conducted, there are, for example, more than 200 contemporary bands that collectively speak fourteen mutually uninterpretable languages, occupy a territory bigger than Western Europe, live in sharply different ecological niches and spiritual worlds, and have radically different histories, both with the current majority culture and with one another.

As new and better evidence begins to accumulate—evidence such as our own—it becomes increasingly apparent that blanket statements created by simply averaging across all of the real cultural diversity that does exist automatically results in what can be called "actuarial fictions." Our own ongoing work on Aboriginal youth suicide provides a clear case in point. While it is true that the overall provincial rate of youth suicide is somewhere between five and twenty times that of the general population, this summary statistic tells us nothing about any particular group or community. This is not to say that either we, or others who report similar findings (e.g., Malchy et al. 1997), somehow got our sums wrong. Rather, what is lost is the fact that youth suicide rates vary radically along almost any dimension one might choose. Figures 1 and 2, for example, display the rates of youth suicide for both British Columbia's Aboriginal and non-Aboriginal populations, first by Health Region and then Census District. What is immediately evident from a quick inspection of these figures is that, in comparison to the general population, the suicide rates on display for Aboriginal youth present a wildly saw-toothed picture. Of course, some of this variability can be laid off to the fact that suicides are rare, even when epidemic, and so are subject to fluctuations due to small sample sizes. Perhaps more meaningful, because they are about groups with something closer to human meaning, are comparable suicide rates by Aboriginal band and tribal council (see Figures 3 and 4). Here, as summarized earlier, it is evident that most Aboriginal communities have no youth suicides in the fourteen-year reporting window, while others have rates a hundred or more times the national or provincial average.

Figure 1:   Youth suicide rate by Health Region, British Columbia, 1987-92

Suicides per 100,000

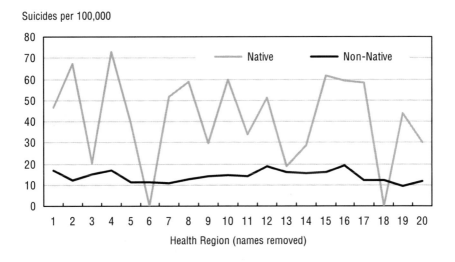

Health Region (names removed)

Figure 2:   Youth suicide rate by Census District, British Columbia, 1987-92

Suicides per 100,000

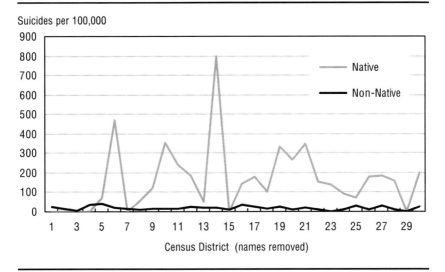

Census District (names removed)

Figure 3:   Youth suicide by band, British Columbia, 1993-00

Suicides per 100,000

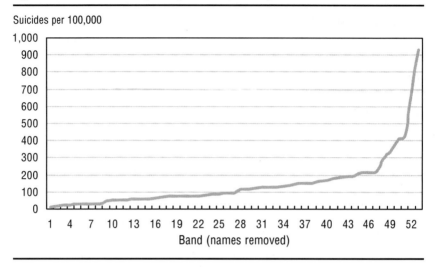

Band (names removed)

Figure 4:   Youth suicide by tribal council, British Columbia, 1993-00

Suicides per 100,000

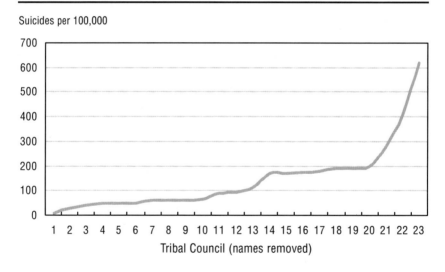

Tribal Council (names removed)

Although similar statistics are becoming available concerning other problems of health and well-being (for example, we now have similar findings concerning school drop-out rates by band), what we hope you will take from our working example is the utter pointlessness and defamatory consequences of envisioning some generic, one-size-fits-all, made in Ottawa/ Victoria solution to the Aboriginal suicide problem. The real truth is that half of the bands in British Columbia—the bands that have no reported youth suicides—scarcely need instruction from the majority culture, which can boast no such claim. Others, tragically, suffer alarmingly high youth-suicide rates, and if we just knew from what quarter help might be forthcoming, they need and very likely want all of the help they can get.

Perhaps the oldest aphorism in medicine is "no differential treatment without differential diagnosis." The point we mean to drive home concerns a similar insight about cultural diversity. There is no monolithic indigene, no "other," and no such thing as the suicidal Aboriginal. The pretense that there is amounts to just another way of running scared before diversity.

Part Two: Indigenous Knowledge, Knowledge Transfer and the Exchange of Best Practices

Talk of "knowledge transfer" and the "exchange of best practices" has become, of late, very much the talk of the town. When you hear it, take special note of who is ordinarily imagined to be on the giving and receiving ends of whatever exchange or transfer is had in mind. Almost invariably, the persons imagined to be taking up a position at either end of this knowledge conduit are both social scientists or health professionals, and the flow of information is almost always "downhill," from positions of higher to lower professional status. Occasionally, communities or community leaders are the intended targets of such new information, but the prospect that useful knowledge might flow "uphill," or even laterally from community to community is ordinarily excluded from the realm of conceivable or legitimate possibilities.

The presumption that all legitimate forms of knowledge transfer follow a one-way street is, of course, especially unfortunate for a long list of reasons. Not the least of these is the fact that, in the case of Aboriginal communities and in the instance of youth suicide, there are very good reasons to believe that some of the bands in question are firmly in possession of knowledge and practices that could be of enormous potential help to others, if these could be exchanged somehow, or transferred from one community group to another. Should it prove possible to "lateral" such best practices back and forth among Aboriginal communities, otherwise seemingly intractable problems might be solved. What we typically have instead is a top-down and insular arrangement that illegitimizes and disqualifies the knowledge forms sedimented within indigenous communities—an arrangement that has little to recommend it. It is, in addition to being frankly unpopular and disrespectful, both strategically unwise, and (if contemporary practitioners of post-colonial theory and colonial discourse analysis are to be believed) it represents a form of "epistemic violence" (Spivak 1985, 126) that is inherently hostile to, and serves to confirm the positional inferiority of, Aboriginal culture. All of these risks, taken singularly or in combination, run so strongly against the contemporary best interests of both governments and their constituencies that the apparent impulse to continue running them deserves closer interrogation.

First, it should hardly come as a surprise, or seem unwarranted, that Canada's Aboriginal people are often suspicious or mistrustful of problem definitions and solution strategies that are invented in Ottawa or even in New York City. However ignorant and beside the point the abstract theorizing of "the academy" may sometimes seem to those who work inside it, such imported ways of thinking appear even more *outré* when lobbed into some Aboriginal community from distant capitals, or parachuted down from some ivory tower. There is, however, more to their problem than simple lack of real expertise. Such educative or "civilizing missions" (Gandhi 1998, 16)— missions in which native "superstitions" are read as naturally "childish" and counterpoised against supposedly "real" scientific knowledge—automatically cast those representing the dominant culture in the role of authorities, while quietly condemning Aboriginal people to a derivative and subjugated epistemic existence. Knowledge invented elsewhere and rudely transplanted root and branch into someone else's backyard is often and rightly understood to be a weapon wielded by those who have it against those who must suffer it, a form of conquest and occupation of minds (Nandy 1983) that serves to further colonize the life worlds of native people (Duran and Duran 1995) and to marginalize indigenous voices.

Second, to imagine that knowledge and problem-solving strategies evolved in native communities over hundreds of years have no legitimate pride of place at the transfer table of contemporary knowledge production and exchange is not only hostile, but makes poor economic and strategic sense. Perhaps there was a time in which the marginalization and intellectual exclusion of traditional practices as legitimate knowledge forms actually served existing purposes of economic domination and the generation of profit, but that was then and hardly now. Instead, ongoing, trickle-down strategies that locate all useful knowledge within the academy now appear to be fighting a losing battle in which current efforts at capacity building are repeatedly overtaken by a rising tide of building social problems.

What all of this would appear to suggest is that, in the place of whatever lingering residue of neo-colonialist thought that, as Fanon (1965, 63) put it, "wants everything to come from it," the usual practice of cancelling or negating or emptying traditional knowledge forms of meaning needs to be cashed out as no longer profitable. In the place of the existing hierarchy of knowledges that equate "otherness" with ignorance, it would now appear to be in the interest of the academy, and society at large, to entertain newly the idea that indigenous knowledge might be real knowledge, and that the best ways of helping those in need of help may be to help them help themselves.

Steps taken in this proposed direction would need to begin, as we have taken pains to emphasize in part one, with serious efforts to determine how various social and health problems are distributed across the diverse whole of the Aboriginal population. This would, as Duran and Duran (1995, 106) point out, have the important advantage of avoiding the obvious waste of spending large sums of talent and money on the business of preventing things that seem not to happen, or that have already happened. More to the present point, such a careful assay of community successes and failures would make it possible to identify and hopefully enlist a wide variety of unrecognized and underutilized cultural resources. As can be seen in our own efforts to identify Aboriginal communities that appear to have already solved their own problem of youth suicide, doing just this would go an important distance towards determining what really counts as "best practices" that are worthy of "exchange," and of identifying, as potential partners in the task of knowledge transfer, whole communities whose indigenous knowledge is less entangled in a history of misused power and authority (Foucault 1980) than is knowledge made in New York City.

Can the Subaltern Speak?

If, as our own data concerning band-level variability in Aboriginal youth suicide rates illustrates, some communities are evidently in possession of forms of knowledge and practices that are currently unknown or unavailable to others, two general sorts of questions immediately arise. One of these asks: "What, exactly, are those knowledges and practices, and who knows about them?" The other has to do with just how deep and declarative such knowledge is, and whether and how it might be shared.

The first of these open questions is relatively the more easily settled through the application of simple, if procedurally involved, epidemiological procedures. Again, in the case of our own data, it is clear enough that those communities that are all or largely free of youth suicide must know and do things that are unknown or left undone by communities where youth suicide is epidemic. Similarly, there is no special mystery in knowing how to go about sorting through available community level descriptors in an effort to distinguish some of what sets more and less successful communities apart. The trick, if there is one, is in having access to useful measures that are common to all of the relevant communities and that capture important differences between them, and in having some workable theory that can guide one in distinguishing potentially relevant descriptors from the chaff that is otherwise available. In our own case, an elaborated developmental theory of individual and community level identity formation allowed us to zero in on a small handful of available "proxy" variables that served to differentially mark those communities that were more or less successful in reconstructing their cultural past, and gaining future control over their evolving civic lives. Figure 5 reproduces a list of eight such variables already shown to distinguish Aboriginal bands with relatively low and high youth suicide rates—variables that, when taken in combination (see Figure 6) are highly predictive of which communities have, and which do not have, the necessary actionable knowledge required to reduce youth suicide rates to zero.

Figure 5:   Suicide rates by community factors

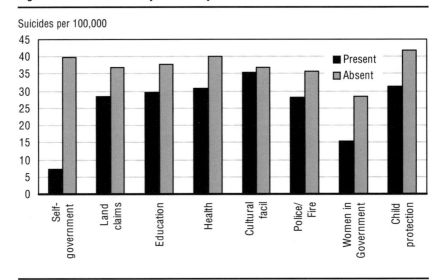

Figure 6:   Suicide rate by number of factors present, British Columbia, 1993-00

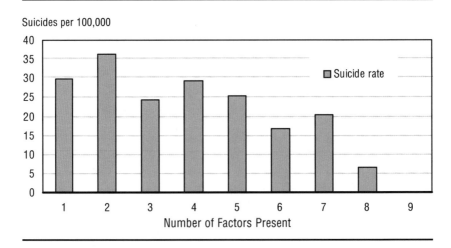

What such figures demonstrate is that we, as social scientists, now know some of what is required to create a world in which Aboriginal youth can find life worth living. Just as obviously, communities that have successfully engineered this considerable accomplishment also "know," in some sense, what they are about, even if, as is likely the case, they were moved to take the various helpful steps that they did without any explicit appreciation that doing so might coincide with achieving a low or absent suicide rate. In short, while both researchers, and the communities they serve, evidently know something of value, it is simply not clear how deep or declarative this knowledge actually is.

All of this is perhaps most obvious in the case of the research community. It is simply an empirical fact that the Aboriginal communities in British Columbia that have, for example, achieved a measure of self-government, or were quick off the mark to litigate for Aboriginal title of traditional lands, have lower or absent youth suicide rates. What remains a mystery is how these broad facts of civic life trickle down into the mental lives of individual Aboriginal youth in such a way that they end up choosing life over death. Until this is better understood—a problem that we are currently working to solve—it will remain unclear what, if anything, is to be recommended. Would it be enough (probably not) to simply urge the same community level actions on other groups that have been slow or unwilling to initiate such actions on their own? Some of our own most recent findings suggest that there is now a significant relation between lower youth suicide rates and actually having withdrawn in protest from British Columbia's treaty process. Clearly, the various proxy variables that have served so well to predict, at some frozen moment in time, rates of youth suicide are exactly that—"proxies" that temporarily stand in lieu of more meaningful and more enduring community actions that we do not yet understand.

The largest and least answered question concerning the especially successful Aboriginal communities that we have studied thus far is just how "declarative" their obvious procedural knowledge is. For purposes of internal consumption, it could be argued (we think mistakenly) that this scarcely matters. Those communities that are enjoying especially low suicide rates could simply soldier on as they have, for whatever reasons may have moved them in the past, all in the hopes that changing circumstances will not undermine their coincidental successes. Where more declarative or accessible knowledge is of more evident and immediate importance is in the world of knowledge transfer, and in any possible future attempt to broker an exchange of best practices. If, as we are currently working to determine, members of Aboriginal communities with variable rates of success in addressing the problem of youth suicide are willing to meet with the aim of being mutually helpful, then efforts, such as our own, to help unmask what lies behind already documented differences in community success rates will need to be a first step in this knowledge transfer process.

References

Berkhoffer, R.F. 1978. *The White Man's Indian.* New York: Vintage.

Chandler, M.J. 2000. "Surviving Time: The Persistence of Identity in This Culture and That." *Culture and Psychology* 6 (2): 209–231.

———. 2001. "The Time of Our Lives: Self-Continuity in Native and Non-Native Youth," in *Advances in Child Development and Behavior.* Vol. 28, ed. H.W. Reese. New York: Academic Press, 175–221.

Chandler, M.J., and Lalonde, C.E. 1998. "Cultural Continuity As a Hedge Against Suicide in Canada's First Nations." *Transcultural Psychiatry* 35 (2): 193–211.

———. 2000a. "Cross Cultural Suicide Prevention." *Visions: BC's Mental Health Journal* 11: 11–22.

———. 2000b. "Cultural Continuity As a Protective Factor Against Suicide in First Nations Youth." *Lifenotes* 5 (2): 10–11.

Chandler, M.J., Lalonde, C.E., and Sokol, B. 2000. "Continuities of Selfhood in the Face of Radical Developmental and Cultural Change" in *Culture, Thought, and Development*, ed. L. Nucci, G. Saxe, and E. Turiel. Mahwah, N.J.: Lawrence Erlbaum Associates, 65–84.

Chandler, M.J., Lalonde, C.E., Sokol, B., and Hallett, D. In press. *Personal Persistence, Identity Development, and Suicide: A Study of Native and Non-Native North American Adolescents.* Monographs of the Society for Research in Child Development.

Chandler, M.J., and Sokol, B. 2003. "Level This, Level That: The Place of Culture in the Construction of the Self" in *Social and Cognitive Development in the Context of Individual, Social, and Cultural Processes*, ed. C. Raeff and J.B. Benson. New York: Taylor and Francis, 191–216.

Duran, E., and Duran, B. 1995. *Native American Postcolonial Psychology.* SUNY series in transpersonal and humanistic psychology, ed. R.D. Mann. Albany: State University of New York Press.

Fanon, F. 1965. *A Dying Colonialism.* Translated by H. Chevaliar. New York: Grove Press.

Foucault, M. 1980. "George Canguilhem: Philosopher of Error." *Ideology and Consciousness* 7: 53–54.

Gandhi, L. 1998. *Postcolonial Theory: A Critical Introduction.* New York: Columbia University Press.

Hodgkenson, H.L. 1990. *The Demographics of American Indians: One Percent of the People; Fifty Percent of the Diversity.* Washington, D.C.: Institute for Educational Leadership, Inc., Center for Demographic Policy.

Kirmayer, L. 1994. "Suicide Among Canadian Aboriginal People." *Transcultural Psychiatric Research Review* 31: 3–57.

Lalonde, C.E. 2003. "Counting the Costs of Failures of Personal and Cultural Continuity." *Human Development* 46: 137–144.

Malchy, B., Enns, M., Young, T., and Cox, B. 1997. "Suicide Among Manitoba's Aboriginal People, 1988 to 1994." *Canadian Medical Association Journal* 156: 1133–1138.

Nandy, A. 1983. *The Intimate Enemy: Loss and Recovery of Self Under Colonialism.* Delhi: Oxford University Press.

Said, E. 1978. *Orientalism.* New York: Pantheon Books.

Spivak, G. 1985. "Can the Subaltern Speak? Speculations on Widow Sacrifice." *Wedge* 7/8: 120–130.

6

Social Capital in First Nations Communities: Concept and Measurement

Javier Mignone, Janet Longclaws, John O'Neil and Cameron Mustard

Introduction

Social epidemiology is motivated by the question "Why is this society unhealthy?" versus the traditional epidemiological question "Why did this individual get sick?"[1] These are two kinds of etiological questions. The latter question seeks the causes of cases, whereas the former seeks the causes of prevalence and incidence, and thus requires the study of population features—not so much the characteristics of individuals.[2] Compositional explanations for variations in health between different communities assume that these areas include different types of individuals, and differences between these individuals would account for the observed difference between places. On the other hand, a contextual explanation would consider that there are features of the social or physical environment that influence the health of those exposed to it (either in addition to or in interaction with individual characteristics). This derives in the key distinction between individual level determinants and ecological level determinants of health. The critical view held by the Royal Commission on Aboriginal Peoples (RCAP) on the individualistic analysis of socioeconomic determinants of health is aligned with this contextual explanation (Royal Commission on Aboriginal Peoples 1996a). It was with this perspective that the Health Information and Research Committee (HIR) of the Assembly of Manitoba Chiefs (AMC), together with the Centre for Aboriginal Health Research (CAHR) at the University of Manitoba, outlined a strategic program of research entitled "Why Are Some First Nations Communities Healthy and Others Are Not? Constituting Evidence in First Nations Health Policy" (O'Neil et al. 1999). The authors of this proposed program indicated that analytical frameworks that attempt to associate factors such as poverty with health outcomes are insensitive to the complex socioeconomic conditions that exist in First Nations communities. Nonetheless, they also suggested that more recent developments in the population health model that include notions of social inequality, social cohesion, and social capital "appear to have more in common with Aboriginal health models." To date, however, there is scarce research on the impact of the social environment on health status in First Nations communities in Canada that include these perspectives.

As mentioned, there are a variety of possible ecological level descriptors for these factors. Social capital is one of these descriptors. It is an elusive concept that, particularly in social epidemiological studies, appears to have been used with little theoretical examination. Thus, if this notion is to be used with any validity to empirically verify its potential as a determinant of health, a conceptual formulation of social capital and the development of culturally appropriate measures for First Nations communities are first required. In essence, this study resulted from the need to scientifically characterize and measure social capital in First Nations communities for subsequent theorization and empirical testing of its potential as a health determinant, as proposed by the research program of the AMC and the CAHR. This is the main contribution of the inquiry.

From the conception of the inquiry to the use of its findings (including all stages in between), the study is a product of the partnership between the HIR Committee of the AMC, three First Nations communities of Manitoba and the CAHR. The study was a team effort that involved numerous individuals in different capacities from these partnering entities. Finally, this research could not have taken place without the funding provided by the Canadian Population Health Initiative of the Canadian Institute for Health Information.

The following were the study's main objectives, specific objectives and questions. The main objectives were to (1) formulate a conceptual framework of social capital for First Nations communities, and (2) develop an instrument, culturally appropriate to First Nations communities, for the measurement of social capital. The specific objectives were to (1) identify the dimensions and components of the concept of social capital in a conceptual framework for First Nations communities, (2) develop culturally appropriate items that capture the identified dimensions within the concept of social capital, (3) conduct pilot testing of the developed instrument to measure social capital in First Nations communities, and (4) conduct psychometric analyses of the social capital instrument and revise accordingly. The research questions asked were: (1) What are the dimensions of social capital in First Nations communities? and (2) What are the estimates of the psychometric properties of an instrument developed to measure social capital in First Nations communities?

Methodology

The study consisted of two phases and was conducted as follows. The HIR Committee chose three Manitoban First Nations communities to be part of the research from seven that had volunteered to participate.

The first phase of the study used ethnographic methodology with two aims: to contribute to the development of the conceptual framework, and to generate a list of survey questions. Over a period of approximately three weeks in each community, primary data collection techniques involved a combination of in-depth interviews, informal focus groups, participant observation, archival research and unobtrusive observations. The total number of interviewees reached 89 individuals. Based on a concept analysis and on the results of the ethnographic study, dimensions of social capital were identified for measurement and a list of questionnaire items was developed. After extensive feedback and seven drafts, a final version of the 137-item questionnaire was pilot-tested during the second phase of the study. A total of 462 randomly selected adults from the three communities were surveyed (Community A, 204; Community B, 135; Community C, 123). Community research assistants administered the survey. This large sample number allowed the study to conduct a series of psychometric analyses to determine how reliable and valid the instrument was. The questionnaire contained three separate scales, one for each of the three dimensions of social capital (bonding, bridging and linkage).

Findings

Study findings are reported in the following two subsections. The first one corresponds to the results of the concept analysis and the development of the conceptual framework that incorporates findings from the ethnographic study. It presents the conceptual structure on which the instrument was developed and addresses the first main objective of the study. The second subsection summarizes the results of the psychometric analyses that assessed the reliability and validity of the survey instrument and addresses the second main objective of the study.

Concept Analysis, Conceptual Framework and Ethnographic Study

An analysis of numerous definitions of social capital concluded that, to the point that it is a property of the social environment, it takes the format of a relational resource. It is a resource composed of a variety of elements, most notably social networks, social norms and values, trust and shared resources. Its function(s) appear(s) related to the enabling of some societal good within the boundary of that specific societal level. A more in-depth analysis of the trajectory of the concept and its different interpretations was then performed.

First Nations Communities' Social Capital Framework

Based on the concept analysis and on results of the ethnographic study, social capital was formulated as constituted by three dimensions: bonding social capital, bridging social capital and linkage social capital. Each dimension was postulated as including three mutually dependent components: socially invested resources, culture and social networks. Is social capital "social" because "capital" is collectively owned, or is it social because the "social" is the "capital"? The identification in this model of "socially invested resources" (the first premise in the question) and of "networks" (the second premise in the question) in a mutually dependent relationship, via cultural enablers or inhibitors, arrives to an understanding of social capital that resolves this apparent ambiguity. This model considers social capital as a feature of communities, with the caveat that the community of which it is a feature must be clearly delimited (e.g., communities can be areal/spatial, of interest, etc.). This study centred its understanding of First Nations communities as those delimited by the political unity of a reserve, but including all inhabitants, both band members and non-band members. In this sense they can be considered communities of place (Flora 1997). However, this definition does not exclude those living off-reserve, but considers them part of the community through their connections with on-reserve community members.

Bonding social capital refers to that within community relations. It addresses the networks, culture and socially invested resources inside the particular society, community, or group in question (i.e., the intracommunity ties). Bridging social capital is essentially a horizontal metaphor, implying connections between societies, communities, or groups (i.e., the inter-community ties). Linkage social capital refers to a vertical dimension. In the words of Woolcock (2001), "the capacity to leverage resources, ideas, and information from formal institutions beyond the community." Specifically to our study, bonding social capital refers to relations within each First Nations community. Bridging refers to horizontal links with other communities, be they other First Nations communities, or other communities of place (e.g., urban centres). Linkage refers to connections between a particular First Nation and institutions such as federal/provincial government departments and public/private corporations (e.g., Manitoba Hydro, banks).

Table 1 summarizes the social capital framework, showing each dimension as consisting of the three components and their descriptors. For Socially Invested Resources (SIR) the descriptors are physical, symbolic, financial, human, or natural. The central notion is that these resources be socially invested, in other words, that they be potentially accessed by, or of potential future benefit to, any member of the specific community. Each descriptor captures the resource investment at that specific stage of being a resource. Physical refers to tangible resources produced by human beings. Symbolic refers to resources that pertain to the identity of the community as such, and for the most part are intangible. Financial are monetary resources in its different forms. Human resources mean human capacity as a product of formal and informal education. Natural resources are those provided by nature, shaped with or without human intervention. Resources are essentially mutable, for example, a financial resource becomes a physical resource when money is used to build houses, or a human resource becomes a financial resource when income is earned due to an education degree. Consequently, these five descriptors seek to capture the different facets of socially invested resources at a given point in time.

Table 1

Bonding		
SIR*	Culture	Networks
Physical	Trust	
Symbolic	Norms of	
Financial	Reciprocity	Inclusive
Human	Collective Action	Flexible
Natural	Participation	Diverse
Bridging		
SIR	Culture	Networks
Physical	Trust	
Symbolic	Norms of	
Financial	Reciprocity	Inclusive
Human	Collective Action	Flexible
Natural	Participation	Diverse
Linkage		
SIR	Culture	Networks
Physical	Trust	
Symbolic	Norms of	
Financial	Reciprocity	Inclusive
Human	Collective Action	Flexible
Natural	Participation	Diverse

SIR* = Socially Invested Resources

The use of the term "culture" as a component of social capital has a particular, albeit related, sense from that of its more common use. It encompasses notions of trust, norms of reciprocity, collective action and participation. Trust is self-explanatory in that it means that community members trust one another as well as community leaders. Existence of norms of reciprocity, although feasible when considered a neutral notion, conveys for this framework the idea that the reciprocity is of a positive nature. Collective action represents the fact that community members may pursue actions that seek the benefit of the collective. Finally, a culture of participation implies the willingness of community members to be involved with others in common activities. The difference with collective action is that the main reason for participation is that of the individual's interest, with no explicit purpose of a collective good.

Networks are understood as "structures of recurrent transactions" (Aldrich 1982), and are described according to their diversity, inclusiveness and flexibility. Higher degrees of these three characteristics would imply higher levels of social capital. Inclusiveness of networks refers to the notion that these structures of interactions are relatively open to the possibility of newcomers and to the exchange of information with newcomers. While there is room for subgroups with high levels of interaction (e.g., communities of interest within a community of place), communities require the existence of diverse networks for higher levels of social capital of the community as a whole. Diversity implies the co-existence of networks that differ from one another, composed of distinct elements or qualities, but that are capable of interacting in a meaningful way. Flexibility of networks implies a ready capability to adapt to new, different, or changing requirements.

Inclusiveness, diversity and flexibility are actually interrelated qualities. They are different aspects of a same phenomenon. In general, a correlation among these three descriptors of networks should be expected. Both bonding and bridging networks refer to horizontal relations. The idea is that lateral learning is critical in networks—communities learn best from each other. The difference between bonding and bridging networks is that the latter refers to those within community relations, whereas the former refers to those between community relations. Networks for the linkage dimension refer to the links of the community to provincial, federal government departments and public/private corporations. Though horizontal links (bonding and bridging) could acquire more or less vertical characteristics due to power inequality dynamics, they are still considered horizontal in nature, whereas linkage refers to relations vertically constituted because the power hierarchy is instituted as vertical (consequently it is possible for these linkages to be more or less horizontal, but from a given vertical nature). However, the same ideas apply in the assessment of the networks, whatever the dimension.

Valences[3] are required to assess the stocks of social capital. These valences are what the framework calls descriptors (they should not be considered sub-components). In the case of culture and networks, they are straightforward in the framework. These descriptors are purposely positive valences. For example, in the case of culture, higher levels of trust would ultimately entail, *ceteris paribus*, higher stocks of social capital. However, this is more indirect for the descriptors of SIR, where the valence is actually the degree to which the resources are socially invested, and the descriptors are specifications of types of resources. Nonetheless, the combined degree to which each specification of SIR is socially invested speaks—other elements being equal—to higher stocks of social capital.

In summary, social capital would be assessed by the combination of its three dimensions, and each dimension by the combination of each component. This brings us to the operational definition of social capital for this study: *Social capital characterizes a First Nation community based on the degree that its resources are socially invested, that it presents a culture of trust, norms of reciprocity, collective action and participation, and that it possesses inclusive, flexible, and diverse networks. Social capital of a community is assessed through a combination of its bonding (within group relations), bridging (intercommunity ties), and linkage (relation with formal institutions) dimensions.*[4,5] Table 2 illustrates these ideas with examples taken from community interviews.

Table 2

Bonding Social Capital

Socially Invested Resources – Symbolic

Cultural camps for children and youth held in one of the communities: "[T] hey'd show the kids how to snare, trap beaver, skin beaver, rats, muskrats, moose anything that tracks…they would always talk Cree….they would make bannock over the fire…you know, what the people used to do a long time ago, that's what they did with the kids."

Culture – Norms of Reciprocity

Illustrated by the following comment:
"There are norms in our community where people do things for other people. It's not written down in stone anywhere, it's just part of the culture. If someone is building a house and says, I need a screw-gun, yeah I have a box, go to my shed and get it. And that person later, the one who loaned the thing may say, I need to borrow an axe off him, and goes back to the guy that borrowed from him."

Networks - Flexible

Families not interacting with other families because of old disputes illustrates lack of flexibility of networks, as per the following comment: "You hear a lot of animosities that are carried forward from years back...I've also heard so and so and his family did so and so to this family and so we are not talking to so and so. There is a lot that is carried on for quite a few years."

Bridging Social Capital

Socially Invested Resources – Natural

An example is the existence of a Natural Resources Secretariat within a First Nations organizations in Manitoba that represents twenty-seven communities, to which two of the communities that participated in the study belong to. A particular illustration was the assistance provided by this First Nations organization to one of these communities in conducting traditional land use and traditional knowledge research and mapping, as well as supporting outstanding claims related to the environmental impact of hydroelectric development.

Culture – Trust

According to the band administrators of one of the communities, they have been for the most part successful in learning from some initiatives of other First Nations communities. "[O]ther [First Nations] communities, they are very open, but depending upon what issues it is..." The openness between First Nations communities in terms of exchanging knowledge and experience in dealing with common issues can be an expression of trust.

Networks – Diverse

A lack of diversity was expressed by an individual from one of the communities: "We have to learn how to network with one another... even network with our First Nations, even the ones that are the most successful, that have all those facilities in their First Nations. How did you do it? Can you lend us a hand over here. There is not too much communication with other communities."

Linkage Social Capital

Socially Invested Resources – Financial

This observation made by one interviewee about the relationship with banks evidences difficulties in this area: "[W]ith the majority of native people I think its either you have poor credit, no credit or bankrupt... and because of that a lot of Band members have limited access or no access to funding to start their own businesses."

Culture – Participation

The loss of participation at a linkage level was made graphic by this interviewee's statement: "Yes, I guess part of our practice, part of our culture is doing a lot of community consultation…and the federal government slashed that piece of it…we used to have community co-ordinators who would do the consultation, set up workshops to inform the people about the changes…the federal government argued what we were doing too much consultation."

Networks – Inclusive

Inclusiveness relates to interactions with institutions. An example of the former from one of the communities is the following statement from a band official: "So I contacted the company representing Indian Affairs …so I dealt with…a gentleman by the name of…a really good guy to deal with…and he was extremely cooperative with all my ideas… providing very useful information that saved money and helped upgrade educational services."

Instrument Development Results

Primary analysis goals were to produce a measurement device that had good discriminatory power among First Nations communities, was made up of internally consistent scales, and had good construct validity. The results of these analyses reduced the number of items in the questionnaire to a total of ninety-nine. The internal consistency of each scale presented coefficient alphas of 0.84 (Bonding), 0.73 (Bridging), and 0.81 (Linkage). For a scale to be deemed internally consistent, 0.70 is the acceptable minimum.

After a number of consultations, the research team had hypothesized that one of the communities would be expected to perform better on the Bonding and Linkage scales, and another on the Bridging scale. If the results corresponded with these predictions it would provide some evidence of construct validity to the instrument. Ninety-seven percent of items from the Bonding scale, 95% of items from the Bridging scale, and 84% from the Linkage scale were in the predicted rank order, thus providing tentative evidence of the construct validity of the scales.

To examine whether empirical support could be found to justify the multi-component conceptualization of each dimension of social capital, factor analyses were run for each scale. Results justified the multi-component conceptualization of each dimension of social capital, but only to a relative extent as to what was predicted in the framework.

The final two steps of the analysis sought to determine if demographic characteristics of respondents accounted for the variance in social capital mean scores of the communities. Subgroup differences within communities were also examined. For these goals, stepwise multiple regression analyses were conducted. The results suggested that the characteristics of respondents, despite not being able to be totally ruled out as having some impact on scores, did not appear problematic in that the respondents' community was in most cases a better predictor. This was an important finding in that it validates the idea that social capital scores may vary over and above subgroup differences within communities.

A comparison between scales suggested that the Bonding scale performed the best in the above assessment, with better reliability and validity, followed by the Linkage scale and finally the Bridging scale.

Research Implications

The study resulted from the need to scientifically characterize and measure social capital in First Nations communities—for subsequent theorization and empirical testing of its potential as a health determinant. Both conceptual and measurement findings faced a series of challenges that require consideration. As well, numerous decisions were based on a series of assumptions. The main ones were that individual scores could be meaningfully aggregated to a community level score, that individuals' perception could be used as evidence, that social capital is a community trait (i.e., with temporal stability), and that results could be generalized to other First Nations communities.[6] The study's conceptual formulation of social capital allowed for these assumptions. The instrument, a survey questionnaire, was composed of three scales, each tapping into a different dimension of social capital. Consequently, its psychometric qualities were assessed separately. After discarding unreliable and non-discriminatory items, the Bonding and Linkage scales evidenced good internal consistency while the Bridging scale showed acceptable internal consistency. This meant that the questionnaire developed on the basis of findings from the first phase of the study was reliable (although test-retest stability was not established due to sample limitations) and discriminated between communities. A further important result was that these differences occurred in the hypothesized order, providing good initial evidence for the construct validity of the instrument. The fact that these individual level data were expected to be aggregated to a community level variable (social capital) meant that we had to determine if individual characteristics of respondents accounted for the variance more than hypothesized community level characteristics. Despite some exceptions, the overall picture was clear that the respondents' community was a better predictor of scores in regression analyses than individuals' characteristics.

So much for the instrument—what did the evidence suggest about the multi-dimensional conceptual framework? The main question in this regard was to determine if there was empirical support to justify the multi-dimensional conceptualization. Results for the three scales had varying degrees of disagreement with this conceptualization. The main implication, from a construct perspective, appears to be that the framework's structure offers dimensional distinctions that are not as distinct as predicted. It raises questions about the validity of the components as formulated in the framework, although not enough to outwardly discard its usefulness. We are then faced with an instrument that appears to be reliable and valid, but at the same time with a construct that has been—only to some extent—validated, and with questions raised about its component structure. As is, the questionnaire can be used in further studies, but the confidence for this use varies between the three scales. This was particularly the case for the Bridging and Linkage scales.

We now have an instrument that evidenced fewer limitations for the Bonding scale and more for the Bridging and Linkage scales. A detailed analysis of non-responses and "don't know" rates demonstrated that they were closely linked to direct or non-direct experience of the respondent with the issue inquired by the item. Community issues would be expected to relate more to individuals' day-to-day experience, whereas intercommunity and institutional topics somewhat less. The differential rates between the Bonding scale and the other two scales were consistent with this expectation. The main consequence appears to be that the use of individual survey data should be supplemented with other sources of evidence to improve the measurement of social capital as conceptually specified in our study. In this sense, further social capital measurement tools would benefit from the development of composite measures, where aggregate data from this questionnaire would be combined with what could be called ecological level data. The latter could come from two sources: key informants survey and community level data. These sources would constitute a structural scale.

Let us consider what the idea of social capital, formulated in this study, can add to the understanding of First Nations communities health determinants. It presents a dynamic way of characterizing communities that enables comparability based on features that encompass both internal and external relations. It captures social elements with varying degrees of tangibility, although all of them are of importance from a First Nations communities perspective. Finally, it offers a meaningful structure from which to hypothesize and empirically study potential pathways to health of social environmental factors. This is enabled by seeking to understand the social energy of communities, precisely because it is based on the assumption that communities cannot be understood as the sum of parts, but as entities that possess global dynamics, both internal and in relation to other social entities. Consequently, a First Nation community may assess itself, both internally and in relation to other communities and institutions, by how well its resources are socially invested; by how good of a culture of trust, norms of reciprocity and collective action it possesses; and by how inclusive, flexible and diverse its networks are.

Two research implications emerge. The line of inquiry that leads to the theoretical development and empirical testing of population health determinants pathway models that incorporate ecological level factors requires precise conceptual formulations of social environmental variables and the use of valid measures. The present study has taken an important step in fulfilling these requirements for First Nations health research. Thus, the first implication is that we now have an initial tool with which to advance along this line of research.[7] We are, to some extent, better placed to proceed, using a nature analogy, to theoretically formulate and empirically examine the ecology of the forest as a determinant of species health based on the understanding that the forest is much more than the sum of trees. Nonetheless, as was repeatedly reiterated throughout the study, construct and measurement validation are part of an ongoing process, which brings us to the second implication—the use of study findings to continue developing the construct of social capital (and maybe other constructs) and improving the tools for its measurement.

A research agenda that would continue this line of inquiry would require the following: First, one further round of measurement refinement and validation, as suggested in the measurement solutions section. Second, based on findings from our current study and from findings from a future study using the revised tools, further adjustments need to be made to the conceptual framework. Third, empirical inquiries need to be conducted to test the hypothesis of social capital as a determinant of health in First Nations communities. Notwithstanding, results from the current study allow for initial steps of the latter by using the current questionnaire in longitudinal studies, for example, with all the cautions already identified. This research agenda would continue to require an effective partnership between First Nations communities, First Nations organizations and academic centres in a research process that, on an ongoing basis, combines conceptual analysis grounded theory development and quantitative evidence.

Policy Implications

The warning that social capital could be a "Trojan horse" for colonization from any side of the ideological spectrum (Labonte 1999) has particular relevance within the First Nations' context. Given the history of relations between First Nations communities and European descendents and their institutions, the risk of furthering colonization by new means merits careful attention. Consequently, policy implications of the study need to be considered from three points of view. First is the innate political nature of the concept of social capital; second, the political utilization of the concept; and third, the potential of policy to impact social capital.

Inherent to the way social capital was conceptualized in our study is the notion of community as an entity of empirical inquiry and policy. The idea of higher or lower levels of community social capital is not value-free, given that it presupposes the good of the community, as a whole, as a base criterion. As an epistemologist argues (Demo 1985), social sciences are intrinsically ideological, meaning that ideology exists in reality itself because social reality is inevitably historical and political. The implication is that empirical inquiries that incorporate the construct of social capital need to make this fact explicit in interpreting their findings. Thus, studies using this construct require that both the methods and the findings be a product of First Nations communities' and organizations' interpretation. This also relates to the second area for consideration, the political use of the concept. The assumption is that findings in this area must be subject to First Nations community and organizations representatives' interpretation. Consequently, the policy decisions would derive from their interpretation of the findings. Lastly, if social capital can be a source of inquiry, then the effects of policy on the social capital of communities could and should be monitored, if not considered from the start. The construct developed here suggests that policy decisions from different levels of government, corporations and First Nations leadership may intentionally or unintentionally impact community social capital stocks for better or for worse. In essence, it highlights the fact that policies that are in the hands of several parties can have profound impacts on First Nations communities, and, consequently, on the health and well-being of their populations.

Endnotes

Funded by the Canadian Population Health Initiative of the Canadian Institute for Health Information.

1. In the words of Kawachi (Kawachi 2002).

2. This paraphrases Rose's ideas (Rose 1985).

3. Valence: the degree of attractiveness an individual, activity, or object possesses as a behavioral goal. *Websters' Dictionary* (Merriam-Webster Inc., 1989).

4. A quote from the Royal Commission on Aboriginal Peoples, referring to Aboriginal societies of the past, offers a clear description of communities that could be understood as possessing high stocks of social capital:

    > The economic relations embedded in traditional cultures emphasized conservation of renewable resources, limiting harvesting on the basis of need, and distributing resources equitably within the community, normally through family networks. Since families and clans owned rights to resources and since everyone was connected in a family, no one was destitute and no one was unemployed. (Royal Commission on Aboriginal Peoples 1996b)

5. A major issue with the use of social capital in population health research has frequently been the lack of a clear distinction from related concepts, or of not identifying the areas where there may be overlaps. Social cohesion suggests both overlapping aspects and distinctions with the understanding of social capital previously formulated. Social cohesion closely approximates the dimension of bonding social capital, in particular, the culture and networks components. However, it does not refer to socially invested resources and networks. In this sense, social cohesion can be considered a concept with overlapping aspects to social capital, or a subset of social capital. The latter perspective would locate social cohesion mostly, though not exclusively, within the dimension of bonding social capital.

    A main difference between social support and social capital relates to what they each characterize. If we consider social capital as an attribute of individuals or families, then there can be some significant overlapping with social support. Social support, in some respect, shares with social capital (more so than social cohesion) the notion of resources and networks. However, contrary to social capital, social support is not a notion that has been formulated as an attribute of a community. The availability of social support appears more individually, or family based and proximal, than social capital.

The concept of social networks presents several common notions with social capital. First, as was examined in the concept analysis, "network" is a component of each dimension of social capital. In this sense, the idea of social networks fits well within social capital. Second, the concept of social networks shares with social capital the double capacity of being an attribute of individuals and families (the "egocentric network approach"), and of being an attribute of a society. The main distinction between social capital and social networks is that the former includes a "resources" component (socially invested resources). The concept of social networks focuses on "the medium," whereas social capital is composed of "the medium and the message" (Woolcock 1998). More so, social capital encompasses the possibility of the medium being the message.

6. Two further assumptions merit brief attention, that individuals understand the boundaries of community in the same way, and that all community members' views should be weighted equally.

7. In fact, the 2002 wave of the Manitoba First Nations Longitudinal Health Survey has already incorporated a significant segment of the Bonding scale in their survey.

References

Aldrich, H. 1982. "The Origins and Persistence of Social Networks" in *Social Structure and Network Analysis*, ed. P. Marsden and N. Lin. Beverly Hills: Sage, 281–293.

Demo, P. 1985. *Investigacion participante: Mito y realidad.* Buenos Aires: Kapelusz.

Flora, C.B. 1997. "Building Social Capital: The Importance of Entrepreneurial Social Infrastructure." *Rural Development News*, Iowa State University (June).

Kawachi, I. 2002. "What Is Social Epidemiology?" *Social Science and Medicine* 54: 1739–1741.

Labonte, R. 1999. "Social Capital and Community Development: Practitioner Emptor." *Australian and New Zealand Journal of Public Health* 23: 430–433.

Merriam-Webster Inc. 1989. *Webster's Ninth New Collegiate Dictionary.* Markham, O.N.: Thomas Allen and Son.

O'Neil, J.D., Kaufert, P.T., Reading, J.R., Kaufert, J., Young, T.K., and Manitoba First Nations Health Research and Information Committee. 1999. "Why Are Some First Nations Communities Healthy and Others Are Not? Constituting Evidence in First Nations Health Policy." Research program proposal presented to the Social Sciences and Humanities Research Council, Northern Health Research Unit, University of Manitoba.

Rose, G. 1985. "Sick Individuals and Sick Populations." *International Journal of Epidemiology* 14: 32–38.

Royal Commission on Aboriginal Peoples. 1996a. *Report of the Royal Commission on Aboriginal Peoples: Gathering Strength.* Vol. 3. Ottawa: Minister of Supply and Services Canada.

_____. 1996b. *Report of the Royal Commission on Aboriginal Peoples: Looking Forward, Looking Back.* Vol. 1. Ottawa: Minister of Supply and Services Canada.

Woolcock, M. 1998. *Social Theory, Development Policy, and Poverty Alleviation: A Comparative-Historical Analysis of Group-Based Banking in Developing Economies.* Brown University.

_____. 2001. "The Place of Social Capital in Understanding Social and Economic Outcomes." *Isuma* 2: 11–17.

Part Three:
Gender Issues

7

Matrimonial Real Property Issues On-Reserve

Wendy Cornet and Allison Lendor

Introduction

For most First Nation reserve communities in Canada, there is currently no applicable law for matrimonial real property disputes from any source—federal, provincial or First Nation governments. The *Indian Act* does not address the issue of matrimonial property rights on-reserve, during marriage or upon marriage or relationship breakdown, or recognize a First Nation law-making authority in the area. In fact, the Act only recognizes a narrow field of First Nation authority over land rights and land management on-reserve, and even less authority over matters relating to family law. The *Indian Act*[1] applies to most First Nation reserve land in Canada. The exceptions are First Nations who have negotiated new legal arrangements replacing the *Indian Act* land management regime through self-government agreements, or through the *First Nations Land Management Act*.[2] These arrangements have provided opportunities for First Nation laws to be adopted addressing matrimonial real property, or for provincial law to be applied.

As a result of the 1986 decisions of the Supreme Court of Canada in the *Derrickson* and *Paul* cases,[3] we know that, while provincial laws relating to matrimonial property apply to *personal* property of "Indians" on-reserve, these laws cannot be applied to modify individual interests on reserve land—such as a family home—under the *Indian Act*. The result is that spouses experiencing a marital breakdown (or breakdown of a common-law or same-sex relationship) are left to resolve property issues affecting the family home largely on their own. There is no applicable body of federal, provincial or First Nation law to guide spouses trying to reach out-of-court settlements, or for courts in dealing with proprietary rights to matrimonial real property issues on-reserve. There is no statement of law recognizing the equal right of spouses on-reserve to the family home, and basic remedies available off-reserve under provincial laws, such as interim exclusive possession of a family home, are not available to spouses on-reserve.

For a number of years, organizations representing First Nation women have urged the Government of Canada to take action to address matrimonial real property issues on-reserve. Litigation has been launched by the Native Women's Association of Canada, and the British Columbia Native Women's Society, over the lack of legal protections respecting matrimonial real property on-reserve (in separate suits against the Government of Canada). They have characterized the lack of applicable legislation recognizing the equal rights of spouses in relation to matrimonial real property as a denial of equality rights. UN human rights bodies have also expressed concerns about equality rights respecting matrimonial real property on-reserve in Canada.[4]

This chapter will provide some general background on the law as it currently stands and identify key policy questions for First Nation women, First Nation[5] governments and the federal government to consider in identifying options for action in this area.

Framing the Issues

Law often reflects specific cultural values. Canadian family law regarding matrimonial real property (statute law and case law) predominately reflects the cultural values of non-Aboriginal people and European-sourced legal traditions.

Use of the term "matrimonial real property" necessarily presumes the application of several European-sourced legal concepts and assumptions, such as

- division of property into "real" (land and things attached to the land, such as houses) and "personal" (cash, vehicles, pension funds, household goods and so on);
- "ownership" of portions of land by individuals providing exclusive rights as against the rest of the world;
- the capacity to place a monetary value on land and things;
- narrow legal definitions of "spouses" (which often exclude couples in Aboriginal customary marriages, common-law relationships and same-sex relationships); and
- an assumption that matrimonial real property issues do not extend to other family members who are not "spouses" or "common-law partners" (however these terms are variously defined in federal and provincial statutes).

In an *Indian Act* reserve context, these concepts and values respecting property and family matters conflict, in many cases, with First Nation laws and values. This presents a challenge for policy-makers wishing to fill the legislative gap respecting matrimonial real property rights on-reserve.

In addition to differences in underlying values and assumptions, there are a number of legal and factual elements that distinguish matrimonial real property issues on-reserve, under the *Indian Act*, from situations off-reserve:

- absence of fee simple ownership, and restrictions on alienation of interests in reserve land to non-band members;
- the decision-making authority of band councils in determining allotments to individual members, and in determining residency rights of non-member spouses;
- conjugal relationships (whether married under provincial law, married under Aboriginal customary law, common-law relationships or same-sex relationships) often consist of persons with different legal, band membership, or land claim beneficiary status under the *Indian Act*, and, accordingly, different residency rights;
- often limited land or housing to accommodate needs of entire membership and their families;
- band-owned housing on common reserve lands, or band-owned housing on land held by allotment to an individual band member; and
- distinctions in the scope of provincial law applicable to real property interests in designated lands relative to real property interests in unsurrendered reserve lands.

For the Government of Canada, gender equality is a key policy value expected to guide the development of all federal policy and legislation.[6] Some First Nation women question whether mainstream equality analysis and gender equality analysis can assist First Nation women striving to reassert their traditional roles and place in First Nation communities, such as the strong and central role of women in matriarchal societies. A different view, held by other First Nations women, is that only when Charter equality values are applied to all legislation, whether federal or First Nation in source, can women be assured of reasserting their rightful place in First Nation communities.

It is clear from judicial decisions and federal policy statements that Charter equality analysis and gender equality analysis are supposed to take into account relevant contextual factors, such as the existence of multiple or compounded forms of discrimination and social inequality. How such analyses of compound discrimination are to be conducted is less clear. It is a relatively untouched area of judicial decision and federal policy analysis in a First Nation context.[7]

In the context of matrimonial real property issues on-reserve, such an analysis would recognize how First Nation women have, historically, experienced racism and sexism—as well as other forms of discrimination— as a result of the *Indian Act*. For example, the imposition of non-Aboriginal concepts of private or individual property rights, combined with numerous forms of patriarchal biases, have led to First Nation men being the primary holders of Certificates of Possession on-reserve. This, in turn, contributed to the displacement of many First Nation women from their traditional roles, and negatively affected their gender relations with men and their relationship to First Nation land. With respect to matrimonial real property, the collective impacts of colonialism (e.g., the displacement or suppression of First Nation cultural values combined with gender bias) have resulted in many women finding themselves in a disadvantageous legal position when their marriage or common-law relationship breaks down. A comprehensive gender equality analysis must also recognize that First Nation women can be negatively affected, in regard to matrimonial real property issues, by the net effect of the *Indian Act* and decision making by Band Councils at the First Nation community level.

Individual Rights to Occupation and Use of Reserve Land

Under the Canadian legal system, legal title to Indian reserve land is held by the federal Crown for the use and benefit of specific First Nations through the "Bands" recognized under the *Indian Act*.[8] Under the *Indian Act*, there is no individual fee simple ownership of reserve land, but a system of allotment of individual rights of possession of specific sections of reserve land.[9] "Allotment" is the term used to refer to the granting of the right to use and occupy reserve land to a member of a First Nation by the council of the First Nation.[10] The *Indian Act* requires that allotments of reserve land to band members be authorized by the Band Council and approved by the Minister of Indian Affairs (or by the Band Council on the Minister's behalf when this authority has been delegated, as mentioned above.) Under the *Indian Act* system of reserve land allotment to individuals, a Certificate of Possession is to be issued following Ministerial approval. Band members may transfer a land allotment to another band member, but the Act requires that the transfer be approved by the Minister. The rights of First Nation individuals holding land allotments by Certificate of Possession have been characterized as unique and not comparable to any legal interest in land off-reserve.[11]

Some First Nations refuse to use Certificates of Possession and instead operate custom systems of allotment. Custom allotment is a right to occupy reserve land granted to an individual by a Band Council or First Nation government outside of the authority of the *Indian Act*, meaning the First Nation does not request approval or registration of the allotment, and a Certificate of Possession is not issued. The Indian Lands Registry, administered by the Department of Indian Affairs, does not accept these transactions—or any subsequent transfers for registration—as they are considered "outside the Indian Act and are not legal interests under the Act."[12]

The fact that transfers by individual band members of reserve lands are often not registered suggests the Indian Lands Registry may not reflect the social reality of land transfers on-reserve, nor the reality of customary law of First Nations using customary allotment. There are, in effect, competing legal systems on-reserve with respect to land allotments, and as a result, disputes often end up in the courts.[13] The uncertainty affecting land allotments, transfers and proof of legal entitlement to occupy specific portions of reserve land can negatively impact efforts to clarify matrimonial real property issues.

Overview of Provincial/Territorial Law on Matrimonial Property

Matrimonial property can be personal and real property owned by either or both spouses. Provincial and territorial laws in Canada set out legal principles for defining exactly what constitutes matrimonial property, and for placing a value on it in order to determine an equitable division upon dissolution of marriage. Provincial matrimonial property legislation is passed under the broad scope of authority provided by s. 92(13) of the *Constitution Act, 1867*, under the head of power titled "Property and Civil Rights in the Province."

Provincial and territorial legislation also, typically, provides for interim remedies, such as exclusive possession of the matrimonial home during a period of separation or in situations of family violence. Some provinces and territories have adopted family violence legislation to address the need for protection of abused family members, and for the right of victims to remain in their home.[14] Off-reserve, orders of interim exclusive possession can be issued in respect to a matrimonial home regardless of whether the home is owned or is being leased, and irrespective of which spouse may be listed on the title or lease. Other grounds on which a spouse can seek an interim order for exclusive possession of the matrimonial home include the best interests of children.

The purpose of today's matrimonial property laws is to recognize the equal position of spouses within marriage, to recognize marriage as a form of partnership and to provide for the orderly and equitable settlement of the affairs of the spouses upon the breakdown of the marriage.

In an off-reserve context, each province and territory has passed legislation addressing the division of matrimonial property—both "real property" (land and buildings on the land) and "personal property" (assets other than real property, such as cash, investments and proceeds from sale of matrimonial real property). This provincial/territorial legislation expresses legal principles that can be used to guide married couples in reaching agreements out of court on the division of their matrimonial property. Where a married couple cannot agree, the courts can apply these principles to grant remedies, and make orders to address the rights of each party.

In several provinces, matrimonial property legislation applies only to married couples and not to common-law relationships. The exclusion of common-law relationships from the definition of "spouse" in a Nova Scotia statute[15] (since changed to include common-law relationships registered as "domestic partnerships"[16]) was unsuccessfully challenged as a violation of Charter equality rights in *Nova Scotia* (Attorney-General) *v. Walsh*.[17] Nevertheless, some jurisdictions have extended their matrimonial property law to include common-law and same-sex relationships.

While there are differences from jurisdiction to jurisdiction, the following are some common elements typically found in most, if not all, provincial and territorial legislation addressing matrimonial real property:[18]

Definition of matrimonial property. All provincial and territorial legislation defines "matrimonial property" (or equivalent term) in terms of personal and real property owned by either or both spouses, and property used for a family purpose. Most legislation includes a specific definition of "matrimonial home" (or equivalent term) (Only British Columbia does not). While the matrimonial home is usually one property (the place where the family ordinarily resides), the definition can encompass other property in some jurisdictions if it is used for a family purpose, such as a summer residence.

Equal rights of possession to matrimonial home during marriage. Regardless of actual ownership (whether one or both spouses' names are on the title to the matrimonial home), provincial/territorial legislation recognizes the right of possession of both spouses to the matrimonial home. This usually means that neither spouse can sell the house or have an encumbrance placed on the title without the other's agreement or a court order to that effect. (However, this does not affect the rights and powers of each spouse to freely dispose of other assets to which he or she has title during the marriage.) The equal right to possession of the matrimonial home is subject to court orders otherwise applicable (e.g., in situations of domestic violence). The value of the matrimonial home is included in the calculation of the overall division of matrimonial property.

Provision for equalization payments based on the value of matrimonial property. Provincial law establishes a formula for dividing the monetary value of matrimonial property, typically based on a presumption of an equal division of the value of the net family property (including real and personal property). In Ontario, for example, the total value of all real and personal property held by each spouse is added up, and an equalization payment of half the difference of the two amounts is made to the spouse with the lesser total. This calculation can be varied by the court if it would cause undue hardship, or if variation would otherwise be just in the circumstances.

Remedies. Provincial law typically provides a range of remedies to spouses in conflict over the matrimonial home, such as

- interim orders of exclusive possession to one spouse upon separation (and pending final resolution), or in cases of domestic violence;
- orders of partition and sale (e.g., as part of a final resolution where parties cannot agree on who should get the matrimonial home if both want it); and
- orders to set aside a transaction where the matrimonial home has been sold or otherwise transferred by one spouse without the other spouse's consent.

Rules respecting agreements. In addition to statutory rules for the division of matrimonial real property, provincial and territorial law contemplates the use of various kinds of agreements between married couples and common-law partners, such as marriage contracts, separation agreements, or cohabitation agreements. Provincial and territorial statute law often prescribes rules respecting the interpretation and effect of such agreements. Most provinces and all territories include provisions governing agreements on property between common-law partners, and a smaller number include same-sex partners in these rules.

Provincial/territorial law respecting the division of matrimonial property *other than land* (personal property) does apply to First Nation people on-reserve as law of general application (subject to the terms of any land claim or self-government agreement). This means courts can use provincial laws to determine how to divide the monetary *value* of matrimonial property on-reserve. All provincial laws of general application respecting real property off-reserve apply to First Nation people.

However, the legal principles, rights and remedies under provincial law applying to matrimonial real property located *off-reserve* are generally not available to married spouses respecting their *on-reserve* real property (nor to common-law partners, couples married by custom, or same-sex partners). The only exception in the case of a married couple is the power of the court to include a valuation of an interest in a reserve land allotment in calculating a compensation order.

Provincial/Territorial Family Violence Legislation

In addition to division of matrimonial property legislation, some provinces and territories have adopted domestic violence legislation to provide civil law remedies in addition to criminal law protections. Family violence legislation has been adopted in Yukon, Alberta, Saskatchewan, Manitoba, Ontario, Nova Scotia and PEI. These laws typically allow people to apply to court for restraining orders against violent spouses or other family members, and for orders of temporary exclusive possession of the matrimonial home and its contents. The intent is to provide some basic protection for victims of violence in terms of personal security while also addressing the need of victims of family violence to stay in their own homes.

Matrimonial Real Property On-Reserve

First Nation reserve communities who have opted to come under the land management provisions of the *First Nations Land Management Act* are required to adopt a code addressing the division of matrimonial real property following adoption of a comprehensive land code. Some First Nations who have negotiated self-government and comprehensive claims agreements also have law-making powers in respect to matrimonial property and related issues.

The vast majority of First Nation reserve communities, however, remain subject to the *Indian Act*. The *Indian Act* does not address the issue of division of matrimonial real property (individual interests in reserve land). Provincial and territorial family law (whether aimed at division of matrimonial property or family violence), which otherwise provides courts certain powers to declare or change rights of possession to matrimonial property, cannot override individual rights of allotment made under the federal *Indian Act*. This has been made clear by two key decisions of the Supreme Court of Canada in 1986.

In *Derrickson v. Derrickson*, both husband and wife were members of the Westbank Indian Band. Mrs. Derrickson brought a petition for divorce and applied for one-half interest in the properties for which her husband held Certificates of Possession. She relied on the application of provincial family law legislation in requesting this order. The Supreme Court of Canada held that provincial family law could not apply to individual rights of occupation in Indian reserve lands. More specifically, the court determined that provincial laws entitling each spouse to an undivided half-interest in all family assets could not be applied to land allotments on-reserve. The court stated: "The right to possession of lands on an Indian reserve is manifestly of the very essence of the federal exclusive legislative power under s. 91(24) of the *Constitution Act, 1867*. It follows that provincial legislation cannot apply to the right of possession of Indian reserve lands." The court was able to make an order for compensation (taking into account the value of the land allotment) for the purpose of adjusting the division of family assets between the spouses under the relevant provincial family law.[19]

In *Paul v. Paul*, the husband and wife—both members of the Tsartlip Indian Band—had been married for nineteen years, and had built a home on land held by the husband by way of a Certificate of Possession issued under the *Indian Act*. The couple had been living in the home for sixteen years. Mrs. Paul applied for an order of interim possession of the matrimonial home. The Supreme Court of Canada ruled that provincial family law could not be used to grant an order of interim occupation of a family residence on-reserve.[20] As in *Derrickson*, the court found that the provincial legislation being relied on to make the requested order was in actual conflict with the provisions of the *Indian Act* (s. 20). In a B.C. case, the court applied *Derrickson* and *Paul* and held that it could not order partition and sale under a provincial statute where a couple jointly held a Certificate of Possession.[21] These are just a few of the cases where courts have struggled to assist the parties, but have had very limited, and, at times, no remedies at their disposal due to the lack of federal legislation in the field.

The result is that provincial family law legislation does not apply to reserve land in any way that can affect individual interests in reserve land. Gaps in applicable law mean very limited remedies are available to married couples on-reserve (and even fewer to common-law and same-sex couples) during marriage or upon marriage breakdown.

First Nation women's organizations have identified the need for action in this area as a priority issue.[22] First Nation women, through their representative organizations, have pointed out that, while First Nation women are not barred by any direct legislative provision from possessing Indian reserve lands, there is a long history of various forms of discrimination aimed at First Nation women through the *Indian Act* (particularly provisions relating to Indian status, band membership and enfranchisement). These often have had the effect of excluding Indian women from reserves or from possessing individual interests in reserve lands.[23]

The consequences of the absence of federal law on matrimonial real property on-reserve are often very negative (as the Special Representative on the Protection of First Nations Women's Rights explains in detail in her report).[24] If a woman's spouse holds the Certificate of Possession for the land on which the matrimonial home is located, her situation can quickly become very vulnerable. If she does not have membership in her husband's band, her right to remain on the reserve may vanish with the breakdown of her marriage. Even if she has membership, should the husband decide to transfer his interest to the band or to another member of the band, or if she is told to leave or has to leave, there is no legal remedy for her to gain possession of the house—not even on an interim basis where she is the primary caregiver to children of the marriage.

The only remedy generally available to a spouse without the Certificate of Possession is an order of compensation based on the applicable provincial formula for division of marital assets (personal and real property). This remedy does not address her immediate need for housing for herself and her children, nor is it very useful unless the spouse has money sufficient to pay out the order.

When women do hold a Certificate of Possession jointly with their partner, but leave the matrimonial home upon separation or due to domestic violence, they can experience difficulty in getting another allotment from Band Councils. This can happen where there is a perception that the family entitlement to land has been filled by the allotment of the matrimonial home, or where there is a shortage of land.

Possession of on-reserve property can often determine the ability to live on-reserve at all. Severe lack of housing on-reserve combined with marital breakdown may lead to a woman having to leave the matrimonial home to live in overcrowded conditions with friends or relatives, or to leave the reserve altogether. The generally low income levels of First Nation women brings a higher risk of becoming homeless, and having their children taken into care if forced to move off-reserve. In other words, dissolution of marriage on-reserve can generate a succession of negative events that can quickly spiral into homelessness for some First Nation women where they are not the sole holder of a Certificate of Possession to the matrimonial home.

First Nations Land Management Act

The *First Nations Land Management Act* (FNLMA) was passed by the federal Parliament in 1999 on the initiative of fourteen First Nations. These First Nations wished to escape the land management provisions of the *Indian Act* in order to improve their opportunities for economic development.

The FNLMA requires each community to establish a community consultation process for "the development of general rules and procedures respecting, in cases of breakdown of marriage, the use, occupation and possession of first nation land and the division of interests in first nation land" among other required elements of the land code.[25] Subsection 17(1) provides that a First Nation shall, following community consultations, "establish general rules and procedures in cases of breakdown of marriage, respecting the use, occupation and possession of first nation land and the division of interests in first nation land." Subsection 17(2) requires each First Nation within twelve months after its land code comes into force to incorporate the general rules and procedures into its land code, or enact a First Nation law containing the general rules and procedures. Under subsection 17(3) the First Nation, or Minister of Indian Affairs, may refer any dispute relating to the establishment of the general rules and procedures to an arbitrator in accordance with the Framework Agreement.

So far, four of the fourteen First Nations to which the *First Nations Land Management Act* applies have adopted a matrimonial property law. These four laws are quite similar to one another. The laws adopted by the Mississaugas of Scugog Island First Nation, Muskoday First Nation, Georgina Island First Nation and Lheidi T'Enneh First Nation under the FNLMA represent a huge step forward compared to the situation under the *Indian Act*. The First Nations under the FNLMA can also call on the assistance and resources of the Lands Advisory Board to further develop and refine laws in this area, as required. However, the lack of an interim regime pending the adoption of specific First Nation matrimonial property laws has been a key point of criticism from First Nations women's organizations.

Matrimonial Real Property under Self-Government Agreements

Under the federal self-government and comprehensive claims policies, several agreements have been reached with various First Nations. These agreements demonstrate a range of different approaches to the question of matrimonial property—from not specifically addressing it, to choosing to have provincial laws of general application apply to the expression of a clear and detailed description of First Nation authority over the matter.

Most self-government agreements do not specifically mention jurisdiction over matrimonial property in provisions listing the law-making authority of First Nations. Where self-government agreements recognize First Nation jurisdiction over reserve land or settlement land, the ability to make laws with respect to matrimonial real property may be included.

Some self-government and comprehensive agreements provide for the application of provincial laws respecting matrimonial real property through general provisions respecting the application of provincial laws of general application to the settlement lands of the First Nation. The Nisga'a Final Agreement deems Nisga'a settlement lands not to be s. 91(24) lands (lands reserved for the Indians). This means that in the absence of a Nisga'a law on the subject of matrimonial real property respecting Nisga'a lands, provincial laws of general application would apply.

Another approach is for the self-government agreement to recognize the power of a First Nation to adopt a provincial or territorial law of general application as its own (see Article 20.1 of the Champagne and Aishihik First

Nation Self-Government Agreement). Still another approach is to address matrimonial real property expressly. In the 2001 Meadowlake First Nation Comprehensive Agreement-in-Principle, the subject of family property is dealt with in considerable detail in Chapter 26, and covers all the basic issues at stake with respect to matrimonial real property. Most self-government agreements recognize First Nations law-making authority with respect to marriage, but do not address, or specifically exclude, jurisdiction over annulment or divorce.

The Aboriginal Self-Government policy adopted by the federal government in 1995 recognizes law-making authority over "marriage"—and over property rights on-reserve—as part of the inherent law-making authority of First Nations that it is willing to discuss through the self-government negotiation process mandated by the policy.[26]

Customary Marriages

The issue of whether and how Canadian law recognizes Aboriginal customary law relating to marriage is an important aspect of considering matrimonial real property law in a First Nation context. First Nation people and courts must be able to accurately identify the relationships to which any division of matrimonial property rules under federal, provincial/territorial, or First Nation law would apply whether on- or off-reserve. It is also important to determine what governmental authorities may determine when, and how, a marriage has been, or can be, terminated.

On the whole, Canadian law has accepted the validity of Aboriginal marriage by custom where the necessary elements identified in the *Connolly v. Woolrich and Johnson* case exist.[27] These elements are: validity in the community, voluntariness, exclusivity and permanence. It is arguable that marriage by Aboriginal custom is an Aboriginal right protected by s. 35 of the *Constitution Act, 1982*, and that a claim based on the resulting marital status is an exercise of that right. However, there is no reported case yet recognizing an Aboriginal customary marriage in the context of matrimonial property issues.

Issues Relating to Aboriginal Customary Law

First Nations scholars have emphasized how difficult it is to explain and relate First Nation notions of law and collectively held values in a way that can be properly understood by Western legal thinkers.[28] Many aspects of First Nation law, values and worldview are radically different from their European-based counterparts.

A challenge for any effort to genuinely respect and recognize Aboriginal customary law is that it is not a system of law based on lists of jurisdictional powers, but rather is a flexible, dynamic and holistic knowledge system. In addition, a discussion of law-making authority over "division of matrimonial property" presumes a certain conception of property and notions of private individual ownership that are often not consistent with the customary law and values of most First Nations.

Conclusion

The need for applicable laws addressing matrimonial property issues on-reserve is especially acute. Many First Nation communities suffer from housing and land shortages. In addition, the upheaval from marriage breakdown and family violence occurs in a larger context of the ongoing legal and cultural impacts of colonialism.

Another important consideration is that women living on-reserve are more often the primary caregivers of young children—and the victims of family violence—than men. The need to ensure shelter for women and children on-reserve, and some degree of stability and continuity in living conditions for children experiencing family upheaval from marriage breakdown or family violence, is especially important. Yet, not a court in the land can offer a resolution of spousal conflict regarding possession of the matrimonial home for most reserves beyond enforcing the rights of a spouse with a Certificate of Possession (where these are used).

There are several factors contributing to this state of the law:

- colonial interference with First Nation values and laws in relation to land, family and conflict resolution (through the imposition of the federal *Indian Act* and a foreign, i.e. non-Aboriginal, system of justice);
- the silence of the antiquated *Indian Act* on matrimonial real property;
- the non-applicability of provincial matrimonial real property law (*Derrickson* and *Paul*); and
- limited access to, or in some cases, interest in, the alternatives within existing federal policy to the *Indian Act* regime—e.g., FNLMA or self-government agreements negotiated within the parameters set by federal policy.

The *Indian Act* has had many negative cultural impacts on First Nation communities, and on the position of women in their communities and their relationship to the land. The introduction and imposition of individual land interests, combined with patriarchal biases in areas such as Indian status, band membership and the granting of individual allotments of reserve land, have created numerous cultural tensions and complex policy issues that affect matrimonial real property issues on-reserve in almost every aspect.

For most First Nations women on-reserve, the collective effect of the Canadian legal system as it currently stands—the colonial and patriarchal biases of the federal *Indian Act* over a long period, the lack of applicable federal, provincial, or First Nations laws on matrimonial real property matters, decisions by Band Councils regarding band membership, housing and land allotments, the lack of housing and land in many reserve communities, and problems related to enforcement of applicable federal, provincial and First Nation laws—results too often in a lack of protection and a lack of very basic legal remedies, relative to the situation of Aboriginal and non-Aboriginal people off-reserve.

There are several distinct legal regimes governing land issues on-reserve—the *Indian Act*, the *First Nations Land Management Act*, and a range of self-government and land claims agreements. There is also an array of legal opinion on the extent to which the Constitution of Canada contemplates the exercise of inherent First Nation jurisdiction over family law matters independent of a self-government agreement between a given First Nation and the federal Crown.

The legal situation of First Nation people across the country, with respect to matrimonial real property, varies according to the specific legal regime governing land issues in their communities, and the extent to which it affords room for the exercise of First Nation jurisdiction (inherent or delegated)— or the adoption or incorporation of provincial family law.

Apart from the question of inherent First Nation jurisdiction, the current state of the law, and of federal policy in respect to matrimonial real property, can be summarized as follows:

- no *Indian Act* provisions specifically address the issue of matrimonial real property rights on-reserve during marriage or upon marriage breakdown;
- provincial/territorial matrimonial property legislation cannot apply to alter any interests granted to individuals under the *Indian Act* in unsurrendered reserve lands, including interests in such lands that fall within the meaning of matrimonial property of the jurisdiction concerned (unless the application of such provincial laws to a given reserve is negotiated through a self-government or land claims agreement);
- provincial/territorial matrimonial property legislation may apply to leasehold interests in designated reserve lands; and
- within the framework of federal policy as it currently stands, the only existing options for First Nations to escape the *Indian Act* status quo and its silence on matrimonial real property is through

negotiation of an agreement to come under the FNLMA, or negotiation of a self-government or claims agreement (where such negotiation processes are available to the First Nation in question).

In considering new policies, programs, or legislative initiatives (whether federal or First Nation) in relation to matrimonial real property issues on-reserve, there are several important policy considerations that flow from the review of legal and policy issues in this chapter. The list below is not intended to be exhaustive.

1. Different Reserve Land Management Regimes

From a national perspective, there are, generally speaking, three different categories of reserve land management situations: (1) reserves that are subject to the *Indian Act* land management regime; (2) reserves that have opted into the First Nations Land Management Act (FNLMA), and operate under First Nation designed land management codes; and (3) reserves belonging to First Nations who have negotiated self-government or land rights agreements with new land management regimes (and other aspects of self-government).

Any initiative to address matrimonial real property rights on-reserve must take into account these different legal regimes, and the different situation and needs of First Nation women in each of them. Another important consideration is that the differences between these different legal regimes means that matrimonial real property issues on-reserve are being addressed more comprehensively in some reserve communities than others.

2. Source and Scope of Law Making

A key question to answer is whether legislative action should be left entirely to First Nations (continuing and extending the approach taken under the FNLMA), or whether any form of national legislation is needed or desirable to meet the policy principles and considerations set out in this paper.

The answer to this question may turn on one's perspective of what constitutes an appropriate use of federal legislative power pursuant to s. 91(24), or any other federal head of power. The Assembly of First Nations, and many other First Nation organizations and First Nation governments, have taken policy positions in the past that the federal government cannot (consistent with its stated commitment to self-government or its constitutional obligations to Aboriginal peoples) enact legislation affecting the rights and interests of First Nations without First Nation consent. On the other hand, some First Nation women's advocates have said the federal government has a duty to ensure that First Nation women have access to the same level and scope of protection and remedies as women off-reserve with respect to matrimonial real property, which includes enacting appropriate federal legislation for this purpose. If First Nations are to be recognized as having law-making powers in this area, the question of the scope of such a power is an important one. If one compares the tiny area of law-making authority recognized under the *Indian Act* in relation to land and family law—to the authority provincial governments enjoy—it is not fair to expect that First Nations will be able to address matrimonial real property issues as effectively as provincial/territorial governments without recognition of a similar scope of authority. Properly addressing matrimonial real property issues on-reserve will involve more than merely adding a line to the by-law powers under the *Indian Act*. Careful thought must be given to the description of the law-making power required, and the implications for First Nation authority over land and family law in general.

3.   Impact on Other Areas of Law

Legislative initiatives in regard to matrimonial real property issues must consider related areas of law, and how these may or should be affected, for example, wills and estates, marriage and divorce.

Any proposed federal reforms would need to contemplate possible legal and policy implications for communities under the *First Nations Land Management Act*, and other communities in the process of negotiating self-government agreements or agreements relating to the *First Nations Land Management Act*.

4.   Gender Equality Concerns

The concept of gender equality raises a number of policy issues, given the diverse views on what it means and its implications for First Nation communities. Gender equality in a First Nation context is especially challenging to "contextualize" in a situation where First Nations are dealing with many other outside legal concepts and policy objectives of other levels of government. Conducting gender equality analysis in a First Nation context will require incorporating the spectrum of equality issues facing First Nation women, and identifying means of empowering women and their communities. For example, it must be recognized that the vulnerability of First Nation women and their children, dealing with the trauma of marriage or relationship breakdown, is made more acute by cultural upheaval, and, in some cases, family violence.

There are also unique issues affecting non-member Aboriginal spouses and non-Aboriginal spouses on-reserve as a result of their different legal rights in relation to residency, land allotments and other matters.

5.   The Interests of Children

The interests of children upon breakdown of a marriage, common-law, or same-sex relationship should be paramount. In this regard, the need for shelter, a stable home environment and parental support are important considerations, as well as the right to stay within the community and have access to the child's culture and community. These goals can be challenging to meet where a custodial parent or guardian does not share the same legal status as the child with respect to band membership. The manner in which the legal principle of the "best interests of the child" is applied in a First Nation context is a key policy concern of First Nation women.

6.   Resource and Capacity Needs of Women at the Community Level

Even where First Nations leadership have specific legal obligations to address the issue of matrimonial property rights on-reserve, the conditions are often lacking to enable women to participate meaningfully in community discussions. Women often do not have the information they need to influence the content of First Nations laws.

First Nations women at the community level require information on the current status of the law in this area, and assistance and support to have input into any process of reform at any level of government. The role of the federal government in funding First Nation women's organizations, or community legal services organizations to carry out such work, needs to be considered.

7.   Scope of Relationships

There is a need to determine the scope of any proposed initiatives affecting the rights of opposite-sex couples on-reserve—whether married under provincial law, married under traditional/Aboriginal law, or living common-law. At the same time, notions of family and the rights of common-law and same-sex couples continue to evolve under provincial and federal law in many areas, including matters in relation to marriage and matrimonial property. The treatment of common-law couples requires consideration of whether matrimonial property law should be applied in the same manner as married couples, and whether common-law couples should be included in matrimonial property legislation on a mandatory or opt-in basis.

The different situation of people on-reserve with respect to Indian status, band membership, or First Nation membership must be considered as it can affect access to certain property interests on-reserve, and the capacity to enforce judgements against an "Indian" spouse resident on-reserve.

8.   Land and Housing Situations

The severe lack of housing and suitable land for housing is a critical reality for many First Nations. In such situations, the need of couples for assistance and guidance on their legal rights and interests, and the best way to address the rights and interests of both parties fairly, is great. The need for clear legal guidelines, whether federal or First Nations in origin, is underlined in situations where housing is a scarce commodity. The varied use of the *Indian Act* land allotment process and custom allotment systems must be taken into account, as well as the situation of people living on leased lands or band lands.

In addition, the different types of housing situations on-reserve must be taken into account—social housing owned by the band, or privately built houses on land held under Certificate of Possession by either or both partners or on band-held land.

9.   Legal Remedies and Alternative Dispute Resolution

The need for speedy access to remedies, such as interim orders for possession of the matrimonial home and issues relating to enforcement, needs to be considered, especially for women in situations of family violence and for women who are the primary caregivers of children. Ultimately, a comprehensive package of remedies and responses (e.g., legal initiatives, programs and housing) should be considered, and not simply one or more legislative options.

The difficulty many First Nation people face in gaining access to the courts is another consideration (e.g., due to distance from home to a major centre with a court, financial limitations, limited access to legal aid resources, lack of knowledge or comfort with European-based legal system, lack of familiarity of Canadian courts with First Nation cultural context). There are a range of views on whether this issue should be addressed by alternative dispute resolution mechanisms established by federal legislation (such as a specialized tribunal that could assist in matrimonial real property issues on-reserve), or in the larger context of First Nations and the administration of justice (such as proposals for a First Nation justice system), or by more limited community initiatives such as elders councils.

10. Community Legal Aid and Mediation Services

The letter of the law is primarily used by those individuals who have the resources to hire legal counsel to advise them on their rights and how to protect their interests. Legislative amendments alone will not address the need to help couples resolve matrimonial real property issues through agreement, as much as possible, without expensive court actions.

The limited access of First Nation women to community legal aid services and to mediation services must also be considered. Cutbacks in such services have occurred in many provinces. Mediation services must take into account the particular cultural context of a given First Nation, and the vulnerability of women in situations of family violence. Where legislation requires mediation, some consideration has to be given to the ability or inability of individuals to pay for such services.

11. Information Sharing and Consultation

The need to raise understanding of matrimonial real property issues at the community level, as well as the timing and manner of consultations in respect to legislative and non-legislative options, are important considerations.

Endnotes

This article is a shorter and edited version of a discussion paper prepared for the Department of Indian Affairs and Northern Development in November 2002 entitled *Discussion Paper: Matrimonial Real Property On Reserve* by Wendy Cornet and Allison Lendor.

1. *Indian Act*, R.S.C. 1985, c. I-5.

2. *First Nations Land Management Act*, S.C. 1999, c. 24.

3. *Derrickson v. Derrickson* [1986] 2 *Canadian Native Law Reporter* 45 (S.C.C.); *Paul v. Paul* (1986), 26 *Dominion Law Reports* (4th) 175 (S.C.C.).

4. See for example, the 1998 Report of the United Nations Committee on Economic, Social and Cultural Rights reviewing Canada's compliance with the International Covenant on Economic, Social and Cultural Rights (UN. E/C.12/1/Add.31, 4 December 1998, at paragraph 29).

5. This paper uses the term "First Nation" or "First Nations" to refer generically to the peoples subject to the *Indian Act*, except where the context requires use of the Indian Act term "Indian." "Aboriginal" is generally used in reference to constitutional rights or issues in accordance with legal practice in this area.

6. Indian and Northern Affairs Canada, *Gender Equality Analysis Policy* (1999); Justice Canada, *Diversity and Justice: Gender Perspectives* (A Guide to Gender Equality Analysis) (1998); Status of Women Canada, *Federal Plan for Gender Equality* (1995).

7. *Rivers v. Squamish Indian Band* [1994] CHRD No. 3, is an example of a case where the B.C. Human Rights Tribunal recognized a case of compound discrimination in a First Nation community.

8 Section 18 provides that reserves are held by Her Majesty for the use and benefit of the respective bands for which they are set apart. Subject to the Act and the terms of any treaty, the Governor in Council may determine whether any purpose for which any lands in a reserve are used, or are to be used, is for the use and benefit of the Band.

9. Under s. 20 Band Councils have a power of allotment of land in a reserve— subject to Ministerial approval. Subsection 20(1) provides that no Indian is lawfully in possession of land in a reserve, unless possession has been allotted by the Band Council with the approval of the Minister of Indian Affairs.

10. Indian and Northern Affairs Canada, *Understanding the Regulatory Environment for On-reserve Lending* (May 1999), 1.

11. *Pronovost v. Minister of Indian Affairs and Northern Development* [1985] 1 F.C. 517, per Marceau J.

12. Indian and Northern Affairs Canada, *Understanding the Regulatory Environment*, 11.

13. See *Lower Nicola Indian Band v. Trans-Canada Displays Ltd.,* [2000] 4 *Canadian Native Law Reporter* 185, 2000 BCSC 1209 (B.C.S.C.); and D. Sanders, *The Present System of Land Ownership*, paper presented to the First Nations' Land Ownership Conference, 29–30 September 1988 at the Justice Institute of British Columbia. Sanders concludes that "the Indian Act attempt to establish a complete and exclusive system of rights in reserve lands has not succeeded." Sanders estimates that half of all bands in Canada do not use the Indian Act system at all, and notes that some bands combine custom allotment systems with some usage of Certificates of Possession.

14. *Alberta Protection Against Family Violence Act*, R.S.A. 2000, c.P-27; Manitoba—*The Domestic Violence and Stalking Prevention, Protection and Compensation Act*, R.S.M. 1998, D.93l; Nova Scotia—*Domestic Violence Intervention Act*, S.N.S. 2001, c.29; Ontario—*The Domestic Violence Protection Act*, 2000, S.O. 2000, c.33. (not yet proclaimed in force); Prince Edward Island—*Victims of Family Violence Act* S.P.E.I. 1996, c.V-3.2; Saskatchewan—*The Victims of Domestic Violence Act*, S.S. 1994, c.V-6.02; Yukon Territory—*Family Violence Protection Act*, S.Y. 1997, c.12.

15. *Matrimonial Property Act,* R.S.N.S. 1989, c. 175, s. 2(g).

16. *Law Reform* (2000) *Act*, S.N.S. 2000, c.29.

17. *Nova Scotia* (Attorney-General) *v. Walsh* (2002), 297 N.R. 203 (S.C.C.).

18. *Matrimonial Property Act*, R.S.A. 2000, c. M-8 (Alberta); *Family Relations Act*, R.S.B.C. 1996, c. 128 (British Columbia); *The Marital Property Act*, R.S.M. 1987, c. M45 (Manitoba); *Marital Property Act*, S.N.B. 1980, c. M-1 (New Brunswick); *Family Law Act*, R.S.N. 1990, c. F-2 (Newfoundland); *Matrimonial Property Act*, R.S.N.S. 1989, c. 275 (Nova Scotia); *Family Law Act,* R.S.N.W.T. 1997, c. 18 (Nunavut); *Family Law Act*, S.N.W.T. 1997, c. 18 (Northwest Territories); *Family Law Act*, R.S.O. 1990, c. F.3 (Ontario); *Family Law Act*, S.P.E.I. 1995, c. 12 (Prince Edward Island); C.C.Q. 1991, c. 64., Division III (Quebec); *Family Property Act*, S.S. 1997, c. F-6.3 as amended by the S.S. 1998, c. 48 and 2001, c. 34 and 51 (Saskatchewan); *Family Property and Support Act*, R.S.Y 1986, c. 63 (Yukon).

19. *Derrickson v. Derrickson* [1986] 2 *Canadian Native Law Reporter* 45 (S.C.C.).

20. *Paul v. Paul* (1986), 26 D.L.R. (4th) 175 (S.C.C.).

21. *Darbyshire-Joseph v. Darbyshire-Joseph* (November 30, 1998), Doc. Vancouver D106124 (B.C.S.C.).

22. The Native Women's Association of Canada has been very active on this issue for some time. The issue received discussion in debate in the House of Commons and in Committee when the ratifying legislation for the Nisga'a Final Agreement was being considered and when the Bill to enact the *First Nations Lands Management Act* was being considered. An earlier version of the latter Act ran into trouble as a result of its silence on the issue. More recently, the NWAC engaged the Minister of Indian Affairs and Northern Development on the subject as it affects the existing *Indian Act*. See, for example, *CBC News*, Saturday, 24 November 2001, "Women want to change the Indian Act" at http://cbc.ca.

23. Native Women's Association of Canada, *Matrimonial Property Rights* (Ottawa, 1991); M.A. Erickson, "Where are the Women? Report of the Special Representative on the Protection of First Nations Women's Rights," 12 January 2001.

24. Erickson, "Where are the Women?"

25. *First Nations Land Management Act*, s. 6(1)(f).

26. Indian Affairs and Northern Development, *Aboriginal Self-Government* (Ottawa, 1995).

27. *Connolly v. Woolrich and Johnson* (1867) 17 R.J.R.Q. 75 (Q.S.C.), affirmed [1869] 1 R.L. 253; *Manychief v. Poffenroth* (1994), 25 Alta. L.R. (3d) 393 (Alta. Q.B.).

28. See, for example, J.Y. Henderson, "First Nations' Legal Inheritances in Canada: The Mikmaq Model" (1996), 23 *Manitoba Law Journal* 1; P.A. Monture-Okanee, "The Roles and Responsibilities of Aboriginal Women: Reclaiming Justice" (1992), 56 *Saskatchewan Law Review* 237; M.E. Turpel, "Patriarchy and Paternalism: The Legacy of the Canadian State for First Nations Women" (1993), 6 *Canadian Journal of Women and the Law* 174.

8

Urban Aboriginal Women in British Columbia and the Impacts of Matrimonial Real Property Regime

Karen L. Abbott

Introduction

Legal provisions for the division of matrimonial real property on-reserve when a marriage breaks down do not currently exist under the *Indian Act*. At the same time, efforts have been made to allow for legislation that supports and respects the determination of First Nations in Canada to develop land and property management rules that best suit their community interests and needs. This effort culminated on June 17, 1999, in the *First Nations Land Management Act* (FNLMA). Fourteen First Nations in Canada opted into this Act in order to formulate their own land management codes outside *Indian Act* regulations. Despite this advance in First Nation determination of land management, critics still have concerns. They believe the FNLMA will have little or no effect on the current lack of rules and procedures surrounding the division of matrimonial real property on-reserve, even though the Act requires such provisions to be implemented. Only time will tell how this situation evolves. In the meantime, anecdotal and testimonial evidence continues to accumulate that documents the experiences and plight of First Nations' women and their children who had to leave their homes on-reserve during marital breakdown.

In the First Nations context, the ways that the matrimonial real property regime on-reserve affects the family have been an outstanding concern of Aboriginal women. When relationships break down, there is not often a fair and equitable division of the marriage's assets. In many respects, this is the direct consequence of a non-existent matrimonial real property regime under the *Indian Act*. However, this situation has not gone unnoticed. For some time Aboriginal women have raised the necessity, in various fora, for a better mechanism to divide matrimonial real property on reserves in the event of marital breakdown.

It is anticipated that this research study can be a first and necessary step in examining the economic, political, and social impact on Aboriginal women faced with marital breakdown, and how this impact affects their personal and family security. Beginning in the urban context in British Columbia, primary research involving Aboriginal women and organizations will help clarify the ways the property regime under the *Indian Act* has affected women's lives and choices.

The geographical context for this research study is centred on the matrimonial real property regime in the province of British Columbia. Vancouver and Victoria, two of British Columbia's largest urban centres, were chosen as natural sites for this research project given their sizable populations of Aboriginal women (6,090 and 3,400 respectively). Using a qualitative research methodology in conjunction with various governmental and NGO partners, Aboriginal women residing in these cities were asked to provide their experiences on how their marital breakdown on the reserve positively or negatively affected them and their children.

The Context: Traditional Roles

Since time immemorial, Native Nations governed all of what is now known as North America, or Turtle Island. Turtle Island was the home of various culturally diverse indigenous nations. To illustrate this point in the current context, today there are over sixty unique First Nations in British Columbia alone. Thus, there were many indigenous ways of being and knowing. Many indigenous communities were matriarchal. In these societies, women typically were actively involved in various forms of tribal governance.

Therefore, in a traditional context, many Aboriginal women held unique and influential positions in their society. Numerous women governed, controlled leadership, owned all community property and had sole responsibility for resolving disputes.[1] Mohawk female elders, or grandmothers, held special positions of power. Due to the fact that Aboriginal women gave life, they held a special and sacred position in the centre of society. Many considered their grandmothers to be the only ones who had "almost walked a full circle."[2] Accordingly, they had the wisdom and power to be solely responsible for the discipline of all community members.

Traditionally, Navajo women had equal rights with Navajo men because women's roles complemented those of men.[3] Historically, Navajo men would move to their wives' family locations after marriage (a matrilocal society).[4] This arrangement prevented spousal abuse since the woman's family would protect her if required.[5] Clan elders and the extended Navajo family would be shamed if one of their men engaged in wife abuse.[6] In the Onondaga Nation, men could not vote or have non-member spouses residing on tribal lands.[7] For indigenous women, leadership roles are "natural extensions of the care taking role."[8] Traditionally, women were central to society, perhaps because of their reproductive powers.[9] "Aboriginal women played equal, significant and respected roles in government-making,"[10] according to McIvor, who also observed that "the role of Aboriginal women was central to the spirituality and existence of the nation."[11] As was custom, divorces were available for Aboriginal women if they were unhappy or if they experienced abuse. They could simply ask the man to leave or just put his belongings outside the door.[12] In traditional Sioux culture, women were considered to be sacred.[13]

Current Social and Economic Situation of Aboriginal Women

Although information exists on the demographic profiles of Aboriginal people, this information is mostly derived from the Census conducted by Statistics Canada, and through the Aboriginal Peoples Survey (APS) that was conducted for the first time in 1991. Indian and Northern Affairs Canada (INAC) collect and maintain several databases on Registered Indians and Land Entitlement Mechanisms on First Nation reserves. However, for the most part, the intent of these databases is not to support ongoing research activities, but to function as administrative and operational tools. This section will briefly outline the results of some research studies and data publications readily available from INAC and Statistics Canada. The focus in this section is on information.

Research and analysis conducted by INAC shows that Registered Indians living on-reserve have both advantages and disadvantages regarding living costs relative to most other Canadians. The advantages include subsidized housing and greater eligibility for government transfer payments. Advantages also include an environment that allows Registered Indians to pursue traditional lifestyles (e.g., hunting, trapping and fishing, assuming that the surrounding lands can sustain this activity) that have given them the potential for lower food costs.

The disadvantages resulting from reserves' isolation from major urban areas include higher costs for many commodities than elsewhere in Canada, and a lack of employment in rural reserve communities. However, many people living on a reserve regard relocation to other areas with better social and economic prospects as less viable and desirable than would other Canadians.

Further data published by INAC show that in British Columbia there were 28,982 off-reserve Registered Indian females as of December 31, 2000. This represents a quarter (25%) of the Registered Indian population provincially. Of these off-reserve females, one-third are under the age of 19, 57.4% are between the ages of 20 and 49, while approximately 17.6% are over the age of 50.

In 1998–99, housing units on-reserve in British Columbia totalled 16,025—although not all people living on-reserve are Registered Indians. The 1991 Census found that only 70% of the people living on-reserve were of Aboriginal origin. Although there were problems with the 1991 and 1996 Censuses due to underreporting of the Aboriginal population, the 1996 Census estimated that the Aboriginal population living on British Columbia Indian reserves was 64,981. This represented a 19.1% growth since the 1991 Census.

Methodology

At the time this research was conducted, very little information or data were available that described the number and extent of issues affecting First Nations women and their children who were experiencing matrimonial breakdown on-reserve. This situation has not changed. For the most part, information on these issues still continues to be anecdotal at best. As a result of this limited information, no efforts were made to determine an appropriate and representative participant sample size for the province of British Columbia, where this study was conducted. No control groups were established to measure any significant differences in experience between First Nations women who left the reserve after marital breakdown and those who were able to stay. Moreover, no efforts were made to stratify the sample by other social and economic factors, such as age, income, with or without children and other relevant factors. In many respects, the research remains highly exploratory. However, because there are no provisions in the *Indian Act* to deal with the issues of the division of matrimonial real property on-reserve, it is highly likely that the events and outcomes for First Nations women experiencing matrimonial breakdown would converge in common experiences. Using this fact, in conjunction with qualitative research methodological criteria, it was determined that an appropriate sample size of no more than thirty-five participants would be enough to satisfy the objectives of this project, given time and cost constraints. In the end, twenty-nine First Nations women living in the Victoria-Vancouver areas of British Columbia, admirably, participated in this research study.

Research Design

At the beginning of the project, considerable time and effort went into designing an appropriate qualitative research instrument before the actual interviews. Efforts focussed on three essential areas, including

- the development of appropriate screening questions for the research sample;
- relevant research questions and/or content and themes to be examined by the study; and
- the determination of a questionnaire pre-test and sample selection strategy.

These key processes were undertaken through various fora and activities in which the principal researcher of this study participated, and collaborated, with other stakeholders involved in the study. These included INAC representatives and Aboriginal NGOs from the study location in British Columbia.

Questionnaire Screening Criteria

The importance of developing efficient and appropriate screening questions for this study cannot be overstated. The following core criteria were used to "screen" Aboriginal female participants into the study:

- the Aboriginal woman participant was married or lived common-law on a reserve in an owned or rented residence;
- her relationship ended or changed through widowhood while living at this reserve residence; and
- she did not have a choice to remain on the reserve when her relationship ended.

If all three criteria were answered affirmatively, then the participant would be "screened in" as part of the sample for this study. No restrictions were placed on how recently a participant's matrimonial breakdown had occurred. All screening sessions were conducted by telephone in order to avoid wasting time on transportation and the participant's time, if it was determined that their experiences were unsuitable for the study. Contacts for potential participants were provided by, and gathered in consultation with, Aboriginal NGOs and other service agencies in the research area. Their knowledge and background in providing services to Aboriginal women experiencing marital breakdown were essential in formulating the sampling and data collection strategy. The principal researcher also solicited participants by distributing pamphlets and brochures to Aboriginal and other service NGOs in the research area where these women might be clients.

Questionnaire Research Content and Themes

Several fora were undertaken to determine and complete the research questions, themes and format of the questionnaire. The main participants in these processes included the primary researcher, officials from INAC and Aboriginal NGOs in the research area.

In mid-December 2001, a focus group session was held in British Columbia with INAC officials participating via conference call. The focus group mechanism accomplished and supported several objectives. First, all Aboriginal NGO officials were introduced to the project and its purpose. Second, the focus group provided the opportunity to gather feedback and suggestions on questionnaire content and themes from various individuals who had direct contact with potential participants for the project. This feedback and insight were important for formulating appropriate and relevant questions for the study. In addition, the focus group provided an opportunity to discuss potential ethical problems or data-collection barriers for disclosing the First Nations women's experiences regarding matrimonial breakdown on-reserve. Finally, all focus group participants were encouraged to participate in and support the project by providing contact information for potential project participants, thus providing direct assistance in forming a sampling strategy.

Based on the suggestions and views presented by the focus group, a set of major themes was formulated to guide the construction and flow of the final questionnaire format. The major research question groupings are as follows:

- screening questions
- background/demographics
- awareness of existing matrimonial real property regime
- participants' stories
- making a difference
- concluding remarks

Questionnaire Pre-Test and Sampling Strategy

A preliminary test of the questionnaire was conducted in order to verify the efficiency and relevancy of the sampling strategy, along with the questionnaire screening questions. As noted above, Aboriginal NGOs were instrumental in providing names and contact information of potential participants as part of the sampling strategy for the project. Several test candidates were contacted by telephone to determine their suitability to participate in the project. Once verified, a test run of the questionnaire was performed to evaluate the efficiency and relevancy of survey questions, and to seek out potentially problematic questions that would result in a high rate of non-response or non-applicable outcomes. This situation was not totally avoidable for certain types of questions. However, the rate of non-response or non-applicability of questions would most likely have been higher if a pre-test had not been performed before the actual participant interviews.

Participant Background Demographic Findings

The average age of the Aboriginal women interviewed was 43 years. They ranged in age from 31 to 63 years. Most participants were originally from British Columbia. However, one-third (ten) came from other provinces or territories of Canada. Two participants came from tribes in the United States. An overwhelming majority of Aboriginal women participants were members of their band of origin and were Registered Indians under the *Indian Act*. Only four women had obtained their status as Registered Indians under Bill C-31 provisions.

In terms of mobility, almost one-quarter of these women indicated that they were raised both on- and off-reserve during their youth. In terms of educational attainment, almost half attended high school, but did not graduate. Only 17% of participants (six women) indicated that they had achieved some post-secondary education. However, on a positive note, one-quarter of the women indicated at the time of the study that they were currently attending or enrolled in an educational institution.

The majority (70%) of participants responded that they were not employed during this study. Of those who were employed, approximately one-third were employed on a part-time basis. Most participants (62%) indicated that their total annual income was below $10,000 per year. This is clearly below the Low-Income Cut-off level as defined by Statistics Canada.[14] However, four participants responded that their annual total income exceeded $40,000 per year.

In terms of secondary sources of income, a majority of participants indicated that they were receiving social or disability assistance. Surprisingly, very few participants indicated that they had received any child or alimony support from their former spouse.

During their relationship with their former spouses, most participants indicated that they were in a common-law relationship followed by the second most common form of relationship—marriage. In addition, the majority (60%) of participants did not share the same First Nation origin as their spouse. However, the vast majority of former spouses (97%) held band membership with their First Nation of origin. In terms of cohabitation, the average time participants lived on-reserve with their former spouses was 6.1 years. Currently, over two-thirds of the Aboriginal women participants identify themselves as single and/or divorced.

As shown in Figure 1, a majority of the participants (72% or 21) held various forms of property interest while cohabiting on-reserve with their former spouses. Interestingly, a majority (76%) responded that they held a joint Certificate of Possession for the property on the reserve with their former spouse. Yet, unfortunately, all of these women left the reserve when their relationship ended. Although eight participants had no children during the period of marital breakdown, there were a total of sixty children whose lives were affected by the participants' estrangement from the reserve.

Figure 1: Property interest with former spouse

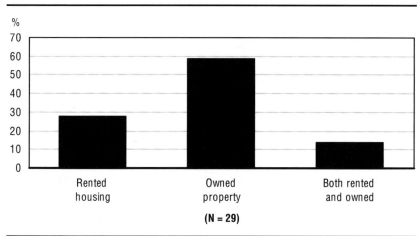

(N = 29)

The various proportions of the types of current home ownership held by the participants is depicted in Figure 2. A majority (97%) of participants indicated that they are renting their current dwelling. Only one participant indicated that she owned her home, which is in direct contrast to the statistics on the participants' former situation on the reserve.

Figure 2:   Current home ownership status of participant

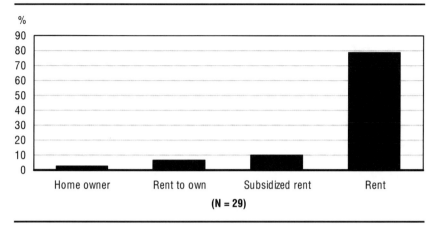

(N = 29)

Awareness of Existing Band Matrimonial Real Property Provisions

Several questions in the interview probed the participants' knowledge about the existence of any First Nation band rules and/or protocols regarding the division of matrimonial real property on the reserve that were directly applicable to their marital breakdown. They were also asked about how the rules, if any, were applied, and if the rules were fairly and consistently applied to their specific case or to any other cases they had seen.

Almost all the women interviewed indicated that before their relationship ended they were unaware of any rules, band by-laws, or protocols in place to guide the division of matrimonial real property on-reserve. Only four participants said they were aware of band property division rules before their marital breakdown. Currently, just over one-fifth (21%) of the participants' bands have rules in place and have made some effort to communicate them to their members. Of these rules, almost half (49%) either give preference to the male spouse or to the band member in matrimonial real property division. At the same time, many participants indicated that it is rare for women to keep the home. Typically, the male spouse retains it after marital breakdown. The participants mentioned other factors that reflect the bias connected to the consistent and fair application of property division rules. These include family status on the reserve and the spouses' relationship to those who control applying the property division rules on-reserve. Participants also reported that most band matrimonial real property division rules on-reserve are silent in the case of widowhood, although only one of the participants in this study left her former reserve home in such a situation.

Participants' Stories

This section of the questionnaire focuses on the experiences of participants on-reserve when the marital breakdown occurred and following the break up. The report examines various aspects of this experience, including the details of the break up, the transitional period from living on-reserve to moving to another location and their life experiences in their new living arrangements.

Most participants' relationships on-reserve ended about eleven years before the interview was conducted. At the time of their marital breakdown, the average age of the participants was 31 years. The average age of their affected children was approximately 10 years. Most participants (80%) retained custody of their children, although very few reported receiving any child support or alimony at the time.

Nearly three quarters (72% or 21) of the participants immediately left their home on the reserve as a consequence of their marital breakdown. The rest remained on the reserve for a short time afterwards, staying either with family members or temporarily in their home. Participants rarely gave a single response for leaving their reserve home. However, as shown in Figure 3, the predominant reason (42%) participants left their home on the reserve was to escape the effects of domestic violence. Other factors included lack of housing, financial concerns and the desire to pursue education and employment in urban areas. Unfortunately, these women reported that there was little or no fair and equitable division of their matrimonial real property on the reserve when their relationship ended.

Figure 3: Reasons for leaving reserve

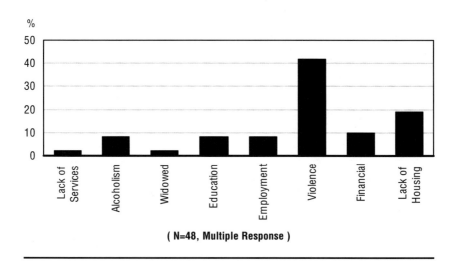

(N=48, Multiple Response)

The majority (79%) reported that their former partner did not provide any financial support after their marital breakdown. Only five participants were successful in securing child support from their former spouses, albeit only for a year or two. However, almost half (45%) of the participants reported that, at the time, their spouse was gainfully employed and most likely capable of providing some level of alimony or child support. Yet very few participants indicated a willingness or motivation to pursue child support. Fear of the former spouse and the risk to personal safety and security were the most common reasons given for this reluctance.

Participants were asked whether they perceived various individuals and organizations as helpful, hurtful, or neutral in their transition process out of the matrimonial home on the reserve. The majority of participants (52%) indicated that they did not use or have Band Council involvement in their situations. They did not indicate why the Band Council was not involved or did not intervene in their case. However, of those who did have Band Council involvement, 21% reported that, overall, the council was more hurtful to their situation than helpful (15%). Reasons cited for these negative perceptions included Band Council indifference and insensitivity to the participants' predicament and the preferential treatment to relatives of Band Council members. However, the participants did not cite Band Councils as the most obstructive element they encountered. Participants overwhelmingly reported that their couple friends, or friends they had made through their relationship together, were the most hurtful element during their transition.

Participants (79%) reported that, by far, their own family was the single most helpful source of overall support during their marital breakdown. In many cases, participants' families provided a place to stay, transportation, emotional support and babysitting services in their time of need. Three participants indicated that their families were neither helpful nor hurtful because they lived so far away.

Of those participants who sought support through various service organizations, roughly half (48%) said they were helpful. Surprisingly, almost half (48%) of the participants also indicated that support service organizations were not applicable to their situation. The main reasons cited for this were lack of awareness and their belief, at the time, that there were no services that could have possibly helped their situation.

In terms of positive experiences resulting from the transition to life in urban areas, participants reported marked improvements in their personal safety (15%), employment (11%), education (11%) and freedom and/or self-esteem (14%). Other positive changes included access to basic living provisions, modern utilities, sobriety and lifestyle changes, and new skills development. The most helpful supports for these women after leaving the reserve were women's shelters (28%) and counsellors (24%), followed by friends (17%) and family (14%).

Although no rigorous methodology was used to analyze the economic and financial impact of the transitional process, participants were asked to comment on the overall changes in their financial situation after leaving the reserve. Participant responses were equally divided between an improvement (38%) and a worsening (38%) of their financial situation. Only three participants (10%) indicated that their financial situation was unchanged after moving off the reserve. Many responses, from those who indicated improvement, were linked to their newly found independence from their former spouses. This indicated conflicts in their former domestic financial situation. For those who indicated a worsening financial situation, reasons included acquiring their former spouses' debt and the lack of access to reserve resources (traditional foods).

A clear majority (80%) of participants indicated that they experienced many unexpected changes in their lives once they left the reserve. These included feelings of loneliness due to isolation, of missing cultural opportunities on-reserve, denial of band-supported educational funding, and financial concerns and worries. Some also indicated that culture shock and the added expense for children's activities in the city were concerns. However, some participants responded that not all changes were negative. Many felt consoled by the fact that they were able to change their lifestyle, function independently and take care of themselves.

Similarly, participants were asked about whether their children were better or worse off in the city than on a reserve in their previous relationships. Over half (59%) reported that they thought their children were better off in the city, citing reasons such as increased resources, training, educational opportunities and increased contact with the maternal family. Only two participants felt their children were not better off in the city. However, overall, most participants indicated that the loss of community, cultural opportunities, and community and/or family gatherings had a negative impact on both them and their children.

Making a Difference

The theme of the questionnaire—Making a Difference—gave participants a forum to express their opinions on measures they felt should be immediately implemented to help Aboriginal women on-reserve and their children facing experiences similar to theirs. In addition, participants were asked to comment on what specific information or resources would have been useful to them and their children during the marital breakdown on-reserve.

The participants provided a wide range of responses (115 answers) to these two questions. Overwhelmingly, participants (72%) stressed the need for resources available on-reserve to support domestic violence intervention and prevention. In particular, the need for Aboriginal-managed shelters, access to information on shelters, transportation and public acknowledgements about violence in the community dominated participants' concerns. For the longer term, some participants also suggested the creation of a "Community Safety Plan" on the reserve that would involve band workers, Royal Canadian Mounted Police (RCMP) and other related staff to respond to and help community members wishing to leave an abusive relationship.

Over half of all participants (59%) indicated that there is a great need for increased public and community education and awareness of overall legal rights on the reserve, including matrimonial real property rights. More specifically, in terms of housing on the reserve, participants indicated (52%) that matrimonial homes should be jointly registered in both spouses' names; that matrimonial homes should remain with the spouse who retains custody of the children; and that there should be more, better quality, affordable housing on the reserve.

Another concern, less often expressed but equally important in the long term, emerged from participants' comments touching on aspects of First Nation governance and horizontal and vertical accountability issues. Specifically, participants suggested that First Nation councils should provide mediation processes to deal better with disputes. They also suggested that First Nation councils should clearly articulate, disseminate and administer band policies and rights in a transparent and fair manner. Participants also mentioned that these policies or contracts resulting from First Nation policies, which include Certificates of Possession, should be legally binding.

The Connection between Domestic Violence and Matrimonial Property Rights

After leaving the reserve, the vast majority of participants are now without property, living in poverty. Making this connection between domestic violence and property rights is important because long after an Aboriginal woman leaves an abusive relationship on-reserve, there are long-term implications for her financial situation. The lack of property rights affects the children of Aboriginal women since they generally remain with their mother, thus negatively impacting one or more generations. In this study, twenty-nine participants were affected, as were their sixty children. We do not know the results, upon the third or subsequent generations, of making these single-parent families homeless and poor. Despite stronger legislation surrounding child support enforcement, very few of the Aboriginal participants received child support. For policy-makers, making this connection between domestic violence and lack of property rights for Aboriginal women is crucial.

This is a situation created by regressive legislation, specifically the *Indian Act*, and this legislation is unique to Aboriginal women. One of the first healing acts is to amend or repeal the regressive portions of the *Indian Act*, which caused Aboriginal women to be deprived of their property rights. If that step is not taken, then many more Aboriginal women and their children will continue to be impacted. However, merely taking that first step to remedying the legislation will not cure all the problems created by the *Indian Act*, and the participants indicated many important holistic measures that need to take place. These measures are direct feedback from the affected women themselves.

Conclusion

All participants who were brave enough to share their experiences and feelings for this study, which centres on a traumatic and negative period of their lives, are to be admired. Through their collaborative efforts, one of the primary objectives of this research study has been met; that is, to qualitatively document the various social and economic impacts on Aboriginal women and their children facing matrimonial breakdown on-reserve. Throughout the study findings, there is evidence of the physical, psychological and spiritual pain that these women had to endure. However, in the end, they ultimately became survivors.

The study's findings relate a consistent thread among participants' narratives along many dimensions. For example, many participants started off as property owners on-reserve with their former spouses, but are now currently living in rental or subsidized housing off-reserve. Only one participant indicated owning her current home. The majority of participants are living in poverty, and are currently unemployed with an annual income below $10,000. The vast majority of participants were unaware, before their relationship ended, of the lack of matrimonial real property provisions in the *Indian Act*, or any band by-laws or procedures regarding the division of matrimonial real property on-reserve. Almost three-quarters of participants immediately left their reserve home upon their marital breakdown. The rest remained on-reserve for a short time thereafter. In the end, however, all participants relocated to urban areas in British Columbia. For those participants who had children with their former spouses, a minority received child support, and only for a limited period after the marital breakdown— even though almost half of the former spouses were employed. However, the most startling finding that resonates throughout this study was the disclosure by over two-thirds of the participants that the main reason for leaving their former spouse was due to domestic violence. For the participants in this study, there is clearly a link between matrimonial real property rights on-reserve and domestic violence.

In the beginning, most participants held some form of property with their former spouse until domestic violence left no alternative except to leave the reserve. Because many of the participants also retained the custody of their children at this time, the result will undoubtedly affect further generations. Research conducted by Hull, analyzing Census data on Aboriginal single mothers and their children, clearly shows that they are particularly disadvantaged in relation to other Canadian families, especially when living in urban areas.[15]

Obviously, there has been a social and economic cost for Aboriginal women and their children for not having matrimonial real property protocols in the *Indian Act* or at the Band Council level of government. Several provincial Supreme Court cases in British Columbia, notably the *Derrickson v. Derrickson* case, have not resulted in any changes to the current situation. Despite these attempts to elicit change, Aboriginal women and their children continue to be at risk of losing their reserve homes and living in poverty, especially if their familial situation was cast in the shadow of domestic violence. Therefore the question remains about how this research can be positioned federally and at the community level so that the momentum for change can continue to flourish and evolve. Perhaps a second, more subtle objective of this research study is to support change in the current thinking of matrimonial real property issues on-reserve from a legal risk and benefits perspective to a open and thorough consideration concerning the associated social, economic and generational costs of doing nothing. We have already witnessed, through the participants of this study, what the qualitative dimensions of some of these costs are. However, the intention of this research was never to be comprehensive, but to be an exploratory and necessary first step in examining all the issues surrounding matrimonial real property on-reserve.

There is much yet to be examined and quantified in order to reach a more fully developed understanding of all issues associated with matrimonial real property rights on-reserve. Further evidence-based research in the areas of legal dimensions and implications of matrimonial real property, current land ownership mechanisms used on First Nation reserves, and other case studies in other jurisdictions—including the international scene—would surely help support and motivate any further federal policy discussion and development. However, as indicated by the participants in their recommendations for change, there is a current need to have resources in place to alleviate some of the immediate crises facing Aboriginal women undergoing marital breakdown on-reserve. It is unknown, at this time, if the current resources committed to this situation, through various federal and provincial agencies, are having any effect in alleviating these crises. Furthermore, a less-mentioned recommendation for change, reported by participants, hints at the long-term and more challenging prospect of Aboriginal communities themselves taking control and ownership of the matrimonial real property issue on-reserve in a holistic, open and inclusive manner to help heal and strengthen community well-being. This point cannot be overlooked in any future process or policy development that strives to come to a better understanding and to support better social and economic outcomes for all those affected by this important issue.

Endnotes

1. P. Monture-Angus, "The Roles and Responsibilities of Aboriginal Women: Reclaiming Justice," in *Thunder in My Soul: A Mohawk Woman Speaks* (Halifax: Fernwood Publishing, 1995), 241.

2. Monture-Angus, "Roles and Responsibilities of Aboriginal Women," 242.

3. J. Zion and E. Zion, "Hozho' Sokee'—Stay Together Nicely: Domestic Violence under Navajo Common Law," *Arizona State Law Journal* 407: 412–413.

4. Zion and Zion, "Hozho' Sokee'—Stay Together Nicely," 414.

5. Ibid., 414.

6. Ibid., 415.

7. G. Valencia-Weber and C.P. Zuni, "Domestic Violence and Tribal Protection of Indigenous Women in the United States," *St. John's Law Review* (1995): 91.

8. Valencia-Weber and Zuni, "Domestic Violence and Tribal Protection," 92.

9. Ibid., 93.

10. S. McIvor, "Aboriginal Self-Governance: The Civil and Political Rights of Women" (Masters of Laws thesis, Queen's University, 1995), 8–9.

11. McIvor, "Aboriginal Self-Governance," 10.

12. Ibid., 33.

13. Valencia-Weber and Zuni, "Domestic Violence and Tribal Protection," 70.

14. Statistics Canada defines the "Low-Income Cut-off" level (or LICO level for short) as total annual income of $32,759 for a family of four.

15. J. Hull, *Aboriginal Single Mothers in Canada, 1996: A Statistical Profile* (Ottawa: Indian and Northern Affairs Canada, 2001).

9

Aboriginal Single Mothers in Canada, 1996: A Statistical Profile

Jeremy Hull

Introduction

Past research has shown that Aboriginal women in Canada experience lower incomes and are less often employed than Aboriginal men or than other women in Canada. In addition, research has shown that single mothers in Canada are more likely than other women to experience employment and income difficulties. However, little research has been done which focuses on Aboriginal single mothers and their families. In order to begin to address this research gap, the Department of Indian Affairs and Northern Development (DIAND) commissioned a study of Aboriginal single mothers based on custom tabulations from the 1996 Census of Canada.

The study takes a descriptive approach, providing tables and figures that are based on two or three-way cross-tabulations. The study seeks to answer the following questions: What is the prevalence of single mothers and single-mother families within the Aboriginal population? What are the educational characteristics of Aboriginal single mothers? Where do Aboriginal single mothers live? Has the prevalence of single mothers been increasing? What are employment income characteristics of Aboriginal single mothers and their families?

Methods

Almost all of the data presented in this study are based on custom 1996 Census tabulations prepared for the DIAND. The study is based on the population who identified themselves as Aboriginal and/or as Registered Indians or members of an Indian Band or First Nation. This population is subdivided into Registered Indians (including members of First Nations) and others with Aboriginal identity. Throughout the study, the Registered Indian population is compared to others with Aboriginal identity and to the non-

Aboriginal Canadian population. The 1996 Census allowed more than one ethnic identity to be indicated. Where an individual has more than one identity, an Aboriginal identity takes precedence over non-Aboriginal identities, and Registered Indian status or First Nation membership takes precedence over other Aboriginal identities in the categorizations used in this study. In 1996 there were 512,755 adults (aged 15 or older) with Aboriginal identity, of whom 303,130 were Registered Indians or members of Indian Bands, and 202,625 were others with Aboriginal identity, based on the definitions above.

An "Aboriginal family" is one in which the lone parent or either the husband or wife has Aboriginal identity as defined above. As with individuals, Aboriginal families have been subcategorized as Registered Indian and other Aboriginal families. For all lone-parent families the identity of the lone parent determines the identity of the family. If either spouse in a husband-wife family has Registered Indian status then the family is categorized as a Registered Indian family. If only one spouse in a husband-wife family has Aboriginal identity, the family is assumed to have this Aboriginal identity. Using these definitions, there were 231,945 Aboriginal families in Canada in 1996, of which 137,500 were Registered Indian families and 94,445 were other Aboriginal families. The study uses standard Census definitions of family types and family status. This information is often combined with whether or not the family has one or more children (0-15 years old) living with them.

There are a number of possible ways of looking at the proportions of lone parents and lone-parent families within the population. When looking at data for individuals this study has documented lone parents as a proportion of all women and as a proportion of women with children. When looking at families, the study looks at lone-parent families as a proportion of all families, and as a proportion of families with children.

This paper is a shortened version of a longer study, available on the Indian Affairs website at: www.inac.gc.ca. It briefly covers such variables as age, educational attainment, labour force characteristics, occupations, individual income and family income. It focuses on female lone parents and their families, but also includes information on male lone parents for comparative purposes. Those interested in greater detail, including data in tabular form and data concerning the Métis and Inuit populations, will find this type of information in the full study.

Effect of "Identity" versus "Ancestry" Definitions

In 1996 the Census identified approximately 1,100,000 people who said they had Aboriginal ancestry, but only 800,000 who said they were themselves Aboriginal. As noted above, this study focuses on the population who identified themselves as Aboriginal, as distinct from the population who say they have an Aboriginal ancestor. The definition that is used has an effect on the socioeconomic characteristics of the population, including the proportion who are single-parents. Figure 1 illustrates this by comparing the prevalence of single-mother families for different population groups. Lone-parent prevalence was highest among Registered Indian families at about 23% of all families, and lower among others with Aboriginal *identity* (the second bar) at about 17%. However, if the "other Aboriginal" population includes all those with Aboriginal *ancestry,* the prevalence falls to 14% (the third bar in the figure). If we isolate only those who have Aboriginal *ancestry* but not Aboriginal *identity* the prevalence falls to 12% (the fourth bar in the figure), which is the same as for the general population (the fifth bar in the figure). The decision to focus on the Aboriginal identity population was made in order to focus on the population that is culturally and socioeconomically most distinct from the Canadian mainstream. It was felt that this population was the focus of greatest concern in the realm of social policy.

Figure 1: Aboriginal definitions and the prevalence of single-mother families, Canada, 1996[1]

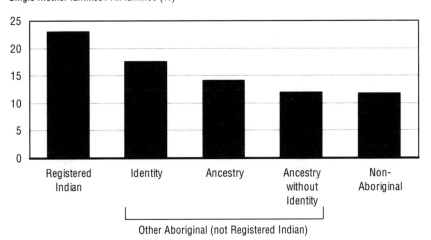

Single mother families / All families (%)

Trends in the Prevalence of Lone-Parent Families, 1981–96

Because of changing Census questions and definitions, it is impossible to compare data on the Aboriginal identity population over the 1981-96 period. However, Census data based on the Registered Indian and Inuit ancestry populations is available, as illustrated in Figure 2 below. The figure shows female lone-parent families as a proportion of all families among the Registered Indian, Inuit ancestry and non-Aboriginal populations. Among Registered Indians this proportion increased from about 20% in 1981 to about 23% in 1996, while among non-Aboriginal Canadians, it increased from 9% to 12% over the same period. Inuit female lone-parent families have also increased as a proportion of all families, from about 12% in 1981 to 17% in 1996. (Comparable data for the non-status Indian and Métis ancestry populations were not available.)

Figure 2:   Female lone-parent families as a percentage of all families selected ancestry groups, Canada, 1981–96

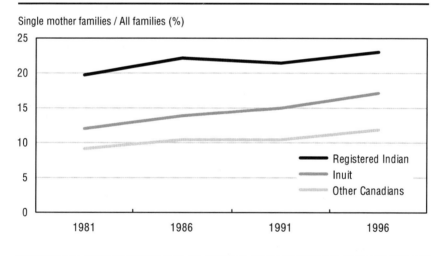

Single mother families / All families (%)

Sources: Statistics Canada 1984; Brecher et. al., 1985; Hagey et. al., 1989; DIAND 1996; Indian and Northern Affairs Canada, custom tabulation based on the 1996 Census of Canada.

Prevalence of Single-Mother Families in 1996

In 1996 there were 945,230 lone-parent families headed by women in Canada, according to the 1996 Census. Of these families, 31,620 were headed by Registered Indian women, and 16,505 were headed by other women with Aboriginal identity.

As shown in Figure 3, single-mother families were almost twice as common in urban areas as in rural areas among all three identity groups. Among Registered Indians, those living off reserves in urban areas had the highest proportion of female single-parent families (29%), while those living off reserves in rural areas had the lowest proportion (12%). Those living on reserves were in the middle (19%). There was a similar pattern among the other Aboriginal identity population, in that there was a much higher proportion of single-mother families in urban areas compared to rural areas. However, the prevalence of single mother families among the other Aboriginal population was substantially lower in urban areas than among the Registered Indian population. The other Canadian population showed a similar pattern of higher rates of single-mother families in urban areas, but the proportions were lower than for the Aboriginal populations in both urban and rural areas. In short, the differences among the three groups were greatest in urban areas.

The proportion of lone parents among families with children 0 to 15 years of age was higher than the proportion among all families. In 1996, 28% of Registered Indian families with children aged 0 to 15 years were female lone-parent families, compared to 24% among the other Aboriginal identity population and 16% among the other Canadian population. Again, the proportions were higher for those living in urban areas than in rural areas. In 1996, in urban areas off reserves, female lone-parent families made up 38% of Registered Indian families with children 0 to 15 compared to 29% of other Aboriginal identity families and 18% of other Canadian families with children. (See Figure 4.)

Number of Children in Lone-Parent Families

The number of children in Census families is important for a number of reasons, including the additional income needs of larger families, and the need for child care and educational services. Figure 5 provides data on the average number of children in families for Registered Indian and other Canadian families. Families that do not have any children 0 to 15 years old are excluded from the figure. It can be seen that, for both populations, husband-wife families had more children than lone parent families, and female lone-parent families had more children than male lone-parent families. In addition, for all family types registered, Indian families had more children than those of other Canadian families.

Figure 3: **Single-mother families as a percentage of all families by Aboriginal identity and location, Canada, 1996**

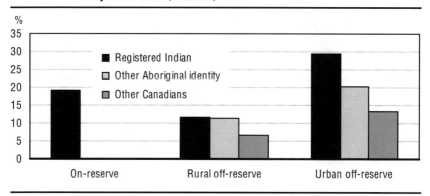

Figure 4: **Single-mother families with children 0 to 15 as a percentage of all families with children 0 to 15 by Aboriginal identity and location, Canada, 1996**

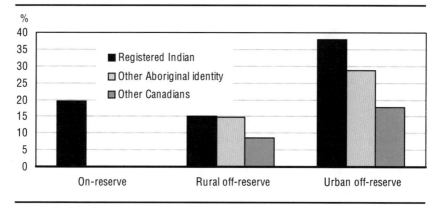

Figure 5: **Average number of children by family type, Registered Indian and other Canadian families with children, Canada, 1996**

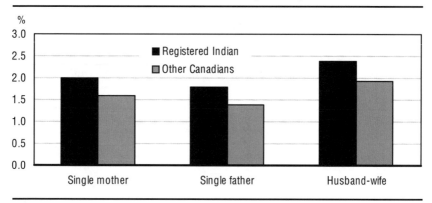

Family Status of Individuals

The proportion of lone parents can also be looked at in terms of individuals. A number of different measures can be used, such as lone parents as a percentage of the adult population or lone parents as a percentage of all parents. Figure 6 is based on the adult female population and shows the proportions of women who are single mothers living with children 0 to 15 years old, other mothers with children 0 to 15, and all other women. In this figure, the Aboriginal identity population is further subdivided between Registered Indians, Métis, Inuit and non-status Indians. Among all of these groups, except for the Inuit, more than half of the women did not have young children 0 to 15 at home. Among Inuit women, about 55% were mothers with children 0 to 15 living at home. All of the Aboriginal identity groups have much higher proportions of single mothers, with the highest proportion (15%) found among Registered Indian women. The proportions among Métis and non-status Indian women were slightly lower, and the proportion of Inuit single mothers was 10%.

We can also look at the proportion of mothers who are lone parents, as opposed to being part of a husband-wife family. Figure 7 reflects this, showing that about one-third of Registered Indian, Métis and non-status Indian mothers are single mothers, compared to about 16% of non-Aboriginal mothers. In other words, twice as many mothers from these three groups are lone parents compared to non-Aboriginal mothers. Inuit mothers are more similar to non-Aboriginal mothers with 19% being single mothers.

As can be seen in Figure 8, the proportion of women who are single mothers varies by place of residence. Among all groups, higher proportions of women living in urban areas were single mothers in 1996. This was especially true for Registered Indian women living in urban areas, 25% of whom were single mothers, compared to about 20% of Métis women, 17% of non-status Indian women and 15% of Inuit women. These figures may be compared to the 9% of non-Aboriginal women living in urban areas who were single mothers. In rural, off-reserve locations, about 11% to 12% of Aboriginal women were single mothers, compared to about 5% of non-Aboriginal women. Among Registered Indian women living on reserves, about 14% were single mothers.

Figure 6: **Distribution of women 15 or older in private households by marital/parental status and Aboriginal identity group, Canada, 1996**

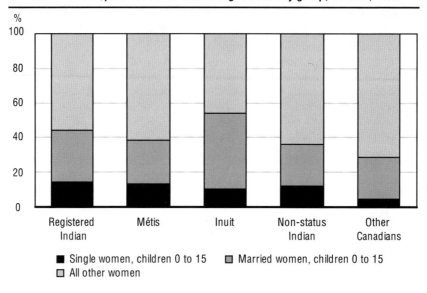

■ Single women, children 0 to 15   ▨ Married women, children 0 to 15
☐ All other women

Figure 7: **Single mothers as a percentage of mothers with children 0 to 15 years old by Aboriginal identity group, Canada, 1996**

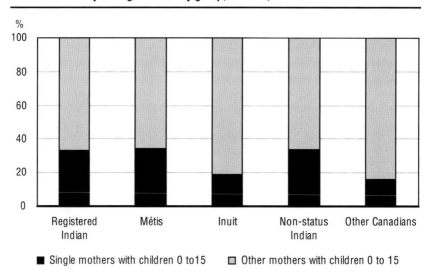

■ Single mothers with children 0 to15   ☐ Other mothers with children 0 to 15

Figure 8: Single mothers as a percentage of women in private households by Aboriginal identity group and location, Canada, 1996

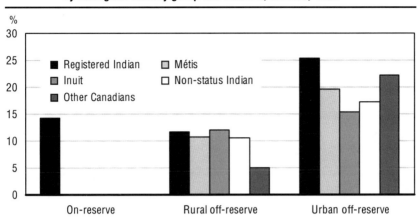

As illustrated in Figure 9, the relationship between the prevalence of single mothers is different for different age groups, and is also different for Aboriginal and non-Aboriginal women. Among Canadians generally, the proportion of mothers who are single mothers is high for the younger (15-24) and older (55-64) age groups, but considerably lower among the age groups in the middle (25-54). Among Aboriginal women (including Registered Indians and others with Aboriginal identity) the proportion of single mothers is again highest for the youngest age group, but it does not decline as much in the older age groups, remaining at or above 30% of mothers.

Single Mothers and Educational Attainment

In addition to age, educational attainment may influence the likelihood of being a single parent. Figure 10 examines this by looking at the relationship between education and the prevalence of single mothers for one age group— those 25 to 44 years old. As the figure shows, among the non-Aboriginal population in this age group, as educational attainment increases, the proportion of single mothers decreases. This is not true of the Aboriginal population, among whom the proportion of single mothers tends to stay about the same or increase slightly with education. For all educational levels, the proportion of single mothers is much higher among Aboriginal women compared to non-Aboriginal women. In short, the relationship between education and being a single mother is not very clear for Aboriginal women and seems to be different from among non-Aboriginal women.

Figure 9: Single mothers as a percentage of mothers of children 0 to 15 among Aboriginal and other Canadian women, by age group, Canada, 1996

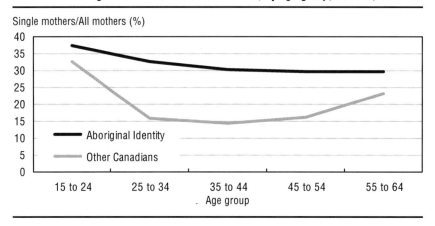

Figure 10: Single mothers with children 0 to 15 as a percentage of all women 25 to 44 years old by highest level of schooling and Aboriginal identity, Canada, 1996

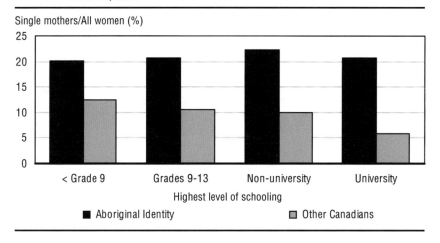

Employment Rates

A number of socioeconomic characteristics may be related to being a single parent, including such things as employment and income. Figure 11 shows the employment rate (percentage of the population that is employed) of four groups defined in terms of gender and parental status: single mothers, married mothers, other women and single fathers. It can be seen that, among the Aboriginal population, single mothers have the lowest employment rates (about 38%) while married mothers and single fathers have the highest employment rates, both at about 51%. Among the non-Aboriginal population the lowest employment rate is found among "other women"—those who are not mothers—and the highest employment rate is found among single fathers. The result is that the gap in employment rates between Aboriginal and non-Aboriginal single mothers is quite large, a difference of about twenty percentage points, and the gap between Aboriginal and non-Aboriginal single fathers is even greater.

As shown in Figure 12, employment is also related to place of residence. This figure shows that Aboriginal single mothers living on reserves or in rural areas had higher rates of employment than those living in off-reserve, urban areas. In all locations there was a large difference in employment rates between Aboriginal single mothers and other single mothers, especially in urban areas where there was a difference of more than twenty percentage points.

Figure 11: Employment rates among the population 15+ not attending school full-time by Aboriginal identity and parental status, Canada, 1996

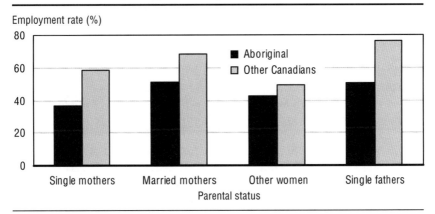

Figure 12: Employment rates among single mothers with children 0 to 15 not attending school full-time by Aboriginal identity and place of residence, Canada, 1996

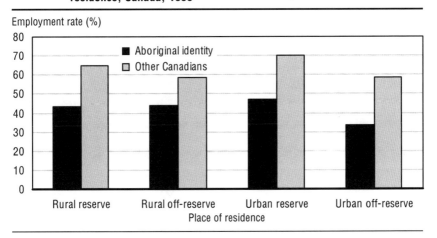

Individual Income

Figure 13 compares the 1995 average incomes of Aboriginal and other single mothers and single fathers across the various age groups. Aboriginal single mothers had the lowest incomes for each age group, followed by Aboriginal single fathers, other single mothers and other single fathers. For all groups incomes increased with age through the 45 to 54 age group. Among Aboriginal single fathers, incomes continued to increase for the 55 to 64 age group, but for the other populations, incomes decreased for this age group. The gaps in average incomes between groups also increased with age so that among the 45 to 54 age group Aboriginal single mothers had incomes which were more than $5,000 less than Aboriginal single fathers and more than $10,000 less than other Canadian single mothers.

Aboriginal single fathers tended to have relatively lower average incomes when compared to those of other Canadian single fathers. For most age groups, Aboriginal single fathers had average incomes that were between 60% and 65% of other Canadian single fathers in both urban and rural areas.

Figure 14 focuses on the educational attainment of different Aboriginal parental/marital groups and the relationship to median income. As the figure shows, in 1995 Aboriginal single mothers' median incomes were lower than those of Aboriginal single fathers, and higher than those of Aboriginal married mothers at most educational levels. Aboriginal married mothers median incomes, however, increased more rapidly with education, so that the incomes of married mothers with a university education surpassed those of single mothers and equalled those of single fathers. Aboriginal married fathers' median incomes were substantially higher than any of the other groups, also increasing rapidly with education.

Figure 15 focuses on the proportion of single mothers whose major source of income is government transfer payments. This figure also compares the various Aboriginal identity groups and on-reserve, rural and urban locations. In general, the figure shows that dependence on government transfer payments is high among single mothers. Almost half of non-Aboriginal single mothers, and 60% or more of Aboriginal single mothers, identified transfer payments as their major income source in 1995. Among the various identity groups, Registered Indian single mothers were most likely to depend on transfer payments. Among Registered Indian women living in urban, off-reserve locations, about 75% identified transfer payments as their major source of income.

Figure 13: Average individual income among single parents by Aboriginal identity, gender and age, Canada, 1995

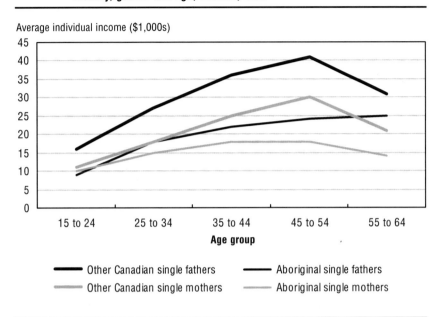

Average individual income ($1,000s)

Age group

— Other Canadian single fathers   — Aboriginal single fathers
— Other Canadian single mothers   — Aboriginal single mothers

Figure 14: Median annual income among the Aboriginal population with income by parental status and educational attainment, Canada, 1995

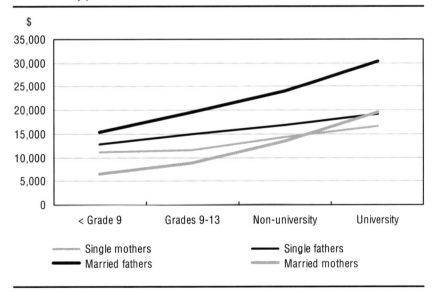

$

— Single mothers   — Single fathers
— Married fathers   — Married mothers

Figure 15: Proportion of single mothers with children 0 to 15 whose major source of income is government transfer payments by Aboriginal identity and place of residence, Canada, 1995

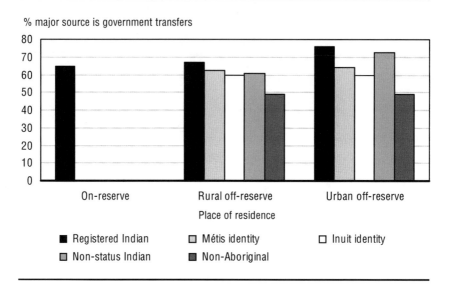

% major source is government transfers

On-reserve   Rural off-reserve   Urban off-reserve

Place of residence

■ Registered Indian   ☐ Métis identity   ☐ Inuit identity
☐ Non-status Indian   ▨ Non-Aboriginal

Family Income

The previous tables and figures have been concerned with individual incomes. Family incomes, however, provide a better indication of relative income and disparities among groups because the family tends to act as an economic unit. In addition, lone-parent families are likely to have fewer income earners than two-parent families and have more dependants than childless couples or unattached individuals.

Figure 16 compares the average incomes among the three identity groups and among three family types in 1995. The figure shows that there were large gaps in incomes between lone-parent families and husband-wife families as well as between Aboriginal and non-Aboriginal population groups. In 1995, Registered Indian single-mother families had an average income of about $15,000 and other Aboriginal single-mother families had an average income only slightly higher at about $17,000. By comparison, non-Aboriginal single-mother families had an average income of about $21,000.

As the figure shows, the income differences between different family types were much greater. Husband-wife families with children had the highest incomes, and these were about three times the average incomes of single-mother families. It can also be seen from the figure that the differences among identity groups are larger for male lone-parent families than for female lone-parent families, and larger still for husband-wife families.

Figure 16: Average annual income of families with children 0 to 15 by identity group and family type, Canada, 1995

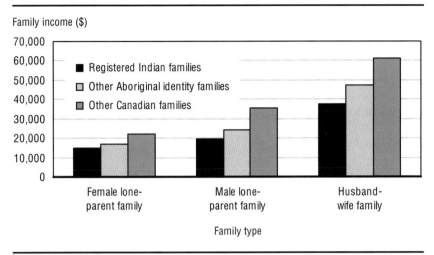

Conclusion

It is clear from the above that Aboriginal women are more likely to be mothers and much more likely to be single parents than other Canadians. In addition, there are differences among various Aboriginal identity groups that show it is a mistake to consider all Aboriginal single mothers as having the same needs. These differences are apparent when comparing Registered Indian, Métis, Inuit and non-status Indian single mothers and when looking at geographic differences, such as comparisons between urban and rural areas.

All Canadian single mothers tend to experience economic disadvantages, including problems in the labour market and low family income, but Aboriginal single mothers experience these problems to a greater degree than do others. The low incomes of single-mother families and high rates of dependency on government transfer payments among Aboriginal single mothers are clearly identified in the data reviewed above.

One of the themes of the study is the high proportion of Aboriginal single mothers in urban areas and the high level of need among them, as shown by their employment characteristics and dependence on transfer income. This is particularly true for Registered Indian single mothers. Urban-rural differences are also found among other Canadian women, but because of the higher proportions of single mothers and their higher levels of need, it is a more significant issue among the Aboriginal population.

The findings of this study point to some preliminary policy-related implications. The relatively large and increasing number of young Aboriginal single mothers suggests a need for housing, parenting support and education. Due to their lower educational and occupational levels, Aboriginal single mothers may have greater difficulty than other single mothers in attempting to enter the labour market and gain employment. Programs that enable Aboriginal single mothers to enter the labour market need to be designed specifically for those with low educational levels who spend longer periods caring for pre-school children.

One of the strengths of Aboriginal single mothers is their willingness to upgrade their education by attending school as mature adults. It appears that existing programs and policies have been effective in helping Aboriginal single mothers pursue post-secondary (university and non-university) education at various age levels. However, there may be a need to do more to improve basic education or to provide educational upgrading for this segment of the population.

Given recent research findings, growing numbers of children living in Aboriginal single-parent families are likely to experience more educational and health problems than other children. These risks seem to be related both to income levels and parenting styles, suggesting that parenting education and support programs are important, in addition to income supports.

The findings also suggest the need for further research in a number of areas. Further work is needed to identify the effects on children of living in single-parent families, particularly for Aboriginal children. A better understanding is also needed concerning how Aboriginal single-parent families are formed, and whether these processes are different from those among the general Canadian population. It seems likely that further analysis will identify distinctly different types of single-parent families based on such things as education, income levels, cultural characteristics, how they were formed, and how long they remain single-parent families. Different types of single-parent families are likely to face different issues. A better understanding of these and other questions will need to go beyond cross-sectional studies to longitudinal research designs.

Endnotes

Presented at the Aboriginal Policy Research Conference, Ottawa, November 2002.

1. Unless otherwise stated, the data source for all figures in this article are from the customized 1996 Census tabulations prepared for Indian and Northern Affairs Canada.

References

Brecher, T., Gauvin, P., Klein, S., and Larocque, G. 1985. *1981 Census Highlights on Registered Indians: Annotated Tables*. Ottawa: Sociodemographic Research Section, Research Branch, Corporate Policy, Indian and Northern Affairs Canada.

Falconer, P. 1990. "The Overlooked of the Neglected: Native Single Mothers in Major Cities on the Prairies" in *The Political Economy of Manitoba*, ed. J. Silver and J. Hull. Canadian Plains Research Centre, University of Regina, 188-210.

Hagey, N.J., Larocque, G., and McBride, C. 1989. "Highlights of Aboriginal Conditions, 1981–2000." Part II of *Social Conditions*. Ottawa: Quantitative Analysis & Socio-demographic Research, Indian and Northern Affairs Canada.

Indian and Northern Affairs Canada. 1996. *Aboriginal Women: A Demographic, Social and Economic Profile*. Ottawa: Information Quality and Research Directorate, Information Management Branch, Corporate Services, Department of Indian Affairs and Northern Development (Catalogue # R32-172\1996E).

Statistics Canada. 1984. *Canada's Native People*. Ottawa: Statistics Canada (Statistics Canada Catalogue # 99-937).

10

La fécondité des Indiennes
à 15 à 19 ans, de 1986 à 1997

Norbert Robitaille, Ali Kouaouci et Eric Guimond

Introduction

Au Canada, la fécondité des Indiennes a été décrite comme plus élevée que celle du reste de la population canadienne avec une tendance à la baisse, voire à la convergence depuis le début des années 60. Cette baisse de la fécondité est perçue comme l'expression d'une volonté chez ces femmes de réduire leur descendance, rendue possible par la diffusion des moyens contraceptifs. Or, jusqu'ici aucune analyse démographique fine de la fécondité selon l'âge, en particulier celle des femmes âgées de moins de 20 ans, n'a été réalisée pour étayer cette thèse. La direction de la recherche et de l'analyse au ministère des Affaires indiennes et du Nord du Canada (MAINC) a senti la nécessité de combler en partie cette lacune en commandant cette étude sur l'évolution de la fécondité des Indiennes adolescentes et ses conséquences socio-économiques. Cette préoccupation reflète les multiples risques liés à la maternité chez les femmes âgées de moins de 20 ans : grossesses non désirées, avortements plus ou moins clandestins, maladies transmissibles sexuellement et SIDA, problèmes sociaux et familiaux, problèmes psychologiques, etc.

L'analyse démographique de l'évolution de la fécondité des Indiennes du Canada est basée sur les données du Registre des Indiens tenu par le MAINC. Cette analyse cible la fécondité des Indiennes inscrites au Registre, âgées de 15 à 19 ans, depuis les modifications apportées à la *Loi sur les Indiens* en 1985. Le travail exploratoire sur les conséquences socio-économiques de la maternité à l'adolescence repose sur des données du Recensement du Canada de 1996. L'analyse dont il est question porte sur les conditions socio-économiques des femmes âgées de 25 à 29 ans devenues mères pendant leur adolescence.

Le présent article comporte quatre sections. À la première section, on définit la population à l'étude et présente succinctement les modifications à la *Loi sur les Indiens* apportées en 1985. Les changements aux règles de transmission du statut légal d'Indien introduits par la *loi C-31* limitent l'analyse démographique de la fécondité à partir du Registre des Indiens. La seconde section est une brève revue de la littérature sur la fécondité des Indiennes du Canada. À la troisième section, on mesure et analyse l'évolution de la fécondité des Indiennes inscrites âgées de 15 à 19 ans au cours de la période 1986–1997. Des estimations nationales et provinciales sont proposées. Enfin à la quatrième section, on s'intéresse aux conditions socio-économiques des Indiennes inscrites âgées de 25 à 29 ans devenues mères entre 15 et 19 ans.

Population à l'étude

Un Indien inscrit est une personne qui possède le statut légal d'Indien défini dans la *Loi sur les Indiens* et dont le nom figure au Registre des Indiens que tient le MAINC. Ce statut est accompagné d'un certain nombre de droits, notamment en ce qui concerne la taxation et l'impôt sur le revenu pour les résidents des réserves indiennes. Des programmes d'éducation post-secondaire, de logement, d'aide sociale et de soins de santé non assurables sont également offerts aux détenteurs du statut légal d'Indien.

La taille et la composition de la population indienne inscrite ont changé considérablement depuis le milieu des années 80. Ces changements démographiques résultent en partie[1] de la réintégration de membres et de l'ajout au Registre des Indiens de nouveaux membres à la suite de modifications apportées à la *Loi sur les Indiens* en avril 1985, communément appelées *loi C-31*. Les effets démographiques des dispositions réparatrices de la *loi C-31*, rapportés ici succinctement, ont été largement documentés par Clatworthy (1993, 1997, 2001, 2002).

La *loi C-31* a modifié les règles définissant le droit à l'inscription au Registre des Indiens. Depuis le 17 avril 1985, une personne peut être inscrite au Registre en vertu de l'une des deux clauses figurant à l'article 6 de la *loi C-31*, à savoir :

- Paragraphe 6(1), quand les deux parents d'une personne sont (ou ont le droit d'être) inscrits; et
- Paragraphe 6(2), quand l'un des parents de la personne est (ou a le droit d'être) inscrit en vertu du Paragraphe 6(1) et que l'autre parent ne l'est pas.

La figure 1 illustre les règles de transmission du droit à l'inscription en relation avec les diverses combinaisons d'ascendance possibles. L'ascendance indienne/non indienne sur deux générations successives aboutit, pour les enfants de la seconde génération, à la perte du droit d'être inscrit au Registre des Indiens.

Figure 1: Règles de transmission du statut légal d'Indien, 1985

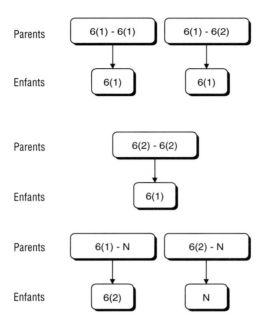

Au 31 décembre 2000, un total de 114 512 personnes nées avant le 17 avril 1985 avaient été (ré-)inscrites au Registre des Indiens selon les termes de la *loi C-31* de 1985. Les « nouveaux » inscrits représentent environ 17 % de la population totale du Registre des Indiens à la fin décembre 2000 (AINC, 2002). Clatworthy (2001) a estimé à environ 60 000 le nombre de personnes nées après le 16 avril 1985 et inscrites au Registre des Indiens qui, au 31 décembre 2000, n'auraient pas été inscrites selon les anciennes dispositions de la *Loi sur les Indiens*.

Dans cette étude, seules les naissances de mères indiennes inscrites en vertu du paragraphe 6.1 de la *loi C-31* sont considérées pour l'analyse de la fécondité des Indiennes adolescentes. La fécondité des Indiennes inscrites en vertu du paragraphe 6.2 ne peut être étudiée puisque seulement une partie des naissances de ces femmes figurent au Registre des Indiens. En effet, les naissances d'une Indienne inscrite en vertu du paragraphe 6.2 et d'un non-indien (N) n'apparaissent pas au Registre parce que non-indiennes (N) selon les règles de transmission du statut.

Revue de la littérature

À notre connaissance, le thème de la fécondité des Indiennes adolescentes du Canada n'a jamais été abordé par les démographes. En règle générale, les démographes se sont surtout intéressés à la fécondité des Indiennes de tous âges. Il existe néanmoins des estimations de la fécondité des Indiennes adolescentes dans quelques publications que nous allons introduire brièvement.

Les principales études inventoriées, toutes de Statistique Canada, ont été produites en vue d'effectuer des projections de la population indienne inscrite pour le compte du MAINC. Ces études représentent des sources intéressantes d'information pour ce travail sur la fécondité des adolescentes. Bien qu'ils contiennent des estimations de la fécondité des Indiennes adolescentes nécessaires au travail de projection, ces travaux n'offrent cependant aucune analyse attentive de leur niveau, ni de leur évolution. Afin d'éviter une certaine redondance, qui est souvent le propre des travaux de projection démographique, nous limitons cette revue de littérature aux analyses réalisées par Ram et Romaniuk (1985) et Loh et al (1998).

La fécondité des Indiennes de tous âges

Ram et Romaniuk ont publié en 1985 une analyse et une projection de la fécondité de la population indienne inscrite par province et pour l'ensemble du Canada. L'étude réalisée à Statistique Canada est basée sur les données du Registre des Indiens du MAINC corrigées des problèmes de non-déclaration et d'enregistrement tardif des naissances.

Un événement ne peut être inscrit au Registre que si son gestionnaire reçoit une copie de l'acte officiel attestant qu'il a eu lieu. Dans le cas du Registre des Indiens, les individus ne sont pas obligés légalement d'enregistrer rapidement les événements, d'où de fréquents délais d'enregistrement. Ce problème d'enregistrement tardif des événements est connu des spécialistes et gestionnaires du Registre des Indiens.

En plus du problème des déclarations tardives, certains événements ne sont jamais inscrits au Registre des Indiens. Par exemple, dans le cas d'un enfant qui décède en bas âge, avant même l'enregistrement de sa naissance, il n'est pas acquis que ces deux événements (naissance et décès) seront un jour enregistrés. Il y a tout lieu de croire que le sous-enregistrement touche plus spécifiquement les événements sans conséquence future sur la vie des gens concernés et de leurs proches. En effet, pour bénéficier de tous les services disponibles auxquels elle a droit (ex : service de santé, école), une personne doit nécessairement procéder, tôt ou tard, à une déclaration de naissance pour fin d'inscription au Registre des Indiens. À l'opposé, il n'y a aucun incitatif à la déclaration d'un décès puisque forcément aucun service n'est par la suite requis par le principal intéressé.

Partant d'informations sur l'année de naissance et l'année d'enregistrement de la naissance contenues dans le Registre des Indiens, Ram et Romaniuk (1985) ont mis au point une série historique ajustée du nombre des naissances à partir de laquelle les indices de fécondité ont pu être calculés. L'analyse a révélé une baisse continue de la fécondité des Indiennes inscrites de 1968 à 1981 (figure 2). À l'échelle du pays, l'indice synthétique de fécondité[2] de la population indienne inscrite a chuté de 6,1 à 3,2 enfants par femme. Au cours de cette même période, la fécondité des Canadiennes est passée de 2,5 à 1,6 enfants par femme. Un indice synthétique de fécondité inférieur à 2,1 enfants par femme est généralement interprété comme un signal que le remplacement des générations n'est pas assuré dans la population concernée et qu'à long terme cela pourrait mener successivement à un vieillissement de la population, puis à une décroissance démographique. Chez la population indienne inscrite, sur la seule base de l'analyse de la fécondité, le remplacement des générations serait largement assuré.

Figure 2: **Indice synthétique de fécondité (ISF) des Indiennes inscrites, Canada, 1968–1996**

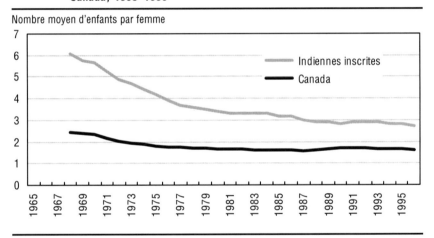

Nombre moyen d'enfants par femme

Sources : Ram et Romaniuk (1985), Loh et al (1998), Statistique Canada (1984).

Loh et al. (1998) ont effectué une révision exhaustive des séries historiques des naissances, des décès et de la population de 1974 à 1996 du Registre des Indiens pour les besoins d'une projection de la population indienne inscrite pour le compte du MAINC. À nouveau, des estimations nationales et provinciales de l'indice synthétique de fécondité ont été produites pour les besoins de l'exercice de projection. D'après ces estimations, la baisse de la fécondité de la population indienne inscrite observée depuis la fin des années 60 s'est poursuivie au cours des années 80 et 90, mais cette baisse se fait de plus en plus modeste. L'indice synthétique de fécondité est passé de 3,2 enfants par femme en 1981 à 2,7 enfants par femme en 1996. Au cours de la première moitié des années 70, la variation annuelle moyenne de l'indice était de -0,1 enfant par femme contre -0,02 enfant par femme pour les cinq premières années de la décennie 90.

En 1981, la région la plus féconde était la Saskatchewan avec 4,1 enfants par femme, et la moins féconde le Québec avec 2,2 enfants par femme. En 1996, le Yukon présente l'indice synthétique de fécondité le plus bas (2,0), alors que le Manitoba présente l'indice le plus élevé (3,5), dépassant celui de la Saskatchewan (3,1). À l'extérieur des Prairies, la fécondité des Indiennes en 1996 est inférieure à 3 enfants par femme.

Tableau 1: Indice synthétique de fécondité (ISF) des Indiennes inscrites, Canada et régions, 1981 et 1996

Région	ISF 1981* (1)	ISF 1996** (2)	Différence (3)=(2)-(1)
Atlantique	2,9	2,4	-0,5
Québec	2,2	2,5	+0,3
Ontario	2,9	2,2	-0,7
Manitoba	3,5	3,5	0,00
Saskatchewan	4,1	3,1	-1,0
Alberta	3,8	3,2	-0,6
Colombie-Britannique	2,5	2,6	+0,1
Yukon	3,6	2,0	-1,6
Territoires du Nord-Ouest	-	2,2	-
Canada	**3,2**	**2,7**	**-0,5**

Sources : * Ram et Romaniuk (1985, 15).
** Loh et al. (1998, 20).

La baisse de la fécondité des Indiennes inscrites observée de 1981 à 1996 pour l'ensemble du Canada est confirmée pour une majorité des régions. Les plus fortes baisses ont été observées en Saskatchewan (-1,0) et dans les Territoires du Nord Ouest-Yukon (-1,6). La fécondité demeure cependant inchangée au Manitoba et aurait augmenté au Québec et en Colombie-Britannique.

La fécondité des Indiennes selon l'âge

La figure 3 présente les taux de fécondité des Indiennes inscrites par groupe d'âge quinquennal (5 ans) pour les années 1975, 1985 et 1995. La baisse de la fécondité des Indiennes inscrites de tous âges (ISF) survenue entre 1975 et 1995 concerne davantage les femmes plus âgées que les plus jeunes. Chez les femmes âgées de 30 ans et plus, la fécondité a chuté de plus de moitié au cours de ces vingt années. Pour les âges les plus féconds (20 à 29 ans), le taux de fécondité a perdu un quart de sa valeur mesurée en 1975. De tous les groupes d'âges, c'est le comportement fécond des adolescentes qui a le moins changé de 1975 à 1995 (<10%).

Comparant la fécondité des Indiennes inscrites et des Canadiennes en 1995, on remarque que les premières se démarquent des secondes seulement chez les moins de 25 ans. D'après les estimations disponibles, la fécondité des Indiennes adolescentes serait 5,5 fois supérieure à celle des Canadiennes. Chez les femmes âgées de 20 à 24 ans, les Indiennes présentent un niveau de fécondité pratiquement 3 fois plus élevé. Au-delà de 25 ans, les niveaux de la fécondité des Indiennes et des Canadiennes en 1995 sont comparables.

Figure 3: Taux de fécondité des Indiennes inscrites selon le groupe d'âge, Canada, 1975, 1985 et 1995

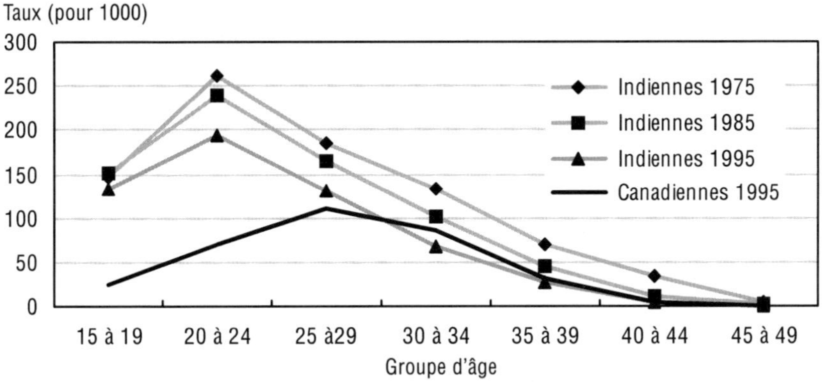

Source : Loh et al (1998). Données non publiées.

Dans les deux études revues (Ram et Romaniuk 1985; Loh et al. 1998), les données du Registre ont chaque fois été corrigées pour deux problèmes : la non-déclaration des naissances et la déclaration tardive des naissances. Étant donné l'objectif premier de ces études de réaliser des projections de population, il est normal de se concentrer sur des indices de fécondité globaux comme l'indice synthétique de fécondité. Les auteurs de ces projections ont donc choisi d'effectuer des corrections globales des effectifs des naissances, sans considérer l'âge de la mère. Or, on s'intéresse ici à la fécondité des femmes âgées de 15 à 19 ans. Une explication vraisemblable à la forme particulière des taux de fécondité selon l'âge des Indiennes inscrites proposés par Ram et Romaniuk (1985) et Loh et al (1998) est que des naissances dont la mère est adulte auraient été attribuées indûment aux adolescentes âgées de 15 à 19 ans.

Au terme de ce bref survol de la littérature, il ressort que la fécondité des Indiennes de 15 à 19 ans est en somme peu connue. Les rares données sur la question proviennent de travaux de projections. Il serait hasardeux d'utiliser ces données en les sortant de leur contexte et c'est pourquoi le présent travail propose de nouvelles mesures de la fécondité de ce groupe d'âge, et de son évolution depuis la mise en application de la *loi C-31* en 1985.

Évolution de la fécondité des Indiennes adolescentes depuis 1985

Données et méthodologie

Pour l'estimation de la fécondité au cours de la période 1986–1997, un fichier non nominatif de données a été élaboré à partir du Registre des Indiens. Le fichier a été structuré de manière à relier tous les Indiens inscrits à leurs parents et à prendre en compte les variables suivantes :

- la date de naissance;
- la date de création du dossier (date d'inscription au Registre);
- le sexe;
- l'inscription au titre de la *loi C-31* (oui, non);
- les détails de l'inscription en vertu de l'article 6 de la *loi C-31* (6.1; 6.2);
- le lieu de résidence (région);
- la date de naissance de la mère et du père;
- la date de création du dossier de la mère et du père (date d'inscription au Registre);
- l'inscription de la mère et du père au titre de la *loi C-31*;
- les détails de l'inscription de la mère et du père en vertu de l'article 6 de la *loi C-31* (6.1; 6.2);
- le lieu de résidence de la mère et du père (région).

Tel qu'indiqué précédemment, seules les naissances de mères indiennes inscrites en vertu du paragraphe 6.1 de la *loi C-31* sont considérées pour cette analyse de la fécondité des Indiennes adolescentes. Il est impossible d'estimer la fécondité des femmes inscrites en vertu du paragraphe 6.2 puisqu'un certain nombre des enfants de ces femmes n'apparaissent pas au Registre des Indiens étant donné l'appartenance non indienne de leur père.

De ce fichier non nominatif, deux séries de données historiques ont été extraites pour l'estimation de la fécondité des Indiennes adolescentes de la période 1986–1997. Ces deux séries sont :

A. l'effectif des Indiennes inscrites au Registre selon l'âge et la région;
B. la distribution des naissances selon l'âge de la mère, l'année de la naissance et l'année de l'enregistrement, par région.

La série B permet de calculer directement les naissances dont les mères sont âgées de 15 à 19 ans et de redresser les effectifs de naissance pour les déclarations tardives. La méthode adoptée pour le redressement des effectifs de naissance est semblable à celle retenue par Ram et Romaniuk (1985), à la différence près qu'on différencie ici les naissances selon l'âge de la mère. De façon globale, cette méthode consiste à déterminer un calendrier-type de déclaration des naissances pour une période de référence donnée, suffisamment ancienne pour que l'on suppose toutes les naissances déclarées, et à l'appliquer aux effectifs de naissance des autres années.

Le calendrier-type de déclaration des naissances utilisé ici est basé sur l'analyse des délais de déclaration des naissances des années 1986 à 1988[3] pour lesquelles on peut raisonnablement considérer que la totalité des naissances ont été déclarées avant l'année 2000, soit 12 ans après l'événement. La figure 4 présente les proportions cumulées pour l'ensemble du Canada et ses régions. Dans la plupart des régions, les déclarations sont négligeables à partir de la huitième année, sauf pour l'Ontario où la part manquante atteint tout de même 9 %. Dans certaines régions (TNO, Yukon, Saskatchewan et Atlantique), les naissances sont pratiquement toutes déclarées à l'intérieur d'un délai de 6 ans. Cependant, si on examine les proportions de naissances déclarées avant le premier anniversaire (délai de 0 an), les régions se distinguent fortement avec un minimum d'environ 10 % au Manitoba et un maximum de plus de 40 % au Yukon. Le tableau 2 suivant traite de l'importance de la correction effectuée pour le délai de déclaration selon la région. Cet indice varie de 39 % pour le Manitoba à 9 % pour la Saskatchewan.

Figure 4: Proportions cumulées des naissances[1] selon le délai de déclaration, Canada et régions, 1986–1988

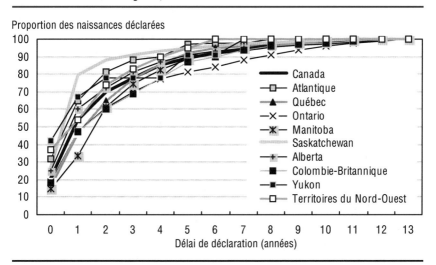

Proportion des naissances déclarées

Délai de déclaration (années)

Canada
Atlantique
Québec
Ontario
Manitoba
Saskatchewan
Alberta
Colombie-Britannique
Yukon
Territoires du Nord-Ouest

Note 1 : Dont la mère est indienne inscrite en vertu du paragraphe 6.1 de la *loi C-31* de 1985.
Source : MAINC, totalisations spéciales.

Aucune correction pour la non-déclaration des naissances n'est effectuée parce qu'elle requiert la formulation d'hypothèses en cascade. Une première hypothèse doit être faite sur la proportion des naissances non déclarées découlant du décès en bas âge. Cette hypothèse repose elle-même sur une proportion forcément inconnue d'événements dont le phénomène, la mortalité infantile, doit à son tour être estimé par des méthodes indirectes et intensives en hypothèses. La portée de la non-correction de l'effectif des naissances pour la non-déclaration des naissances sur l'analyse de la fécondité serait modeste puisque la mortalité infantile estimée par Nault et al (1992) est de 15 pour 1 000 en 1990. Quelle que soit la proportion de naissances non déclarées pour cause de décès, l'impact sur l'effectif des naissances ne peut guère dépasser 2 % (Robitaille et al. 2003).

Tableau 2: Importance de la correction pour la déclaration tardive des naissances[1], Canada et régions, 1986–1997

Région	Effectif des naissances déclarées (1)	Effectif corrigé des naissances (2)	Importance de la correction (2)-(1) / (1)
			%
Atlantique	935	1 054	12,73
Québec	2 654	3 348	26,15
Ontario	5 322	6 775	27,30
Manitoba	6 927	9 651	39,32
Saskatchewan	7 217	7 874	9,10
Alberta	5 241	6 107	16,52
Colombie-Britannique	4 348	5 581	28,36
Yukon	186	213	14,52
Territoires du Nord-Ouest	537	609	13,41

Note 1 : Dont la mère est indienne inscrite en vertu du paragraphe 6.1 de la *loi C-31* de 1985.
Source : MAINC, totalisations spéciales.

Résultats

Contrairement à ce que les études disponibles laissaient présager, la fécondité des Indiennes inscrites âgées entre 15 et 19 ans est en hausse de 1986 à 1997 : de 98 à 123 pour 1 000 femmes de 15 à 19 ans (figure 5). L'analyse d'indicateurs globaux de fécondité tel l'indice synthétique de fécondité (figure 2) masque donc la situation particulière des adolescentes. Comparant la fécondité des Indiennes inscrites âgées de 15 à 19 ans à celle de l'ensemble des Canadiennes du même groupe d'âge, on constate que l'écart s'est creusé entre ces deux groupes : le taux de fécondité des premières serait six fois celui des secondes en 1997, alors que le rapport n'était que de 1 à 4 en 1986. À l'échelle régionale (figure 6), la fécondité a eu tendance à augmenter dans toutes les régions au cours de la période post-C31. Le niveau de fécondité varie cependant selon la région de résidence. Les Indiennes inscrites résidentes du Manitoba, de la Saskatchewan, et de l'Alberta présentent des niveaux de fécondité généralement supérieurs à la moyenne canadienne. Au Manitoba, une Indienne adolescente sur six aurait eu un enfant en 1997. Les populations de l'Atlantique et du Yukon présentent les taux de fécondité les plus faibles.

Il est possible que la hausse observée des taux de fécondité estimés soit en partie attribuable aux hypothèses utilisées pour la correction des déclarations de naissance tardives. Si les délais de déclaration ont diminué au cours des dix dernières années, alors il est possible que la méthode utilisée (un calendrier-type de déclarations des naissances) conduise à une surestimation du nombre total des naissances dont la mère est adolescente. Néanmoins, qu'importe la tendance réelle quant aux délais de déclaration, la fécondité des Indiennes adolescentes demeure extrêmement élevée en comparaison avec celle des autres Canadiennes adolescentes.

Cette analyse soulève donc quelques questions intéressantes : pourquoi le taux de fécondité des Indiennes est-il si élevé, comparé au taux canadien ? Pourquoi la tendance est-elle à la hausse alors que pour l'indice synthétique de fécondité la tendance est à la baisse, esquissant une convergence avec le taux canadien ?

Figure 5:   Taux de fécondité des Indiennes inscrites et de l'ensemble des Canadiennes âgées de 15 à 19 ans, Canada, 1986–1999

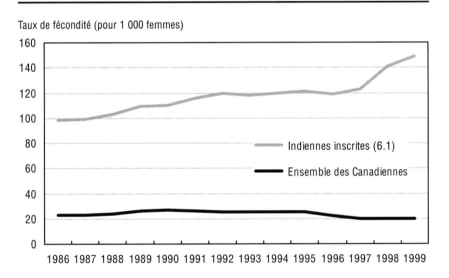

Taux de fécondité (pour 1 000 femmes)

Source : MAINC, totalisations spéciales.

Figure 6: Taux de fécondité des Indiennes inscrites âgées de 15 à 19 ans, Canada et régions, 1986–1997

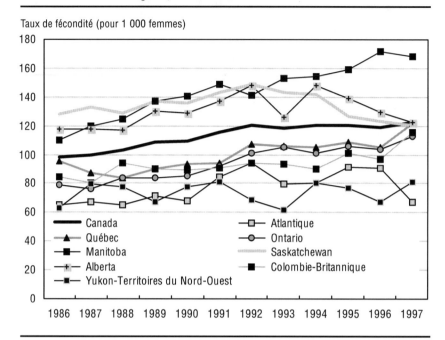

Taux de fécondité (pour 1 000 femmes)

Legend:
— Canada
▲ Québec
■ Manitoba
+ Alberta
■ Yukon-Territoires du Nord-Ouest
□ Atlantique
● Ontario
Saskatchewan
■ Colombie-Britannique

Note :   Les estimations pour la période 1986–1997 ne valent que pour les Indiennes inscrites selon les termes du paragraphe 6.1 de la *Loi sur les Indiens*.

Source :   MAINC, totalisations spéciales.

Profil socio-économique des mères adolescentes au recensement de 1996

Une fois l'évolution de la fécondité des Indiennes adolescentes mesurée et analysée, il importe d'en évaluer les conséquences pour la qualité de vie de la mère et de ses enfants. Le Recensement du Canada constitue l'unique source de données disponibles pour l'analyse des conséquences socio-économiques de la maternité précoce chez les Indiennes inscrites. Le groupe ciblé est celui des Indiennes inscrites âgées de 25 à 29 ans au moment du recensement et qui étaient devenues mères entre 15 et 19 ans. Il s'agit donc de femmes âgées de 25 à 29 ans avec un enfant âgé de 10 à 14 ans.

Les données disponibles permettent de répondre aux questions suivantes :

- Ces femmes ont-elles du fait de leur maternité précoce plus ou moins de chance de se retrouver monoparentales ?
- Sont-elles en plus ou moins grandes proportions dans les réserves ?

- Résident-elles en plus ou moins grandes proportions en ville ?
- Ont-elles plus ou moins de chance de poursuivre leur scolarité ?
- Ont-elles un revenu plus ou moins élevé ?

Pour répondre à ces questions, on compare dans un premier temps les Indiennes inscrites âgées de 25 à 29 ans avec enfant de 10 à 14 ans à celles qui ont un enfant de 0 à 9 ans, c'est-à-dire celles qui sont donc devenues mères après leur vingtième anniversaire, et à celles sans enfant. Dans une seconde étape, la comparaison se limite aux femmes de 25–29 ans avec un enfant de 10 à 14 ans selon l'origine et l'inscription au Registre des Indiens.

Mères adolescentes et monoparentalité

Selon les données du Recensement du Canada de 1996, la maternité à 15 à 19 ans chez les Indiennes ne semble guère augmenter la probabilité de se retrouver monoparentale une dizaine d'années plus tard (figure 7). La proportion de mères monoparentales parmi les Indiennes inscrites âgées de 25 à 29 ans devenues mères à l'adolescence (30 %) est même inférieure à celle des femmes devenues mères après 20 ans (35 %).

La monoparentalité chez les femmes devenues mères à 15–19 ans concerne les Indiennes inscrites (30 %) et les non-autochtones (28 %) dans des proportions comparables. Cependant, pour les femmes devenues mères après 20 ans (c'est-à-dire avec un enfant de 0 à 9 ans), il en va autrement puisque la proportion de mères seules diminue à 18 % chez les non-autochtones alors qu'elle augmente à 35 % chez les Indiennes inscrites. Chez les Indiennes non inscrites, l'âge à la maternité n'a aucun effet sur la probabilité d'être monoparentale. La proportion de mères monoparentales parmi les femmes devenues mères à l'adolescence est à quelques décimales près identique à celle des femmes devenues mères après 20 ans (35 %).

Figure 7: **Proportion de femmes monoparentales âgées de 25 à 29 ans, par groupe d'âge de l'enfant, Canada, 1996**

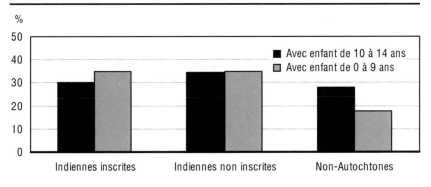

Source : Statistique Canada, Recensement du Canada de 1996, totalisations spéciales.

Résidence dans/hors réserve

Les Indiennes inscrites âgées de 25 à 29 ans devenues mères au cours de leur adolescence habitent une réserve indienne (47 %) dans une proportion supérieure aux autres mères indiennes (40 %) et aux Indiennes sans enfant (27 %). Dans tous les cas cependant, la majorité des femmes âgées de 25 à 29 ans vivent à l'extérieur des réserves (tableau 3).

Tableau 3: **Répartition (%) des Indiennes inscrites âgées de 25 à 29 ans selon le lieu de résidence dans/hors réserve, par groupe d'âge de l'enfant et état matrimonial, Canada, 1996**

| | Sans enfant | Avec enfant de 0–9 ans | | | Avec enfant de 10–14 ans | | |
		Parent seul	En union	**Total**	Parent seul	En union	**Total**
Réserve indienne	27	26	48	**40**	29	55	**47**
Hors réserve indienne	73	74	52	**60**	71	45	**53**

Source : Statistique Canada, Recensement du Canada de 1996, totalisations spéciales.

Chez les mères, la situation familiale des femmes semble davantage discriminante que la maternité précoce en ce qui a trait au lieu de résidence. Tant pour les femmes devenues mères à l'adolescence que pour les autres mères, plus de 70 % vivent à l'extérieur des réserves, alors que près de la moitié des mères en union habitent une réserve.

Résidence urbain/rural

Les Indiennes inscrites âgées de 25 à 29 ans ayant eu un enfant au cours de leur adolescence résident en milieu urbain (figure 8) dans une proportion de 41 %, sensiblement moins que les autres mères indiennes inscrites (49 %) et les Indiennes inscrites sans enfant (59 %). Pour tous les groupes d'appartenance ethnique, la proportion de femmes en milieu urbain est la plus faible chez les mères adolescentes, suivies dans l'ordre des autres mères et des femmes sans enfant. Les non-autochtones sont les plus urbaines (72 %) d'entre toutes les femmes devenues mères à l'adolescence.

Figure 8:   Répartition (%) des femmes âgées de 25 à 29 ans selon le lieu de résidence rural/urbain, par groupe d'âge de l'enfant, Canada, 1996

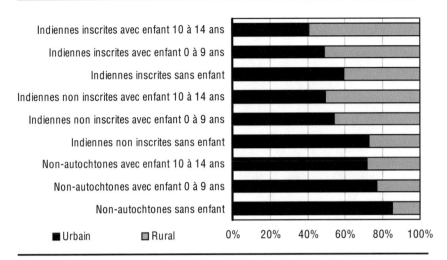

Source : Statistique Canada, Recensement du Canada de 1996, totalisations spéciales.

En comparant la résidence selon le type de famille (tableau 4), on constate chez les Indiennes inscrites que 40 % des mères adolescentes vivant seules résident en milieu rural contre 67 % des mères adolescentes vivant en union. Ainsi, la monoparentalité chez les Indiennes inscrites devenues mères entre 15 et 19 ans se retrouve essentiellement concentrée en milieu urbain, en dehors des réserves.

L'appartenance indienne opère une nette différenciation pour les mères en union. Vivre en union est un fait urbain pour 68 % des non-autochtones âgées de 25 à 29 ans avec un enfant de 10 à 14 ans, ce qui n'est pas le cas pour les Indiennes inscrites (33 %) ou non inscrites (40 %). La majorité des mères adolescentes monoparentales habitent la ville, peu importe l'appartenance ethnique. Les proportions varient de 60 % pour les Indiennes inscrites à 67 % pour les Indiennes non inscrites et à 82 % chez les non-autochtones.

Tableau 4:   Répartition (%) des femmes âgées de 25 à 29 ans avec un enfant âgé entre 10 et 14 ans selon le lieu de résidence rural/urbain, par état matrimonial, Canada, 1996

	Indiennes inscrites		Indiennes non inscrites		Non-autochtones	
	Parent seul	En union	Parent seul	En union	Parent seul	En union
Rural	40	67	33	60	18	32
Urbain	60	33	67	40	82	68

Source : Statistique Canada, Recensement du Canada de 1996, totalisations spéciales.

La scolarité

La maternité précoce affecte clairement la probabilité de poursuivre des études puisqu'en bas âge, le nouveau-né dépend fortement de la mère. Parmi les Indiennes inscrites âgées de 25 à 29 ans (figure 9), ce sont celles sans enfant qui présentent le profil scolaire le plus avantageux : plus de 24 % des Indiennes inscrites âgées de 25 à 29 ans sans enfant ont atteint le niveau universitaire et moins de 8 % n'ont pas atteint la 9e année. La proportion d'universitaires est la plus faible chez les femmes devenues mères pendant l'adolescence (12 %).

Parmi l'ensemble des femmes devenues mères à l'adolescence, les Indiennes inscrites présentent néanmoins une proportion d'universitaires (12 %) supérieure aux non-autochtones (9 %) et aux Indiennes non inscrites (5 %). Cependant, ce sont également les Indiennes inscrites qui présentent la plus forte proportion de femmes n'ayant pas complété une 9ième année : 20 % chez les Indiennes inscrites, comparativement à 13 % chez les Indiennes non inscrites et 8 % chez les non-autochtones.

Figure 9: **Répartition (%) des femmes âgées de 25 à 29 ans selon le plus haut niveau de scolarité atteint, par groupe d'âge de l'enfant, Canada, 1996**

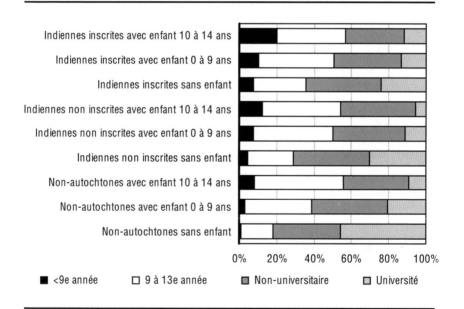

Source : Statistique Canada, Recensement du Canada de 1996, totalisations spéciales.

Tableau 5: Répartition (%) des femmes âgées de 25 à 29 ans avec un enfant de 10 à 14 ans selon le plus haut niveau de scolarité atteint, par état matrimonial, Canada, 1996

	Indiennes inscrites		Indiennes non inscrites		Non-autochtones	
	Parent seul	En union	Parent seul	En union	Parent seul	En union
Moins de 9ᵉ année	17	22	8	15	9	8
9 à 13ᵉ année	34	38	51	37	45	49
Non-universitaire	34	30	34	43	38	34
Université	15	11	7	5	8	9

Source : Statistique Canada, Recensement du Canada de 1996, totalisations spéciales.

Est-ce la situation familiale ou l'appartenance ethnique qui cause les plus grands écarts en terme de scolarité chez les femmes âgées de 25 à 29 ans devenues mères à l'adolescence ? L'information obtenue du recensement de 1996 indique que l'appartenance ethnique serait davantage discriminante que la situation familiale en regard de la scolarité (tableau 5).

Voyons d'abord les différences de scolarité des femmes d'une même appartenance ethnique selon la situation familiale. Les femmes de 25 à 29 ans avec un enfant âgée entre 10 et 14 ans présentent quelques différences de scolarité selon le type de famille, habituellement à l'avantage des mères seules, ce qui en soit constitue une surprise. Ainsi chez les Indiennes inscrites et les non-autochtones, les mères monoparentales comptent 4 % de plus de femmes avec une formation supérieure non-universitaire que les mères en union. Toujours chez les Indiennes inscrites, la proportion de mères avec des études universitaires est de 4 % plus élevée chez les mères monoparentales. Au bas de l'échelle de scolarité, on observe que la proportion d'Indiennes monoparentales avec moins d'une 9ᵢᵉᵐᵉ année est inférieure (-5 %) à celle des Indiennes en situation de couple.

Les différences de scolarité sont nettement plus importantes lorsqu'on compare les femmes d'une même situation familiale selon l'appartenance ethnique. Les Indiennes inscrites monoparentales (15 %) présentent une proportion d'universitaires deux fois supérieure à celle des non-autochtones (8 %) et des Indiennes non inscrites (7 %). La proportion d'Indiennes inscrites monoparentales (17 %) n'ayant pas complété une 9ᵢᵉᵐᵉ année est également le double de celle des non-autochtones (9 %) et des Indiennes non inscrites (8 %) dans la même situation.

L'écart de scolarité le plus marqué entre Indiennes et non-autochtones est observé chez les mères en union : 22 % des Indiennes inscrites, en union et avec un enfant âgé entre 10 et 14 ans ont un niveau de scolarité inférieur à une 9ᵢᵉᵐᵉ année, comparativement à seulement 8 % chez les non-autochtones et 15 % chez les Indiennes non inscrites. Il n'empêche que la proportion d'universitaires est plus élevée chez les Indiennes inscrites (11 %) que chez les non-autochtones (9 %) et les Indiennes non inscrites (5 %).

Ainsi, chez les femmes âgées de 25 à 29 ans ayant eu un enfant durant l'adolescence, les différences de scolarité entre Indiennes inscrites et non-autochtones sont plus grandes (plus de 2 fois) que les différences entre les mères en union et les mères seules au sein même de ces deux groupes d'appartenance ethnique (tableau 5).

La proportion relativement élevée d'universitaires parmi les Indiennes inscrites pourrait donc être liée à la monoparentalité qui inciterait ces jeunes mères à chercher des ressources en dehors des réserves. En d'autres mots, l'éducation serait un moyen d'accéder à des ressources. L'engagement dans des études peut aussi traduire la difficulté de se trouver un emploi.

Le revenu des mères adolescentes

L'analyse des données du Recensement du Canada de 1996 sur le revenu individuel des femmes est compliquée par le fait que la législation et les politiques familiales canadiennes accordent certains avantages fiscaux ainsi qu'un programme de supplément de revenu aux personnes monoparentales, à majorité des femmes. Une étude du MAINC a établi que, pour 72 % des mères seules autochtones, les transferts gouvernementaux constituaient la principale source de revenu (Hull 2001). De plus, le revenu individuel des femmes peut être influencé par la présence ou non d'un revenu de conjoint.

Figure 10: Revenu moyen et revenu médian des femmes âgées de 25 à 29 ans par groupe d'âge de l'enfant, Canada, 1995

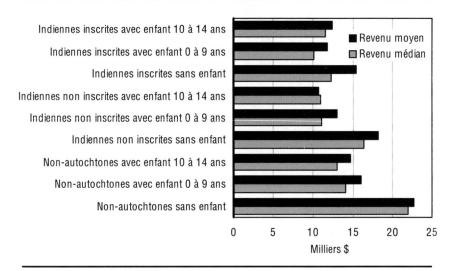

Source : Statistique Canada, Recensement du Canada de 1996, totalisations spéciales.

Les Indiennes inscrites de 25 à 29 ans ont obtenu des revenus systématiquement inférieurs à ceux des non-autochtones, quelle que soit leur situation : sans enfant, mère à l'adolescence ou mère après vingt ans (figure 10). Cependant, tant pour les Indiennes que pour les non-autochtones, les femmes âgées de 25 à 29 ans sans enfant ont eu en 1995 un revenu individuel supérieur aux mères du même groupe d'âge. Le revenu moyen le plus élevé appartient aux non-autochtones sans enfant ($22 712). Parmi les mères avec un enfant âgé entre 10 et 14 ans, le revenu des Indiennes inscrites ($12 357) se situe entre les mères non autochtones ($14 639) et les Indiennes non inscrites ($10 697).

Tableau 6: Revenu moyen et revenu médian des femmes âgées entre 25 et 29 ans avec un enfant entre 10 et 14 ans, par état matrimonial, Canada, 1995

	Indiennes inscrites		Indiennes non inscrites		Non-autochtones	
	Parent seul	En union	Parent seul	En union	Parent seul	En union
	$	$	$	$	$	$
Revenu médian	14 218	10 040	12 279	9 993	14 631	11 971
Revenu moyen	14 378	12 436	13 688 $	12 045	15 483	14 301

Source : Statistique Canada, Recensement du Canada de 1996, totalisations spéciales.

Tant pour les mères seules que pour les mères en union, les Indiennes inscrites âgées entre 25 et 29 ans et devenues mères à l'adolescence ont eu en 1995 des revenus systématiquement inférieurs à ceux des non-autochtones, et supérieurs à ceux des Indiennes non inscrites. Cependant, tant pour les Indiennes que pour les non-autochtones, les femmes monoparentales ont eu des revenus systématiquement supérieurs à ceux des femmes en union. Le revenu moyen le plus élevé se trouve être celui des non-autochtones monoparentales ($15 483), et le moins élevé celui des Indiennes non inscrites en union ($9 993). Ces données sont cohérentes avec les résultats publiés par Hull (2001) sur la situation des mères autochtones seules.

Conclusion

La fécondité des Indiennes adolescentes est très nettement supérieure à celle des autres Canadiennes adolescentes. Selon les données du Registre des Indiennes ajustées pour les délais de déclaration des naissances, la fécondité des Indiennes âgées de 15 à 19 ans au cours des années 1990 serait de l'ordre de 100 à 120 enfants pour 1 000 femmes, un taux de cinq à six fois supérieur à celui des autres adolescentes canadiennes (20 à 25 p.1000). Depuis 1985, la fécondité des Indiennes adolescentes serait à la hausse, avec pour résultat que l'écart avec les autres Canadiennes s'est agrandi. Une fécondité élevée chez les adolescentes est généralement perçue comme un indice de sous-développement d'une nation.

Dans l'ensemble, l'analyse des caractéristiques socio-économiques des femmes âgées de 25 à 29 ans qui avaient eu un enfant pendant leur adolescence indique que la situation de ces femmes semble légèrement défavorable en comparaison avec celles des autres femmes, i.e. les autres mères et les femmes sans enfant. L'analyse révèle par contre deux surprises de taille. La première surprise vient du fait que les Indiennes qui ont été mères à l'adolescence sont « moins monoparentales » (30 %) que les autres femmes indiennes (35 %). Le deuxième élément de surprise ressortant de l'analyse concerne le niveau d'éducation de ces femmes. Selon les statistiques sur le plus haut niveau de scolarité atteint, la proportion d'universitaires chez les Indiennes inscrites mères à l'adolescence est supérieure à celle des autres Canadiennes mères à l'adolescence. Cette proportion d'universitaires chez les Indiennes inscrites mères à l'adolescence est même deux fois supérieure à celle des Indiennes non inscrites.

Il n'est pas aisé d'interpréter les résultats de cette analyse et de les situer dans leur contexte plus large. L'information disponible permet de soulever un coin seulement du voile d'une situation sociétale vaste et complexe. De cette analyse ressort néanmoins une question fondamentale : est-ce que les Indiennes et les autres Canadiennes perçoivent de la même façon les conséquences positives et négatives liées à l'arrivée d'un enfant avant la vingtaine? À la lumière de ces résultats, trois scénarios de vie de mères adolescentes semblent émerger, lesquelles histoires co-existent sans doute au sein de la population amérindienne.

Intuitivement, il est relativement aisé d'imaginer le scénario d'une jeune fille devenue mère de manière « accidentelle », non planifiée. Certaines de ces filles-mères affichent sans doute des comportements sexuels à risque, d'où cette naissance non planifiée. Il est également possible que le contexte social dans lequel évoluent ces adolescentes devenues mères comporte des situations de violence et d'abus. Le caractère « non planifié » de la naissance pourrait être en partie responsable du taux de paternité non déclarée plus élevé chez les jeunes mères (Clatworthy 2000). Les programmes en place serviraient donc à améliorer quelque peu le quotidien de ces jeunes femmes et de leurs enfants. Dans un tel scénario, il y aurait un besoin de programmes axés sur la planification familiale, le contrôle des naissances et les comportements sexuels volontaires et protégés.

Un scénario « plus positif » où les adolescentes indiennes ont voulu et planifié un enfant est également plausible. Les comportements observés en matière de fécondité précoce chez ces jeunes femmes seraient alors le reflet de valeurs et d'attitudes vis-à-vis le tandem famille/carrière qui seraient différentes de celles du reste de la société canadienne. Dans un tel scénario, il y aurait un besoin de programmes d'éducation secondaires et postsecondaires qui tiennent compte de la réalité familiale des jeunes adultes amérindiens.

Un troisième scénario doit être considéré à la lumière des résultats d'analyse. La maternité précoce serait voulue et planifiée comme dans le second scénario, mais l'objectif poursuivi ici serait en partie différent : la maternité serait une stratégie pour « échapper » à une situation sociale et/ou économique précaire. La violence, l'abus sexuel, l'absence de logement et d'emploi pousseraient certaines jeunes femmes à choisir la maternité afin d'accéder à des programmes de supplément de revenu, d'accès aux logements sociaux et de formation/éducation. La maternité précoce pourrait donc être une manière de survivre. Ainsi, la présence même des programmes existants de support aux mères indiennes adolescentes (et probablement monoparentales) ne favoriseraient pas les changements de comportement en matière de fécondité précoce.

Rien dans les données disponibles ne permet de confirmer ou d'infirmer l'un ou l'autre de ces scénarios. Seule une enquête détaillée, de préférence longitudinale, permettra de préciser davantage la nature des motivations de ces jeunes femmes indiennes ainsi que les déterminants de leur maternité précoce. Pour l'heure, il faut se contenter des parcelles d'information que nous accordent le Registre des Indiens et le Recensement du Canada.

Notes de fin de chapitre

1. L'autre partie étant attribuable à la fécondité et à la mortalité.

2. L'indice synthétique de fécondité (ISF) représente le nombre moyen d'enfants nés vivants qu'aurait une génération fictive de femmes au cours de sa vie féconde, c'est-à-dire de 15 à 49 ans, si elle avait affiché la fécondité observée au cours d'une période donnée, le plus souvent une année civile. L'ISF est sensible aux conditions du moment ainsi qu'aux modifications dans le calendrier de la fécondité au sein des générations impliquées.

3. L'année 1985 n'a pas été retenue étant donné les modifications à la *Loi sur les Indiens* survenues cette année-là.

Bibliographie

Affaires Indiennes et du Nord Canada. 2002. *Données ministérielles de base 2001*. Ottawa: Direction générale de la gestion de l'information, 76.

British Columbia Vital Statistics Agency. 2001. *Regional Analysis of Health Statistics for Status Indians in British Columbia, 1991–1999*. Victoria: Ministry of Health Services.

Clatworthy, S.J. 2000. *Paternal Identity and Entitlement to Indian Registration: the Manitoba Context*. Ottawa: Pour le compte du ministère des Affaires Indiennes et du Nord Canada, Direction de la recherche et de l'analyse, 60.

Clatworthy, S.J., Hull, J., et Loughren, N. 1997. *Implications of First Nations Demography*. Ottawa: Pour le compte du ministère des Affaires Indiennes et du Nord Canada, Direction de la recherche et de l'analyse.

Clatworthy, S.J., et Smith, A. 1992. *Population Implications of the 1985 Amendments to the Indian Act*. Ottawa: Pour le compte du ministère des Affaires Indiennes et du Nord Canada, Direction de la recherche et de l'analyse, 123.

Hull, J. 2001. *Les mères seules autochtones au Canada, 1996: Un profil statistique*. Ottawa: Pour le compte du ministère des Affaires Indiennes et du Nord Canada, Direction de la recherche et de l'analyse, 134.

Loh, S., Verma, R.B.P., Ng, E., Norris, M.J., George, M.V., et Perreault, J. 1998. *Population Projections of Registered Indians, 1996–2021*. Statistique Canada, Division de la démographie, 199.

Nault, F., Chen, J., et Norris, M.J. 1992. *Demographic Time Series Data of Births, Deaths and Population for Registered Indian Population, Canada, 1973–1990*. Statistique Canada, Division de la démographie.

Nault, F., Gauvin, P., et George, M.V. 1995. « Projections de la population des Indiens inscrits du Canada, 1991–2015 ». *Cahiers Québécois de démographie* 24 (1): 109–127.

Normandeau, L., et Piche, V. 1984. *Les populations amérindiennes et inuit au Canada: Aperçu démographique*. Montréal: Presses de l'université de Montréal, 282.

Piche, V., et George, M.V. 1973. « Estimates of Vital Rates for the Canadian Indians, 1960–1970 ». *Demography* 10 (3): 367–382.

Pressat, R. 1979. *Dictionnaire de démographie*. Paris: PUF.

Ram, B., et Romaniuk, A. 1985. *Projections de la fécondité des Indiens inscrits, 1982–1996*. Statistique Canada, Division de la démographie, 35.

Robitaille, N., et Choiniere, R. 1985. « La croissance des groupes autochtones du Canada au 20ᵉ siècle ». *Document de travail*. Université de Montréal, Département de démographie, 27.

Robitaille, N., Kouaouci, A., et Guimond, E. 2003. *La fécondité des Indiennes à 15 à 19 ans, 1980–1999*. Rapport de recherche présenté à la direction de la recherche et de l'analyse, Affaires Indiennes et du Nord Canada, Ottawa.

Romaniuk, A. 1981. « Increase in Natural Fertility during the Early Stages of Modernization : Canadian Indians Case Study ». *Demography* 18 (2): 157–172.

Statistique Canada. 1993. *Statistiques choisies sur la natalité et la fécondité, Canada, 1921 à 1990*. Ottawa: Centre Canadien d'information sur la sante, Catalogue 82-553, Occasionnel, 83.

11

Unstated Paternity: Estimates and Contributing Factors

Stewart Clatworthy

Introduction

This report provides a summary of the main findings of two recent research studies, sponsored by the Research and Analysis Directorate of Indian and Northern Affairs Canada, concerning unstated paternity among First Nations children. An initial study, completed in 2001, provided estimates of the incidence and prevalence of unstated paternity during the 1985–99 time period, and examined variations in levels of unstated paternity by region, location of residence and the age of mothers at the time of childbirth.[1] A second study was undertaken to gather and analyze information from several parties involved in the processes of birth and Indian Registration.[2] This information is believed to be central to gaining a better understanding of why unstated paternity is occurring, and what may be done to ensure that First Nations parents are better able to comply with the requirements of the birth and Indian registration processes.

Implications and Prevalence of Unstated Paternity

Why Is Unstated Paternity Important?

Unstated paternity refers to the situation where a child's father is not reported for purposes of birth registration and Indian registration. Interest in this issue emerges, in large part, from changes to the rules governing entitlement to Indian registration that were introduced as part of the 1985 amendments to the *Indian Act* (Bill C–31). Prior to these changes, children with unreported fathers were allowed to register provided that their registration was not successfully protested within twelve months (i.e., the father was proven to be non-Indian).

Under the rules introduced by the 1985 *Indian Act*, a child's entitlement to registration is based on the registration characteristics of the child's parents. Section 6 of the 1985 *Indian Act* allows for children to be registered under one of two sub-sections:

Section 6(1), where both parents of the child are entitled to registration; and

Section 6(2), where one of the child's parents is entitled to registration under Section 6(1) and the other parent is not registered.

When a child's father is not reported, the child's registration entitlement can only be based on the mother's entitlement. In cases where the father is unreported and the mother is registered under Section 6(1), the child would be entitled to registration under Section 6(2). Where a child's mother is registered under Section 6(2) and the father is unreported, the child is not entitled to registration. Under the current rules, *failure to report a registered Indian father results in either inappropriate registration of the child (i.e., under Section 6(2) as opposed to 6(1)), or denial of registration and loss of associated entitlements, benefits and privileges.*

How Common Is Unstated Paternity?

The Indian Register has been recording data on children with unstated fathers since 1983, although unstated paternity data for the 1983–88 time period are believed to be incomplete. The Register is also subject to late reporting of events, including births. Procedures have been used to adjust the Register data for late reported births.[3] Unless otherwise noted, all estimates of incidence and prevalence of unstated paternity presented in this report have been based on the adjusted Register data.

Direct estimates of the incidence and prevalence of unstated paternity can only be developed for children born to women registered under Section 6(1). Unstated paternity may also occur among children born to Indian women registered under Section 6(2) of the *Indian Act*. These children, however, are not entitled to Indian registration, and, as a consequence, a record of their birth is not contained in the Indian Register. As a result, this dimension of the issue cannot be addressed *directly* with the Register data.

Based on analysis of the Indian Register data from April 17, 1985, to December 31, 1999, roughly 37,300 children born to women registered under Section 6(1) have unstated fathers. This number represents about 19% of all children born to Section 6(1) women during this period.

Data from the Indian Register also allows one to identify the trend in the annual incidence (or rate) of unstated paternity over the 1985–99 time period.

Annual estimates for this time period are presented in Figure 1. As revealed in the figure, the annual rate of unstated paternity among children born to women registered under Section 6(1) peaked in 1990 (at nearly 24%). Since that time, the annual rate of unstated paternity has fallen to about 18% (in 1999), a level slightly lower than the average for the 1985–99 time period.

Figure 1:   Percent of children with fathers unstated as a proportion of all children born to Section 6(1) mothers, Canada, 1985-99

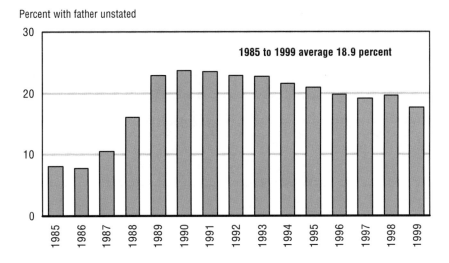

Percent with father unstated

Source: 1999 Indian Register, adjusted for late birth reporting.

Regional level data, which are presented in Figure 2, reveal that the prevalence of unstated paternity varies widely by region and is especially high in the provinces of Manitoba, Saskatchewan and the Northwest Territories. In these regions, more than one in every four children born to women registered under Section 6(1) during the 1985–99 period have unstated fathers.

Empirical research has also shown that unstated paternity is highly correlated with the age of mothers at the time of birth. As illustrated in Figure 3, rates of unstated paternity among children born to teenaged mothers greatly exceed the national average. During the 1985 to 1999 period, about 30% of all children with unstated fathers were born to mothers under 20 years of age.

Figure 2:   Percent of children with fathers unstated among children born to mothers registered under Section 6(1) by province/region, Canada, 1985-99

Percent of fathers unstated

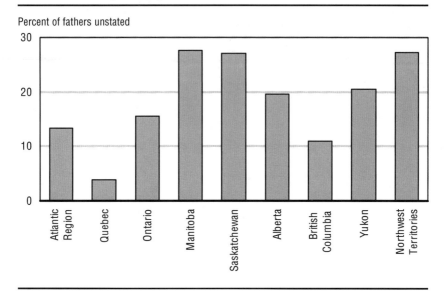

Source: 1999 Indian Register, adjusted for late birth reporting.

Figure 3:   Percent of children with fathers unstated among children born to mothers registered under section 6(1) by age of mother at birth of child, Canada, 1985-99

Percent of children with unstated fathers

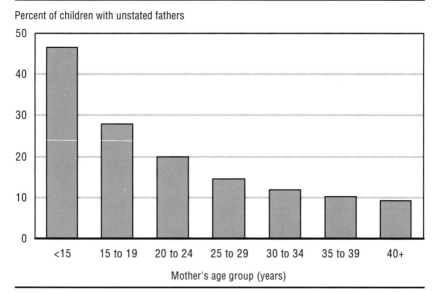

Source: 1999 Indian Register, adjusted for late birth reporting.

Rates of unstated paternity also vary widely among individual First Nations. For the 1985–99 period, sufficient data concerning births were available to prepare estimates of the prevalence of unstated paternity for 599 First Nations. As revealed in Figure 4, unstated paternity is quite common among children born to many First Nations. Two hundred and five (about 34% of all) First Nations reported rates of unstated paternity of 20% or more. Sixty-two of these First Nations, representing about 10% of all those for which estimates could be prepared, reported rates of 30% or more.

Figure 4:   Distribution of First Nations by prevalence of unstated paternity, Canada, 1985-99

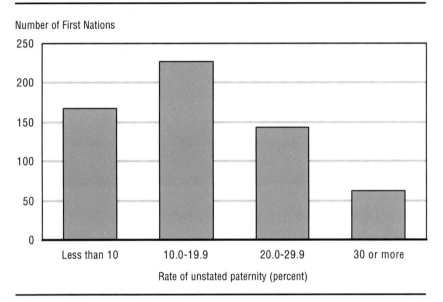

Number of First Nations

Rate of unstated paternity (percent)

Source: 1999 Indian Register, unadjusted for late birth reporting.

Although direct measures of unstated paternity cannot be developed for children born to women registered under Section 6(2), indirect estimates for the 1985–99 period suggest that as many as 13,000 of these children may have unstated fathers and do not qualify for Indian registration.[4]

Factors Contributing to Unstated Paternity

The widespread and persistently high levels of unstated paternity among First Nations children clearly raises many questions about why this is occurring. In designing this aspect of the research it was recognized that although unstated paternity may reflect the intentions of one or both parents, it may also result from a lack of knowledge or understanding of the issue and/or difficulties in complying with the requirements of the birth registration and

Indian registration processes. A large number of actors are involved in the birth and Indian registration processes, including parents, community health care staff, hospital maternity ward staff, provincial Vital Statistics, First Nations registration administrators (who administer the Indian registration process in First Nations communities) and regional INAC managers of Indian registration. All of these actors have some role in the process and may be in a position to provide information, which may be useful in understanding what is happening.

Efforts were made to obtain input from each of these groups, through either focus groups, structured telephone interviews, or e-mailed questionnaires. However, difficulties were experienced in obtaining (first hand) the views of First Nations parents. In this regard, the study attempted to arrange two focus groups with recent mothers and registration administrators for five First Nations were contacted to explore opportunities to conduct sessions in their communities. Two administrators reported that they were unable to obtain the support of their chief and council to hold focus groups. The remaining three administrators reported that few mothers were willing to participate in a focus group over the summer period. To partially compensate for the lack of direct input from recent mothers, the survey of First Nations registration administrators was increased from a sample of 100 to 135.

Telephone interviews were conducted with three groups, including

- a national sample of First Nations registration administrators concerning their role/practices in relation to the Indian registration process, paternal non-disclosure and perspectives concerning the reasons for paternal non-disclosure;
- regional INAC registration managers concerning the requirement of the Indian registration process and training of First Nations registration administrators;[5] and
- provincial/territorial Vital Statistics department representatives (except in Prince Edward Island and Ontario)[6] concerning their policies and procedures related to birth registration, paternal non-disclosure, requirements related to birth registration amendment, and fee and charges.

Resources available to the study did not permit a broad survey of community health staff or hospital maternity ward staff. Telephone interviews were held with three community health nurses and three unit managers responsible for hospital maternity wards. The interviews with community health nurses focussed on their role with respect to providing information to expectant parents about the requirements of the birth registration process. Interviews with maternity ward unit managers focussed on the nature of supports/assistance provided to parents in relation to registering their child's birth.

The Survey of First Nations Registration Administrators

The telephone survey of First Nations registration administrators constitutes the key source of information reported in this study. The interviews were designed to address the following issues:

- duration of employment as a registration officer;
- perceptions concerning the prevalence of unstated paternity among children born to members of their community;
- awareness and estimates of the numbers of children denied registration and First Nations membership as a result of unstated paternity;
- actions taken (and protocols) in relation to registration applications with unstated fathers;
- information provided to applicant's parents (or guardians) concerning birth registration amendment;
- the nature and sources of birth and Indian registration information provided to community members and expectant parents;
- perceived needs (and responsibilities) for provision of additional information or education concerning the unstated fathers issue;
- where most births to community members occur (i.e., within or outside the community) and the distance (degree of accessibility) to the nearest maternity facility;
- perceptions concerning why paternity information is not reported; and
- perceptions concerning parental intentions versus compliance difficulties.

The survey's sample was structured to capture the viewpoints from a broad cross-section of First Nations that have assumed responsibility for administering Indian registration. Three groups of First Nations were excluded from the sample, including:

- First Nations located in the Northwest Territories[7] (where Indian registration is administered directly by the regional INAC office);
- First Nations where Indian registration is administered by a tribal council office; and
- First Nations who reported less than ten registered Indian births during the 1985-99 time period.

The remaining 414 First Nations were assigned to one of three groups based on their measured rate of unstated paternity during the 1985-99 period. The initial group (Group 1) included 113 First Nations with rates of unstated paternity below 10.0%. A second group (Group 2) included 260 First Nations where rates of unstated paternity ranged from 10.0 to 29.9%. Forty-one First Nations with rates of unstated paternity of 30.0% or more formed a third group (Group 3).

Samples of 24.8%, 33.1% and 51.2% were drawn at random from the three groups, respectively, resulting in a total sample of 135 First Nations. Interviews were completed for 95 First Nations, representing a response rate of 70.4% at the national level. Group response rates ranged from 67.9% (for Group 1) to 71.4% (for Group 3). Response rates for all provinces/regions exceeded 50% (Figure 5).

The survey of First Nations registration administrators did not experience any refusals. Interviews could not be completed for forty First Nations (included in the sample), primarily as a result of difficulties in contacting the registration administrator.

Figure 5:   Response rates for First Nations registration administrator survey by province/region, 2001

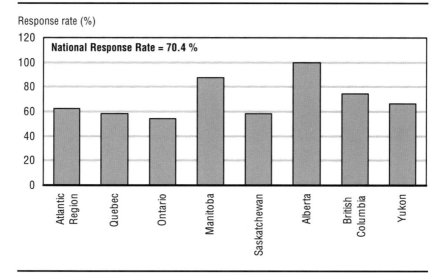

Select Research Findings

Recognition and Perceived Impacts of Unstated Paternity

All of the INAC regional registration managers interviewed for this study reported that unstated paternity was common within their region. This view was shared by a sizable majority (70.3%) of the First Nations registration administrators who participated in the survey. Not surprisingly, registration administrators in First Nations with higher measured rates of unstated paternity were more likely to report unstated paternity to be common in their community (Figure 6).

Rates of unstated paternity estimated by First Nations registration administrators varied widely and averaged 28% at the national level. This estimate is about 10% higher than that measured from data contained on the Indian Register. As expected, estimated rates of unstated paternity were clearly patterned over survey groups (Figure 7), and were reported to be substantially higher among First Nations with high (i.e., Group 3), as opposed to low (i.e., Group 1), measured rates of unstated paternity.

Figure 6: Proportion of First Nation registration administrators reporting unstated paternity to be common in their community by survey group, Canada, 2002

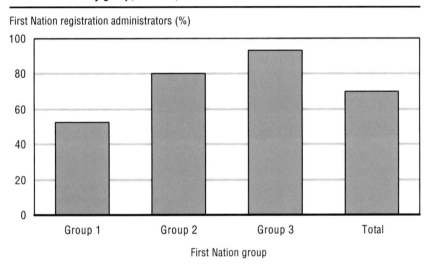

Unstated paternity is also widely believed by First Nations registration administrators to have resulted in loss of Indian registration entitlement among some children in their community. More than two-thirds of survey respondents reported that they knew of children who failed to qualify for registration due to unstated paternity. For First Nations with high measured rates of unstated paternity, loss of registration entitlement among children with unstated paternity was noted by more than 86% of the survey's respondents.

Figure 7:   Rate of unstated paternity estimated by First Nations registration administrators by survey group, Canada, 2002

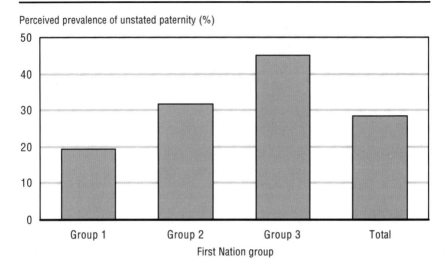

Perceived prevalence of unstated paternity (%)

First Nations registration administrators surveyed for this study reported 1,271 children with unstated fathers who have been denied registration. Based on the estimates provided by survey respondents, about 4,480 children with unstated fathers have failed to qualify for Indian registration at the national level.

Paternal information may also be a critical factor in determining a child's eligibility for First Nations membership, especially in First Nations that use *Indian Act*, blood quantum or two-parent membership rules. Unstated paternity was identified by more than 37% of the respondents to this study's survey to have resulted in loss of eligibility of First Nations membership for some children. For First Nations with high measured rates of unstated paternity (i.e., Group 3), loss of membership eligibility among children with unstated fathers was reported by two-thirds of survey respondents (Figure 8).

Training, Experience and Resources of First Nations Registration Administrators

First Nations registration administrators receive training through INAC's Indian Registration and Band Lists (IRBL) unit. Among other things, this training covers the rules surrounding entitlement, required documentation and related forms, and includes the topic of unstated paternity. According to the INAC regional registration managers surveyed for this study, First Nations administrators have the knowledge and training necessary to accurately inform and assist parents in relation to complying with the requirements of birth and Indian registration. Some INAC regional managers have arranged special information sessions on the topic of unstated paternity.

In addition to training, most of the survey's respondents reported considerable job experience as a registration administrator. Roughly three-quarters of those surveyed indicated that they had been employed as a registration administrator for more than three years. Nearly one-half of respondents reported employment at their job for at least six years. In general, lack of training or inexperience on the job does not appear to be a contributing factor to unstated paternity.

Although trained and experienced at the job, many First Nations registration administrators identified a shortage of resources in relation to responding to the needs of parents and the broader community on the issue of unstated paternity. More than 40% of survey respondents indicated that print materials (e.g., pamphlets and handouts) concerning birth, Indian registration and unstated paternity were needed. About 29% of respondents also felt that print materials needed to be augmented by other awareness and educational initiatives, such as group workshops or information sessions, and through personal contact with expectant parents. The need for additional resources to support increased awareness and educational initiatives was echoed by a majority of the INAC regional managers interviewed for this study.

Figure 8:   Proportion of First Nations registration administrators reporting loss of membership eligibility among children with unstated fathers by survey group, Canada, 2002

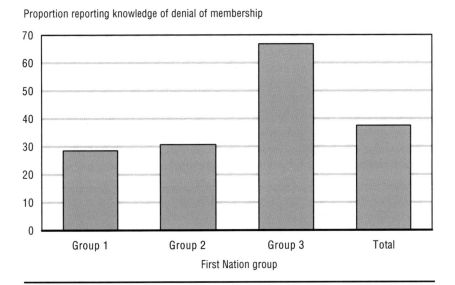

Proportion reporting knowledge of denial of membership

Parental and Community Awareness and Knowledge

Based on the responses of First Nations registration administrators, some efforts are underway to inform expectant parents (specifically mothers) about birth and Indian registration in most (about 78% of) First Nations communities. Initiatives were most frequently undertaken by registration administrators themselves (57% of respondents) and by community health staff/nurses (32% of respondents). Several other agencies (mostly involved in social service provision) were also identified by a smaller number of respondents. Although some actions are being taken in most communities, most (90% of) respondents noted that their community did not have a comprehensive system in place for conveying information to all expectant parents. Eighty-nine percent of respondents did not view current information and educational efforts for expectant parents concerning the requirements of birth and Indian registration (and the consequences of unstated paternity) to be satisfactory.

The survey's findings also suggest that most communities presently lack a focal point or locus of responsibility related to awareness, information and educational activities pertaining to the issue of unstated paternity. About 40% of the First Nations registration administrators surveyed believed that they should assume the lead role in this regard. About 23% of respondents, however, thought that information should be delivered through community health staff as part of prenatal care programs. However, the latter view was not shared by the community health nurses interviewed for this study. They cited lack of adequate training on the issues and little time to take on additional job responsibilities.

A significant proportion (more than 25%) of respondents also stated that awareness and educational initiatives were required not only among parents but also among other segments of the community. There is a widespread perception among respondents that most people in their community do not understand the rules related to Indian registration, the distinction between registration under Section 6(1) and 6(2), and the impact of unstated paternity on a child's registration entitlement. Several respondents (about 20%) noted the need for a special focus on early teens and pre-teens, a concern that appears to be linked to frequent births to teenaged parents.

Requirements Concerning Birth and Indian Registration Processes

Information on the requirements and process of birth registration was obtained through telephone interviews with representatives of provincial/regional Vital Statistics departments in all provinces/regions, except Prince Edward Island and Ontario. Most of the required information for Ontario and

Prince Edward Island was available on their departmental websites. This sub-section of the report provides a brief description of the processes followed in relation to birth registration in each region, as well as the requirements associated with amending paternal information once a birth has been registered.

Birth Registration

In general, the process of registering a birth is similar across provinces/regions. Up to three forms may be required to register a child's birth. A *notification of live birth* form, completed by medical facility staff, records information concerning the time and place of birth, the mother (including Indian registration status) and the baby (e.g., gender, birth weight, etc.). This form does not record information concerning the child's father. Copies of this form are forwarded to Vital Statistics and Health Canada within five days of the birth. A copy of the form is also provided to the mother.

A *registration of birth* form, completed by the parent(s), records information on the date and place of birth, the mother and (if reported) father, marital status of the parents and the name given to the child. Most provinces/regions (except Quebec) require that this form be completed prior to leaving the hospital. If the birth occurs outside of a medical facility, it must be filed within thirty days. Maternity ward unit managers contacted for this study indicated that their staff endeavours to be available to provide instructions to parents with respect to completing the required forms. It was also noted, however, that staff do not always have sufficient time to provide explanations, nor to ensure that the registration forms are being completed properly.

The requirements for parental identification on the registration of birth form differ among provinces/regions. In Ontario, Quebec, Saskatchewan, British Columbia, Prince Edward Island, New Brunswick and Alberta, this form must be signed by both parents in situations where the mother and father are not married. If the mother does not wish to identify the father, a declaration to that effect (signed by the mother) is required in Prince Edward Island, Saskatchewan, Quebec and Ontario. In all of these regions, when both parental signatures are required (but are not present) on the birth registration form, Vital Statistics informs the parent(s) of this requirement by mail (normally within thirty days). If all information and signatures are not submitted within roughly sixty days, the father's information (if present on the original form) is stricken from the birth registration.[8]

In other provinces/regions (including Manitoba, Yukon Territory, Nova Scotia and the Northwest Territories) only one parental signature is required on the birth registration form. In these regions, if information concerning the father is not reported on a birth registration form that has been signed by the mother, it is interpreted to mean that the mother does not wish to disclose the father's identity. If the parents are unmarried and wish to have the father's information included, a *joint request form*, signed by both the mother and father, must also be submitted. This form must be filed within thirty days (although some flexibility appears to be exercised in some regions). In these regions, if the joint request form is required but not received within thirty days, Vital Statistics sends a letter reminding the mother of the requirement to submit the form (a copy of which is included in the letter). If the joint request form (signed by both parents) is not returned within roughly thirty days from the date of reminder, the father's information is stricken from the child's birth registration.[9]

Efforts to promote compliance with birth registration information requirements is shared between Vital Statistics and INAC in the Northwest Territories. In this region, INAC is notified (by Vital Statistics) of all births to Registered Indians and assumes some of the functions related to ensuring that required birth registration information is completed by parents.

Amending Birth Registration Information

In general, procedures for amending or adding to information contained on a birth registration are also similar among provinces/regions. Vital Statistics departments in most provinces/regions allow for changes to birth registration information to be made free of charge during the initial sixty days following the date of registration. After this time, paternity information may be added by filing a joint request form, affidavit, or declaration of paternity document identifying the father's particulars (e.g., name, current address, place and date of birth) and signed by both the mother and father. In all regions (except Saskatchewan, Manitoba, Prince Edward Island and Nova Scotia) documentation must be witnessed and signed by a notary or some other person authorized to take oaths.

Administrative fees are charged by all provinces/regions for birth registration amendments. The charges range from $20 to $70. In the province of Quebec, the addition of paternal information to a birth registration may also require posting the amendment in a gazette. This would require an additional charge reported to be about $100. In British Columbia, amendments to paternity information made after six years have an additional requirement of medical (DNA) proof and an administrative fee of $27. In all provinces/regions, birth registration information can also be amended pursuant to a court order.

Indian Registration

Similar requirements exist across all INAC regions with respect to Indian registration. These requirements include

- parental consent forms requesting the child's registration;
- a "framing size" birth certificate for the applicant which identifies both the mother and father (if reported); and
- statutory declarations and guardianship papers (if applicable).

With the exception of the Northwest Territories, information needed for purposes of registration is compiled by First Nations registration administrators and forwarded to the regional INAC office where it is vetted for completeness and entered into the Register. Regional offices also receive registration requests and applications directly via mail, fax and "walk-in," as well as through provincial child and family services agencies (who have entitled children in their care).

The Indian registration process in the Northwest Territories continues to be administered entirely through the regional INAC office. The regional office receives documentation from Vital Statistics for all birth registrations involving a Registered Indian parent and the office arranges to acquire the remaining documentation (e.g., parental consents, etc.) from the parent(s). The regional office also provides resources for notarizing birth registration amendment documents.

Compliance with Birth and Indian Registration Requirements

As noted previously in this report, a substantial majority of survey respondents noted that many parents are unaware of (or do not understand) the birth registration requirements and the importance of paternal information. Not surprisingly, difficulties experienced by parents in complying with the requirements of the birth registration process are widely viewed to be a contributing factor to unstated paternity. Slightly more than one-half (53%) of the respondents to the First Nations registration administrator survey attributed unstated paternity to birth registration compliance problems. As illustrated in Figure 9, the proportion of respondents that identified compliance difficulties was higher for communities with higher measured rates of unstated paternity (i.e., Groups 2 and 3). The most common explanation in this regard derives from the logistics of obtaining required signatures on registration forms. Most (more than 77%) of the First Nations contacted for this study reported that births normally occur at medical facilities located outside of the home community. In many cases (and especially in more remote communities), fathers do not accompany the mother and are not available to sign the required documents at the medical facilities following the child's birth. This results in birth registration documents, which lack the father's signature, being forwarded to Vital Statistics by medical facility staff.

Figure 9:   Proportion of registration administrators reporting birth registration compliance difficulties as the cause of unstated paternity by survey group, Canada, 2002

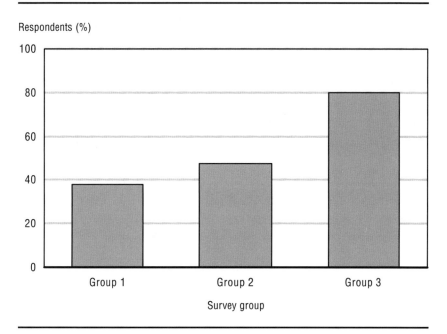

Respondents (%)

Survey group

Vital Statistics staff in all of the regions contacted for this study confirm that they receive many birth registrations that contain the father's identity, but which have not been signed by the father or accompanied by a signed joint request form. Subsequent efforts by Vital Statistics to obtain signed documents frequently meet with no response.

Data collected in the study's survey of registration administrators concerning proximity to the nearest maternity facility lend support to the above explanation of events. As illustrated in Table 1, communities that display higher measured rates of unstated paternity (i.e., Groups 2 and 3) are more likely to lack community-based maternity facilities, and are more distanced from maternity facilities.

Table 1: First Nations respondent community showing proportion lacking community-based maternity facilities and average distance to nearest maternity facility, Canada, 2002

Accessibility Indicator	Group 1	Group 2	Group 3
Number of respondent First Nations	19	61	15
Percent lacking community facility	68.4	78.7	86.7
Average distance to nearest facility (km)	112.1	169.9	213.5

In many First Nations, lengthy delays between the time of birth registration and Indian registration are common. These delays in registration are believed by many respondents to result in additional barriers to paternal disclosure as they contribute to increased difficulties in relation to amending birth registration documents. These difficulties can result from many factors including

- dissolution of relationships between mothers and fathers;
- requirements for additional paternal evidence and document notarization; and
- administrative charges for changes requested after amendment deadlines have past.

The breakdown of relationships between parents and between the time of birth and the time of Indian registration was noted by 80% of the survey respondents as a factor resulting in unstated paternity.

Although difficulties related to complying with the requirements of the birth registration process are widely believed to be a frequent cause of unstated paternity, a large minority (about 47%) of First Nations registration administrators expressed the view that unreported paternity most often reflects the intentions of one or both parents (most commonly the mother). Many specific factors were noted in this regard, including

- unstable family and partnering relationships (e.g., mother wants nothing to do with the father, 80% of respondents);
- father's denial of paternity (21% of respondents);
- confidentiality concerns of the mother (e.g., mother does not want the father's identity to be known to other community residents, 17% of respondents);
- child custody concerns (e.g., mother afraid of father gaining access to the child, 10% of respondents);
- mother afraid of losing Indian registration or First Nations membership (3% of respondents); and
- unwillingness to pay administrative fees for birth registration changes (2% of respondents).

Other Possible Factors

Although the surveys conducted for this study were not designed to probe for the role of culture or traditions as possible causes of unstated paternity, this issue was raised within the specific context of some First Nations in the Northwest Territories. By tradition, some First Nations in this region do not name their children at birth. Names are given later—by grandparents—at the time of baptism or at ceremonies. For purposes of birth registration, a child is initially registered as "unnamed" and will remain unnamed (on the official birth registry system) unless an amendment is subsequently filed to name the child. This can give rise to situations where a father is (for legal purposes) "unnamed," and lead to the requirement for the father's birth registration to be amended in order to have his identity included on his child's birth registration.

Conclusion

Changes introduced by the 1985 amendments to the *Indian Act* have altered the consequences of unreported paternity for the registration of First Nations children. Statistical evidence reported in this study suggests that nearly one in every five children born to Registered Indian women during the 1985–99 time period has an unreported father. Although unstated paternity is most common among First Nations in specific regions (Manitoba, Saskatchewan and the Northwest Territories), the issue is clearly of national significance. More than 37,000 children born to First Nations mothers registered under Section 6(1) during the 1985–99 period have unreported fathers. An additional 13,000 children, born to women registered under Section 6(2), are also estimated to have unreported fathers and do not qualify for registration under the rules of the 1985 *Indian Act*. Many of these children are believed to have been denied First Nations membership and its associated privileges and benefits.

Based on the evidence provided by respondents to the study's surveys, unstated paternity frequently results from difficulties experienced by parents in complying with the requirements of the birth registration process. In many instances, these difficulties appear to be associated with a lack of awareness and understanding of the requirements and importance of paternal identity in the process of establishing a child's registration entitlement.

At the same time, it is clear that a significant portion of unstated paternity reflects the intentions of parents. These intentions, however, are influenced by the social conditions of the community and by personal circumstances, especially the nature of the relationship between parenting partners. In the context of many First Nations communities, partnering frequently involves births to young and unmarried couples, and unstable and occasionally violent relationships. These situations can, in turn, lead parents to believe that paternal non-disclosure is the best course of action. While it is recognized that interventions to promote constructive changes to community social conditions and relationships between parents are clearly needed, it is also clear that such changes are likely to be very difficult to achieve quickly.

Endnotes

1. S. Clatworthy, *Paternal Identity and Entitlement to Indian Registration: The Manitoba Context* (Indian and Northern Affairs Canada, 2001).

2. S. Clatworthy, *Factors Contributing to Unstated Paternity* (Indian and Northern Affairs Canada, 2003).

3. See note 1.

4. Estimates of the number of children with unstated fathers who have been born to women registered under Section 6(2) have been based on the assumption that rates of unstated paternity are similar among children born to these women. At the present time, there are no data available to substantiate this assumption.

5. Interviews were held with all INAC regional registration managers except in Saskatchewan and the Atlantic region.

6. Several unsuccessful efforts were made to contact Vital Statistics representatives in Ontario.

7. Not all First Nations have assumed the responsibility for administering Indian registration. In the case of First Nations in the Northwest Territories, the process is administered by the regional INAC office. A special interview was conducted with the INAC registration manager of the Northwest Territories to obtain information for First Nations in that region.

8. One additional reminder is provided in the province of Alberta.

9. One additional reminder is provided in the province of Manitoba.

Part Four:
Crime, Victimization and Healing

12
Childhood Experiences of Aboriginal Offenders

Shelley Trevethan and John-Patrick Moore

Introduction

The disproportionate involvement of Aboriginal persons in the criminal justice system has been recognized for some time. Various inquiries and reports have noted that Aboriginal people are overrepresented in virtually all aspects of the criminal justice system (Correctional Service of Canada 2000; Henderson 1999; Royal Commission on Aboriginal Peoples 1996; Saskatchewan Indian Justice Review Committee 1992; Solicitor General of Canada 1988; Solicitor General of Canada and Attorney General of Alberta 1991; Task Force on the Criminal Justice System and Its Impact on the Indian and Métis People of Alberta 1991; Trevethan, Tremblay and Carter 2000). As reported by the Royal Commission on Aboriginal Peoples (1996), "Reports and inquiries . . . have not only confirmed the fact of over-representation [of Aboriginal offenders in the criminal justice system] but, most alarmingly, have demonstrated that the problem is getting worse, not better."

The reasons for the overrepresentation of the Aboriginal people within the criminal justice system are complex and multi-faceted. Often, a neglected area for examination is the effect that childhood experiences have on criminal behaviour. More specifically, to what extent does lack of attachment or stability during childhood affect criminal behaviour and future relationships? The research concerning family attachment, particularly to a primary caregiver, shows that lack of attachment often results in maladaptive and antisocial behaviour among children and adolescents (Cernkovich and Giordano 1987; Loeber 1991; Paolucci, Violato and Schofield 1998; Sim and Vuchinich 1996; Towberman 1994; Widom 1991).

Research has demonstrated that family disruption due to placement in a foster or group home can have negative effects on children and adolescents (Blome 1997; Brand and Brinich 1999; Chinitz 1995; Kendrick 1990; Kim et al. 1992; McMillen and Tucker 1999; Roy, Rutter and Pickles 2000; Westad 1994). Negative effects can take various forms, such as externalizing problems, intellectual and academic functioning, and internalizing behaviours.

Adoption studies have identified some of the same negative effects as foster/group homes, although not to the same extent. According to Brand and Brinich (1999), while children in foster care have significantly more behavioural problems, the vast majority of adopted children show patterns of behaviour problems similar to those of non-adopted children.

There is a lack of information on attachment and family relationships as it relates to Aboriginal people. This present study was conducted to examine the living situations of Aboriginal offenders while growing up—including adoption, foster care and group homes. Information was also included on family disruption, attachment to caregivers, stability of home life and current relationships. The study also examined whether Aboriginal offenders were raised in Aboriginal or non-Aboriginal cultures.

Information was gathered from data sources. First, structured interviews were conducted with a random sample of 175 Aboriginal and 148 non-Aboriginal offenders from seven federal prairie institutions in Canada (two maximum security, three medium security and two women's multi-level security). The largest proportion of Aboriginal offenders were First Nations (n=106). Smaller numbers were Métis (n=39) and Inuit (n=3). Interviews focussed on a number of key areas, including background, involvement in the child welfare system, attachment, childhood stability and current family relationships. Second, data were collected from offender files stored in Correctional Service of Canada's (CSC) Offender Management System. In particular, information pertaining to the offender's criminal history, offence characteristics, risk and needs were examined.

Involvement in the Child Welfare System

As illustrated in Figure 1, significantly larger proportions of Aboriginal than non-Aboriginal offenders were involved in the child welfare system when they were children. Overall, 63% of Aboriginal offenders said they had been adopted or placed in foster or group homes at some point in their childhood, compared to 36% of non-Aboriginal offenders. Larger proportions of Aboriginal than non-Aboriginal offenders had been placed in foster care (49% versus 24%) or placed for adoption (16% versus 6%). Although larger proportions of Aboriginal than non-Aboriginal offenders were placed into group homes (34% and 27%, respectively), the differences were not statistically significant.

Figure 1:   Involvement in the child welfare system

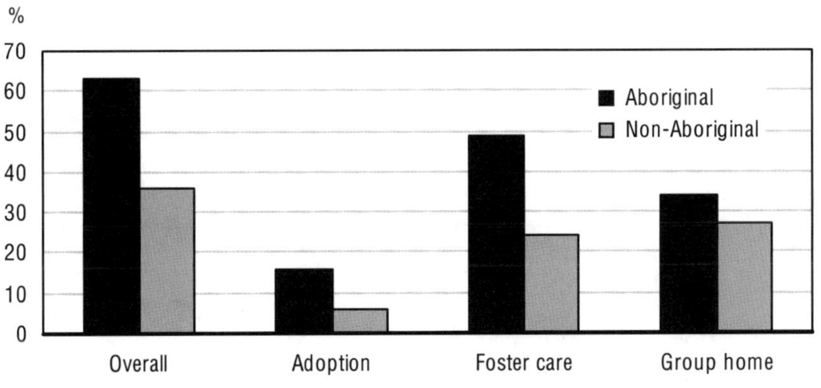

The findings from this study are similar to other studies—finding large proportions of offenders with past involvement in the child welfare system (Johnston 1997; MacDonald 1997). Furthermore, the proportions of both Aboriginal and non-Aboriginal offenders who had been involved in the child welfare system is substantially higher than among those outside the criminal justice system. For instance, according to studies conducted in the 1980s (Hepworth 1980; Loucks and Timothy 1981; Special Committee on Indian Self-Government 1983), approximately 1% of children overall and about 4% of Aboriginal children are involved in child welfare services. However, this is clearly an important issue to be addressed among Aboriginal offenders, since about two-thirds have been involved in the child welfare system.

Stability of Childhood

Another important question is whether Aboriginal offenders had a more unstable childhood than non-Aboriginal offenders. As indicated in Figure 2, a significantly larger proportion of Aboriginal than non-Aboriginal offenders said they had an unstable childhood (36% versus 26%). This difference was most obvious during the teenage years—one-half (50%) of Aboriginal offenders reported an unstable adolescence, compared to one-third (32%) of non-Aboriginal offenders. There were no significant differences in perceived stability during early childhood—30% of Aboriginal and 25% of non-Aboriginal offenders said it was unstable.

Figure 2:   Stability of childhood

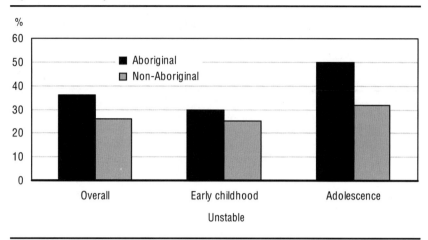

Other indicators of stability were also examined. Significantly larger proportions of Aboriginal than non-Aboriginal offenders had family violence and drug and/or alcohol problems in the home environment, a poor economic situation, and family members involved in criminal activity. These results highlight the lack of security and reliability in the homes of many Aboriginal offenders. In particular, Aboriginal offenders appear to have experienced a considerable amount of difficulty during their teenage years.

In examining only those involved in the child welfare system, the differences in childhood stability between Aboriginal and non-Aboriginal offenders disappeared. Among both Aboriginal and non-Aboriginal offenders, significantly larger proportions of those involved in the child welfare system reported an unstable childhood compared to those not involved in the child welfare system (Aboriginal, 43% versus 25%; non-Aboriginal, 40% versus 18%). These analyses appear to demonstrate that involvement in the child welfare system is related to instability during childhood and adolescence. This is the case for both Aboriginal and non-Aboriginal offenders. Since larger proportions of Aboriginal offenders were involved in the child welfare system, this seems to contribute to the differences between Aboriginal and non-Aboriginal offenders in stability of childhood. However, it is important to note that it is not clear whether placement in the child welfare system caused instability, or whether placement in the child welfare system was a result of other factors in the home or involvement in the criminal justice system.

Attachment during Childhood

Most offenders said that the primary person who cared for them was a parent. However, this was much more often the case among non-Aboriginal (80%) than Aboriginal (50%) offenders. A significantly larger proportion of Aboriginal, as opposed to non-Aboriginal, offenders were cared for by other relatives (29% versus 9%), such as a grandmother.

Both Aboriginal and non-Aboriginal offenders reported a great deal of attachment to their primary caregiver during childhood (90% and 91%, respectively). However, as indicated in Figure 3, those who reported an unstable childhood were less attached to their primary caregiver than those who reported a stable childhood. This was the case among Aboriginal (82% versus 94%) and non-Aboriginal offenders (71% versus 98%).

Figure 3:   Attachment to primary caregiver—unstable and stable childhood

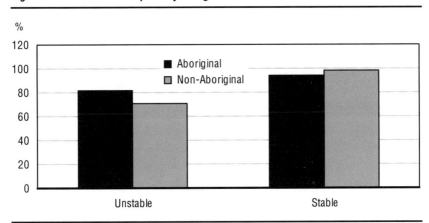

No significant differences existed in attachment to their primary caregiver between those involved and not involved in the child welfare system. Overall, the findings suggest a link between the extent to which offenders felt loved and cared for as a child and perceived instability in youth.

Current Relationship with Family

Early childhood experiences did not seem to impact on the relationship offenders currently have with their spouse or children, but did impact on their relationship with their family of origin. No significant differences were found in current contact with, or attachment to, a spouse/partner between those who reported a stable adolescence compared to those who reported an unstable adolescence. This was the case for both Aboriginal and non-Aboriginal offenders. Stability of adolescence also did not seem to affect the current relationship with children. However, differences were found among Aboriginal offenders when examining contact with their children. Aboriginal offenders with an unstable adolescence reported significantly less regular contact with their children than those who had a stable adolescence (52% versus 71%).

Offenders with an unstable adolescence tended to have a more negative relationship with parents and siblings. This was the case for both Aboriginal and non-Aboriginal offenders. Among Aboriginal offenders, those who had an unstable adolescence reported significantly less regular contact with their birth father than those with a stable adolescence (28% versus 50%). Interestingly, those with an unstable adolescence actually reported more regular contact with their grandmother than those with a stable adolescence (63% versus 36%). This may be because as a child they lived with their grandmother and maintained this relationship over the years. In terms of attachment, those who had an unstable adolescence said they had less attachment to their birth mother (67% versus 92%) and birth father (46% versus 66%).

Overall, it appears that those with a great deal of instability during the teenage years felt less connected to their families and had distant relationships with parents and siblings. However, Aboriginal offenders who experienced difficulty in adolescence also developed enduring relationships with their grandmothers.

Attachment to Aboriginal Culture

A large number of Aboriginal offenders are currently attached to Aboriginal culture and participate in Aboriginal activities. Almost three-quarters (74%) of the Aboriginal offenders said that they were currently attached to Aboriginal culture; that is, they considered it part of their everyday life and felt a sense of belonging. Furthermore, 80% said that they were currently involved in Aboriginal activities, such as circles, ceremonies, sweat lodges and smudges.

Attachment to Aboriginal culture was examined for Aboriginal offenders to determine whether those with little attachment and/or an unstable childhood were more detached from Aboriginal culture than those with a great deal of attachment or a stable childhood. Interestingly, attachment to a primary caregiver during childhood did not seem to influence current attachment to Aboriginal culture. It may not be the attachment per se that influences the cultural attachment, but more so with whom the person was living. If the person was living in a home without access to traditional activities, there may be less attachment to Aboriginal culture. Since large proportions of Aboriginal offenders who were put in care were placed with non-Aboriginal families, they may not have had access to Aboriginal culture.

No significant differences were found in understanding or speaking an Aboriginal language, current attachment to Aboriginal culture, or current involvement in Aboriginal activities between those who had stable and unstable childhood experiences. However, significantly fewer of those who had an unstable childhood said that they were involved in traditional Aboriginal activities while they were growing up (38% versus 59%). It seems that involvement in Aboriginal activities and attachment to culture may have been redeveloped once the offenders entered the correctional facility. These results emphasize the extent to which Aboriginal offenders feel connected to their culture. In addition, culture plays a strong role in the daily lives of Aboriginal offenders.

Conclusion

The findings from this research demonstrate that Aboriginal offenders have unstable childhood experiences, including a great deal of involvement in the child welfare system. Furthermore, involvement in the child welfare system is associated with instability. However, it is unclear whether involvement in the child welfare system is the cause of the instability, or the result of it.

The study also indicates that those with an unstable childhood were less attached to their primary caregiver while growing up, and are less attached to parents and siblings currently. This was similar for both Aboriginal and non-Aboriginal offenders.

It is clear that attachment to Aboriginal culture is fairly strong among the Aboriginal offenders. However, it seems that the attachment to Aboriginal culture is gained during the institutional experience.

This research helps to demonstrate the importance of offering Aboriginal-specific programs in a correctional setting tailored to the unique developmental experiences of Aboriginal offenders. Programs may need to focus more on the effects of childhood trauma and address issues associated with involvement in the child welfare system. Moreover, findings underscore the importance of culture in correctional programming. Delivering institutional services and programs in a culturally sensitive manner and providing access to cultural practices may serve to heighten responsiveness to treatment among Aboriginal offenders.

References

Blome, W.W. 1997. "What Happens to Foster Kids: Educational Experiences of a Random Sample of Foster Care Youth and a Matched Group of Non-Foster Care Youth." *Child and Adolescent Social Work Journal* 14 (1): 41–53.

Brand, A.E., and Brinich, P.M. 1999. "Behavior Problems and Mental Health Contacts in Adopted, Foster, and Non-Adopted Children." *Journal of Child Psychology and Psychiatry* 40 (8): 1221–1229.

Cernkovich, S.A., and Giordano, P.C. 1987. "Family Relationships and Delinquency." *Criminology* 25 (2): 295–321.

Chinitz, S.P. 1995. "Intervention with Children with Developmental Disabilities and Attachment Disorders." *Developmental and Behavioral Pediatrics* 16 (3): 17–20.

Henderson, J.Y. 1999. *Changing Punishment for Aboriginal Peoples of Canada*. Presented at the Canadian Institute for the Administration of Justice, Saskatoon, Saskatchewan.

Hepworth, P. 1980. *Foster Care and Adoption in Canada*. Canadian Council on Social Development.

Johnston, J.C. 1997. *Aboriginal Offender Survey: Case Files and Interview Sample*. Prepared for Correctional Service Canada, Research Branch, Report No. R-61.

Kendrick, M. 1990. *Nobody's Children: The Foster Care Crisis in Canada*. Toronto: MacMillan.

Kim, W.J., Zrull, J.P., Davenport, C.W., and Weaver, M. 1992. "Characteristics of Adopted Juvenile Delinquents." *Journal of the American Academy of Child and Adolescent Psychiatry* 31 (3): 525–532.

Loeber, R. 1991. "Risk Factors and the Development of Disruptive and Antisocial Behaviour in Children." *Forum on Corrections Research* 3 (3): 22–28.

Loucks, B., and Timothy, A. 1981. *Justice Related Children and Family Services for Native People in Ontario: A Discussion Paper*. The Ontario Native Council on Justice.

MacDonald, M. 1997. "Perceptions of Racism in Youth Corrections: The British Columbia Experience." *The Canadian Journal of Native Studies* 17 (2): 329–350.

McMillen, J.C., and Tucker, J. 1999. "The Status of Older Adolescents at Exit from Out-of-Home Care." *Child Welfare* 78 (3): 339–360.

Roy, P., Rutter, M., and Pickles, A. 2000. "Institutional Care: Risk from Family Background or Pattern of Rearing?" *Journal of Child Psychology and Psychiatry* 41 (2): 139–148.

Royal Commission on Aboriginal Peoples. 1996. *Bridging the Cultural Divide: A Report on Aboriginal People and Criminal Justice and Canada.* Ministry of Supply and Services Canada.

Saskatchewan Indian Justice Review Committee. 1992. *Report of the Saskatchewan Indian Justice Review Committee.*

Sim, H.O., and Vuchinich, S. 1996. "The Declining Effects of Family Stressors on Antisocial Behavior from Childhood to Adolescence and Early Adulthood." *Journal of Family Issues* 17 (3): 408–427.

Solicitor General of Canada. 1988. *Correctional Issues Affecting Native Peoples.* Correctional Law Review, Working Paper No. 7.

Solicitor General of Canada and Attorney General of Alberta. 1991. *Justice on Trial: Report of the Task Force on the Criminal Justice System and Its Impact on the Indian and Métis People of Alberta.*

Special Committee on Indian Self-Government. 1983. *Second Report: Indian Self-Government in Canada.* Chair: K. Penner, Canada.

Task Force on the Criminal Justice System and Its Impact on the Indian and Métis People of Alberta. 1991. *Justice on Trial: Report of the Task Force on the Criminal Justice System and Its Impact on the Indian and Métis People of Alberta.* Vol. 1.

Towberman, D.B. 1994. "Psychosocial Antecedents of Chronic Delinquency." *Journal of Offender Rehabilitation* 21 (1/2): 151–164.

Trevethan, S., Tremblay, S., and Carter, J. 2000. *The Over-Representation of Aboriginal People in the Justice System.* Ottawa: Canadian Centre for Justice Statistics, Statistics Canada.

Westad, K. 1994. *The God-Sent Child: The Bitter Adoption of Baby David.* Toronto: Penguin Group.

Widom, C.S. 1991. "The Role of Placement Experienced in Mediating the Criminal Consequences of Early Childhood Victimization." *American Journal of Orthopsychiatry* 61 (2): 195–209.

13

Aboriginal Resource Access in Response to Criminal Victimization in an Urban Context

Raymond R. Corrado, Irwin M. Cohen and Jesse L. Cale

A disproportionate number of Aboriginal people, on- and off-reserve, experience a wide range of criminal victimizations from minor property offences to serious personal violence. While victimization generally can have severe consequences, Aboriginal victims are particularly susceptible to both social exclusion and more problematic access to resources, services and programs to assist their recovery and reintegration. Unlike the United States, where considerable research has been conducted on minority groups, crime and victimization (Greenfeld and Smith 1999), little similar research has been conducted in Canada, with the exception of the General Social Survey (GSS). However, the GSS did not specifically explore Aboriginal victimization. Consequently, little is known about how these victims respond generally to their victimization experiences and specifically in terms of their accessing available resources.

The rate of Aboriginal crime and victimization varies widely across communities (Roberts and Doob 1994). A consistent observation is that violence in Aboriginal communities is usually directed at family members, particularly women. In La Prairie's (1994) study of Aboriginal people in the inner cities, the majority of Aboriginal women interviewed reported a violent victimization. Additionally, crime is predominately intraracial since most perpetrators and victims are Aboriginal (Silverman and Kennedy 1993; Trevethan 1991; Roberts and Doob 1994; Griffiths et al. 1995).

As mentioned above, Aboriginal violence typically involves family members (Frank 1992). The Aboriginal Justice Inquiry of Manitoba found that approximately one-third (33%) of Aboriginal women had been abused—at some point in their relationships—by their intimate partner. A report by the Ontario Native Women's Association revealed that 80% of the Aboriginal women surveyed had personally experienced family violence. In British Columbia, the Beyond Violence Report by the Helping Spirit Lodge concluded that 86% of respondents experienced or witnessed family violence. In addition, approximately 40% of respondents identified all family members as suffering from some form of abuse. The report from the British Columbia Task Force on Family Violence (1992) found that Aboriginal women not only face a much greater risk of family violence than non-Aboriginal women, but also are typically afraid to access non-Aboriginal victim-based services, resources and/or programs because of Aboriginal people's historical experiences with non-Aboriginal governmental and non-governmental departments, agencies and services.

The Royal Commission on Aboriginal Peoples (1996) also examined family violence in Aboriginal communities. They defined family violence as "a serious abuse of power within the family, trust or dependency relationships" (RCAP 1996, 54–55). Violence includes spousal assault, violence against children and sexual abuse, as well as more general forms of psychological and emotional abuse. While family violence exists in mainstream society, the Royal Commission on Aboriginal People (1996) suggests that there are three distinct features in the Aboriginal context: (1) family violence effects the entire community; (2) in part, family violence is an outcome of government interventions that disrupted and/or displaced Aboriginal families; and (3) violence is sustained by a racist social environment (RCAP 1996). For example, in the case of sexual abuse, if the perpetrator is from an older generation, the Aboriginal victim may be hesitant to acknowledge the abuse, confront the offender and seek help. Moreover, the entire family may experience shame as a result of the victimization and directly or indirectly pressure the victim to remain silent (RCAP 1996).

Despite a growing acceptance within Aboriginal communities that violence is a serious problem requiring prevention and intervention policies, too many victims remain fearful and are prevented from seeking resources, services and programs. Accordingly, these victims do not report to the police or seek medical, social, or mental health assistance. Particularly troublesome are victims of physical or sexual abuse whose sense of shame and fear prevent them from seeking assistance. The Royal Commission on Aboriginal People concluded that "fear is behind the violence. Fear allows it to continue. Fear prevents people from doing something to stop the cycle of violence" (RCAP 1993, 35).

The Royal Commission on Aboriginal People found considerable consistency in the Aboriginal research literature concerning the reasons why many Aboriginal women do not report family violence. The most common reasons are: (1) family violence is viewed as normative behavior; (2) a general lack of self-esteem, shame and acceptance of the victim; (3) a fear that children will be removed from the victim's home; (4) women do not want to see their partners charged; (5) a fear of the potential loss of income if their partner is convicted and incarcerated; (6) a general lack of faith in the system to effectively intervene on the victim's behalf; and (7) a fear of retaliation from the perpetrator (RCAP 1996). Finally, McEvoy and Daniluk (1995) argue that, in general, much of the clinical and research literature on the outcomes and intervention strategies associated with sexual abuse assumes a relative homogeneity in the abuse experience.

Given the general lack of systematic Canadian research into Aboriginal victimization, and particularly the ways in which Aboriginal victims of crime access and use services, programs and resources in response to these experiences, the National Community Research Project (NCRP) surveyed Aboriginal people's access to services, primarily in an urban context, in response to their most serious lifetime criminal victimization. The NCRP involves an innovative approach to policy and research. It is based on intricate working partnerships among individuals from government departments, academics, community workers and First Nation's communities to initially identify specific policy issues, and then to construct research instruments to collect, analyze and disseminate policy information relevant to all of the research partners.

Between April 2001 and April 2002, using a snowball sampling technique, 1,047 Aboriginal people from the Greater Vancouver Regional District in British Columbia participated in a two-hour, semi-structured, in-depth, one-on-one interview on a wide range of issues, including: (2) mobility and housing issues; (2) social cohesion and collective efficacy; (3) lifetime and recent criminal victimization experiences and outcomes; (4) access, use and satisfaction with programs, services and resources in response to their victimization experiences; (5) cultural identity and family history; (6) health and mental health issues; and (7) alcohol and drug use.[1] While this sample appears to be representative of the Aboriginal people who live in the downtown core of Vancouver on several key demographic indicators, this sample should not be considered representative of Aboriginal people in Canada.

Of the entire sample of 1,047 Aboriginal people, 76.5% stated that they had been the victim of a crime they defined as having a serious impact on them. Only these respondents (n=801) are included in the following analyses. This sample is nearly equally divided by gender with 53.4% of respondents being female and 46.6% of respondents being male. The respondents in this sample are overwhelmingly self-identified as Status Indians (82%). The mean age of the sample was 39 years with a range of 18 to 75 years. More specifically, 37.1% of the sample was between 18 and 35 years old, 47.2% was between 36 and 50 years old, and 15.6% of the sample was more than 50 years old.

In terms of education attainment, only a small percentage (7.2%) had only an elementary education. The majority of the sample had either completed some secondary school or graduated from secondary school (58%). Nearly one-fifth of the sample (19.6%) had either some post-secondary schooling or graduated from post-secondary school. Moreover,

15.1% had some other form of schooling, such as having attended or graduated from a vocational or trade school.

Based on the level of education evident in this sample, it is not unexpected that 60.5% of the sample had an annual household income of less than $20,000 in the previous twelve months. Slightly more than one-quarter of respondents (28.8%) reported household earnings between $20,000 and $40,000, while 10.7% reported earnings in excess of $40,000. Approximately one-fifth of the sample reported that they worked for themselves, on average from two to three months of the year, and this provided 20%–30% of their annual income. Others exclusively engaged in seasonal work (16.4%).

While the majority of the sample experienced more than one criminal victimization, respondents were asked to identify the one victimization that had the greatest negative impact on their lives (see Table 1). Approximately one-fifth (19.5%) of the sample mentioned a violent offence as the most serious victimization. A gender difference is evident since 23.4% of the males versus 16.4% of the females reported a non-violent criminal victimization as having the greatest negative impact on their lives.

Table 1:   Most serious lifetime criminal victimization

	Total (n = 801) %	Males (n = 373) %		Females (n = 428) %	
Personal theft	3.2	4.6	*	1.9	*
Breaking and entering	7.6	9.7		6.1	
Threats or stalking	8.7	9.1		8.4	
Assault without a weapon	19.9	16.1	***	22.9	***
Assault with a weapon	18.5	25.3	***	12.4	***
Robbery	7.9	14.2	***	2.6	***
Attempted sexual assault	12	8.1	***	15.7	***
Sexual assault	18.7	8.6	***	27.6	***

* p = .05; ** p = .01; *** p = .001

Assaults had the greatest negative impact on the lives of the males in this sample. Approximately one quarter (25.3%) reported an assault with a weapon and 16.1% reported an assault without a weapon. While 22.9% of the females were assaulted without a weapon, 27.6% indicated that a sexual assault had the greatest negative impact on their lives. The prevalence of attempted sexual assaults (15.7%) and assaults with a weapon (12.4%) is also high for the females in this sample. Aboriginal people in this sample have experienced serious forms of criminal victimization.

For all types of serious personal criminal victimization, the majority of respondents accessed at least one service, program, or resource (see Table 2). More than one-third (35.3%) of the respondents who identified a property offence as having had the greatest negative impact on their lives accessed a resource, service, or program in response. Of these respondents, slightly more females (37.8%) than males (34.8%) accessed a resource. The highest access occurred for those who identified a personal theft (57.7%) as the victimization that had the greatest negative impact.

Table 2:   Resource access based on most serious lifetime victimization

	Total (n = 801) %
Personal theft	57.7
Breaking and entering	33.9
Threats or stalking	49.0
Assault without a weapon	75.2
Assault with a weapon	78.0
Robbery	67.2
Attempted sexual assault	68.0
Sexual assault	78.9

Most respondents (74.8%) who identified a violent victimization as having had the greatest negative impact on their lives accessed at least one service, resource, or program. As with those who reported a property offence, again, slightly more females (79.4%) than males (69.1%) indicated that they accessed resources. Most of those who reported being the victim of a sexual assault (78.9%) or experienced an attempted sexual assault (68%) accessed resources. Equally expected, high access rates are evident for the remaining violent victimization categories.

In terms of the specific types of programs, services, or resources that respondents accessed in response to their most serious victimization, all of the responses were collapsed into six distinct types: (1) health, (2) mental health, (3) police-based, (4) community-based, (5) government, and (6) Aboriginal (see Table 3). In interpreting Table 3, it is important to keep in mind that people can access more than one type of resource in response to a single victimization.

Table 3:   Type of resource accessed by gender and most serious lifetime victimization

	Property Victimization		Violent Victimization	
	Males %	Females %	Males %	Females %
Health resources	0.0	4.4 ***	47.5 ***	49.9 ***
Mental health resources	10.1	13.3	28.3 ***	49.3 ***
Police-based resources	4.3	6.7	10.4 ***	33.1 ***
Community-based resources	7.2	15.6	16.0 **	25.6 **
Government resources	13.0	13.3	16.4 ***	19.0 ***
Aboriginal resources	8.7	11.1	8.20	9.2

* p = .05; ** p = .01; *** p = .001

While the percentage of respondents who accessed any type of resource in response to a property offence is quite low for all of the different types of resources, they are more likely to access an Aboriginal resource to deal with a property offence than a violent offence. Moreover, when a resource is accessed in response to a property offence, the most common resources are community and government-based programs, services and resources. As reported above, the females in this sample were more likely to access a resource than males. While the rates of accessing a health resource to deal with a violent victimization were similar for males and females, many more females accessed a mental health resource (49.3%) than males (28.3%). An even larger gender ratio is evident regarding accessing police-based resources since three times as many women resorted to this type of resource than males in response to their most serious violent victimization.

A substantial percentage of victims (38.2%) did not access any resources, programs, or services in response to the criminal victimization that had the greatest negative impact on the respondent. The most common reason given is that the respondent did not want any help (57.6%). Other reasons given for not accessing services included: victimization was not considered serious enough (41%); lack of awareness of resources that could assist victims (27.1%); sense of being ashamed or embarrassed (26.4%); and concerns that they would not be believed (13.3%). However, when one considers only those respondents who identified a violent victimization and did not access any resources, the reasons provided for not accessing any assistance provides a number of important policy implications (see Table 4).

Table 4: Reasons for not accessing any resources in response to a violent victimization

	Assaults (n = 72) %	Robbery (n = 20) %	Sexual Offences (n = 32) %
Respondent did not know of any resources	29.6	25	18.2
Resources were not available	8.6	0	27.3
Respondent felt that the incident was too minor	43.2	45	18.2
Respondent was ashamed or embarrassed	24.7	25	81.8
Respondent felt they would not be believed	11.1	5	36.4
Respondent was prevented by the offender	6.2	0	0
Respondent did not want or need any help	64.2	55	90.9
Location of service was inconvenient	9.9	5	9.1

In terms of those respondents who identified an assault with or without a weapon, 23.1% did not access any resources in response. Specifically, nearly two-thirds (64.2%) reported that they either did not feel that they required any help or did not want any help. As expected, nearly half of those who identified an assault (43.2%) felt that the incident was too minor to access any services. Very few respondents (8.6%) attempted to access victim services and found none. In contrast, nearly one-third did not know of any victim programs.

Nearly one-third of all respondents (31.3%) who identified a robbery as their most serious victimization did not access any resources. Nearly half of those respondents (45%) felt that the incident was too minor. In addition, a slight majority (55%) did not want, or felt they did not need, any assistance. However, a quarter of respondents reported that they did not know of any resources that could assist them. It is possible that these respondents did not consider the police a possible resource.

Slightly more than one-fifth (21.1%) of those individuals who identified a sexual assault where intercourse occurred did not access any resources. A major policy concern for service providers and community leaders is the finding that 90.9% of those respondents either did not want help or felt that they did not need help. As discussed in the research, 81.8% report that they did not access any resources because they felt ashamed or embarrassed. More than one-third (36.4%) felt they would not be believed by service providers. Equally problematic for service providers is the finding that 18.2% of victims did not know of any resources that could have assisted them and 27.3% could not access any resources because none were available. It is also troublesome that nearly one-fifth of those respondents (18.2%) who were sexually assaulted—where intercourse occurred—felt that the assault was too minor to access any resources.

There are many negative impacts associated with the criminal victimization experienced by respondents. In order to assess any negative impact, a five-point scale was created based on respondents' self-reported feelings that their most serious victimization made them feel: angry, fearful, emotional harm, shocked, or caused physical injury. Using this measure, those respondents with a higher score experienced a greater negative impact as a result of their victimization. The mean negative impact score was higher for those who accessed a resource, service, or program compared to those who did not access any kind of resource. Specifically, the mean negative impact score for those who accessed a resource was 4.1, while those who did not access a resource had a mean negative impact score of 3.5. This difference was statistically significant (p=.001). Moreover, the odds of accessing a service versus not accessing a service was 2.95 times greater for those respondents who reported "more of or a stronger" negative impact from the victimization experience than those who reported "less of or a weaker" negative impact from the victimization experience.

In addition to the finding that those who felt a greater negative impact from the victimization were more likely to access at least one type of service, respondents also reported a significant benefit from accessing resources.

Respondents who accessed at least one of the service types indicated in Table 3 were 1.5 times more likely to have expressed a positive outcome from the victimization experience in terms of greater self-reliance or strength than those who did not access any services, resources, or programs (see Table 5).

Table 5:   Odds ratio – Positive outcome based on type of resource accessed

	Odds Ratio
Health resources	1.1
Mental health resources	1.5 **
Police-based resources	1.8 **
Community-based resources	1.7 **
Government resources	1.4
Aboriginal resources	0.9

* p = .05; ** p = .01; *** p = .001

Accessing a police-based resource, a community-based resource, or a mental health resource is associated with statistically significant differences in positive outcomes compared to those who did not access any services. Those who accessed a police-based service were 1.8 times more likely to state that they felt more self-reliant or stronger following their victimization experience. Similarly, those who accessed a community-based resource were 1.7 times more likely than those who did not access a resource to report feeling more self-reliant or strong, while those who accessed a mental health resource were 1.5 times more likely to report a positive outcome. While not statistically significant, those who accessed at least one government resource were 1.4 times more likely to have expressed a positive outcome compared to those who did not access resources. Those who accessed an Aboriginal resource were more likely to have expressed a positive outcome in terms of greater self-reliance or strength compared to those who did not access any services. However, this relationship is the weakest among the various resource types.

This initial analysis of the NCRP victimization data confirms that both property and personal victimization is not uncommon. Most troubling are the high frequencies of violent victim experiences and the large number of these victims who either did not report them to the police or did not seek any assistance. Moreover, there are many individuals who sought help from service providers and were unsuccessful. What is encouraging is that many victims who accessed resources viewed them positively and, equally important, reported significantly more positive outcomes than those who did not access any resources, services, or programs.

There are, however, the policy challenges of convincing many victims who did not seek services that their victim experiences are important enough, and serious enough, to be provided assistance. It may also be necessary to better publicize the availability of resources to increase awareness among victims. In addition, it appears that male victims are substantially more reluctant than female victims to access most types of resources. In particular, male victims were more than three times less likely to turn to police-based resources in response to their most serious lifetime victimization experience. Given this, more must be done to encourage male victims of crime to access resources, services and programs that can be beneficial to them in dealing with their often serious victimization experiences.

Endnotes

This research was funded by the Social Science and Humanities Research Council (SSHRC); the Department of Indian Affairs and Northern Development (DIAND); the federal Department of Justice; the National Crime Prevention Centre (NCPC); and the Law Commission.

1. For a full description of the research project and the methodology please see: R.R. Corrado, I. M. Cohen, and M. Boudreau, *The National Community Research Project: Vancouver Urban Sample: Report 1—Overview of the Research*, Department of Indian Affairs and Northern Development, 2002.

References

British Columbia Task Force On Family Violence. 1992. *Is Anyone Listening?* Victoria: Queen's Printer for British Columbia.

Canadian Centre for Justice Statistics. 2001. *A Profile of Criminal Victimization: Results of the 1999 General Social Survey.* Ottawa: Statistics Canada.

Corrado, R.R., Cohen, I.M., and Boudreau, M. 2002. *The National Community Research Project: Vancouver Urban Sample: Report 1—Overview of the Research.* Department of Indian Affairs and Northern Development.

Frank, S. 1992. *Family Violence in Aboriginal Communities: A First Nations Report.* Victoria: Canadian Cataloguing in Publication Data.

Greenfeld, L.A., and Smith, S.K. 1999. *American Indians and Crime.* Office of Justice Programs, U.S. Department of Justice.

Griffiths, C.T., Zellerer, E., Wood, D.S., and Saville, G. 1995. *Crime, Law and Justice among the Inuit in the Baffin Region, N.W.T. Canada.* Criminology Research Center, Simon Fraser University.

La Prairie, C. 1994. *Seen but Not Heard: Native People in the Inner City.* Ottawa: Department of Justice.

McEvoy, M., and Daniluk, J. 1995. "Wounds to the Soul: The Experiences of Aboriginal Women Survivors of Sexual Abuse." *Canadian Psychology* 36 (3): 221–235.

Moyer, S. 1992. *Race, Gender and Homicide: Comparisons between Aboriginals and Other Canadians.* Ottawa: Ministry of the Solicitor General.

Roberts, J.V., and Doob, A.N. 1994. "Race, Ethnicity and Criminal Justice," in *Crime and Ethnicity, Crime and Justice.* Annual vol. 21, ed. M. Tonry. Chicago: Chicago University Press.

Royal Commission on Aboriginal Peoples. 1993. *The Path to Healing: Report of the National Round Table on Aboriginal Health and Social Issues.* Ottawa: Ministry of Supply and Services Canada.

_____. 1996. *Gathering Strength.* Report of the Royal Commission on Aboriginal Peoples. Vol. 3. Ottawa: Minister of Supply and Services.

Trevethan, S. 1991. *Police-Reported Aboriginal Crime in Calgary, Regina and Saskatoon.* Ottawa: Canadian Centre for Justice Statistics.

14

Aboriginal Sexual Offending in Canada: A Review of the Evidence

John H. Hylton

Introduction

Sexual offending is a serious problem in Canada.[1] Despite a downward trend in the number of reported incidents since the early 1990s, victimization surveys indicate that as many as 600,000 offences still occur in Canada each year (Hylton 2002). Although 95% of sexual crimes do not involve any physical injury, these offences often do cause serious, lifelong trauma to victims, families and communities (Statistics Canada 2000).

Responding to sexual offending is one of the most vexing challenges for the criminal justice system. Although sexual offences make up about 1% of crimes reported to the police, 90% or more of sexual crimes never come to the attention of the authorities. This underreporting rate is higher than for any other crime category (Hylton 2002). Thus, while the consequences of widespread sexual victimization are very serious, at present, the criminal justice system addresses only the tip of a proverbial iceberg. Moreover, even when offences are detected and cases are brought before the courts, there is much that remains to be understood about effective methods for deterring and rehabilitating offenders who have committed sexual crimes.[2]

The impact of sexual offending is particularly devastating in small communities. Victims and offenders involved in sexual crimes are generally known to one another in any event (Statistics Canada 2000), but this is even more likely to be the case in smaller communities. In these communities, victims and offenders—as well as families—may be friends, acquaintances, or even members of the same extended families.

It is well documented that crime rates and rates of involvement in the criminal justice system are higher in many Aboriginal communities (e.g., La Prairie 1996; Wood and Griffiths 1999). A number of reasons for this overinvolvement have been examined elsewhere and will not be repeated here, except to say that these reasons are complex and relate to a long historical process that has placed the Aboriginal people of Canada at a significant social, economic and cultural disadvantage relative to the general population (see, Royal Commission 1995; Hamilton and Sinclair 1991).

Concerns about high rates of sexual offending within some Aboriginal communities has been expressed for at least the past thirty years, particularly by a number of the leading national Aboriginal women's organizations (Indian and Inuit Nurses Association 1987, 1990, 1991; Pauktuutit 1989, 1991a, 1991b, 1991c). Despite these concerns, however, there has been little attempt to examine the problem systematically. Little is known about the extent to which Aboriginal people are victims of sexual offences, and even less is known about the numbers, characteristics and needs of victims or offenders.

The purpose of this chapter is to consider the available evidence about Aboriginal sexual offending, to analyze this evidence with respect to the prevalence of sexual offending in Aboriginal communities, to consider gaps in available information, and to discuss priorities for future research.

Much of the available information about the prevalence of sexual offending in Aboriginal communities is anecdotal. This information is based on case histories, the testimony of community leaders, grant proposals, briefs prepared by Aboriginal organizations and, occasionally, community case studies. There have also been some government reports that have described the concerns, identified gaps in information, and suggested directions for the future. This anecdotal information is reviewed elsewhere (Hylton 2002).

What little systematic research is available about Aboriginal sexual offending has mostly been sponsored by criminal justice agencies, particularly the correctional agencies that are responsible for the management and treatment of sex offenders. Chief among these are the Solicitor General Canada and Correctional Service of Canada. These organizations have a long history of involvement in sex offender research, particularly research relating to risk prediction and treatment effectiveness. Over the past several years, some resources have been directed towards examining specific issues pertaining to Aboriginal sexual offenders. However, even within the criminal justice system, Aboriginal sexual offending has only very recently come onto the "radar screen" in any significant manner. Fortunately, a number of research projects are currently underway that will help to shed more light on patterns of Aboriginal victimization and Aboriginal offending. These projects will be discussed later in the chapter.

Aboriginal Sexual Offences Reported to the Police

As mentioned previously, very few sexual offences are reported to the police. Nonetheless, relative to correctional data, policing statistics are a somewhat truer indication of crime volumes in the community because the attrition of cases that normally occurs through subsequent stages of justice-system processing has not yet occurred. Unfortunately, policing statistics do not usually record whether victims or offenders are Aboriginal. Therefore, policing data is generally of limited utility for assessing the prevalence of sexual offending in Aboriginal communities.

Uniform Crime Reports from Provincial and Territorial Jurisdictions

Some indication of higher crime and victimization rates for sexual offences in Aboriginal communities can be gleaned from Table 1. As the data in that table indicates, the rates of sexual offences reported to the police are highest in the jurisdictions that also have the highest proportions of Aboriginal people in the general population. This is true, for example, in Manitoba, Saskatchewan, the Yukon, the Northwest Territories (NWT) and Nunavut. While it would be a stretch to attribute the higher rates in Manitoba and Saskatchewan to the victimization of Aboriginal people (since Aboriginal people make up less than 12% of the general population in those two provinces), such an association is on safer grounds in the Territories, where the Aboriginal proportion of the population is much higher.

Table 1:   Sexual assaults in Canada, 1999

| | Offences | | Persons Charged | | | |
| | | | Adults | | Youth | |
	Number	Rate	Male	Female	Male	Female
Newfoundland	644	119	213	3	45	2
Prince Edward Island	105	76	30	0	6	0
Nova Scotia	844	90	249	6	43	2
New Brunswick	775	103	205	4	43	3
Quebec	3,434	47	983	25	181	8
Ontario	8,270	72	2,580	65	534	11
Manitoba	1,307	114	480	7	81	5
Saskatchewan	1,375	134	373	-	83	-
Alberta	2,715	92	736	16	149	5
British Columbia	3,907	97	1,301	20	189	10
Yukon	90	294	47	2	4	1
Northwest Territories	202	486	82	1	10	-
Nunavut	204	754	82	5	5	-
Canada	**23,872**	**78**	**7,361**	**154**	**1,373**	**50**
Total Criminal Code	2.36m	7,733	310,021	66,991	77,142	22,604

Source: Statistics Canada (2000).

In the Yukon, for example, the Aboriginal proportion of the population is about 20%, while the sexual offence rate is about four times the national average. In the NWT, the proportion of the Aboriginal population was about 60% prior to the creation of Nunavut, while the sexual offence rate is about six times the national average. In Nunavut, it has been estimated that about 85% of the inhabitants are Aboriginal, while the sexual offence rate in that territory is about ten times the national average (Aboriginal Issues Branch 2001).

Kowalski's Examination of First Nations Policing Statistics

Some limited research is available that provides a more direct measure of sexual offence reporting rates in Aboriginal communities. In particular, Kowalski (1996) has examined offences reported to a number of First Nations police forces across Canada.

For a number of years, First Nations police forces have been submitting reports to the national Uniform Crime Reporting system maintained by Statistics Canada. These reports are important since these First Nations forces are exclusively involved in providing policing services to First Nations communities. Therefore, an analyses of these data, and comparisons with corresponding data for non-Aboriginal jurisdictions, provides some insight into comparative incident levels of various types of offences. Using 1996 data, Kowalski (1996) carried out just such an analysis.

In Table 2, Kowalski's results for violent offences and for assaults are shown. These data show that violent offences and assaults make up a much larger proportion of the offences reported to the police in Aboriginal communities than they do in a comparison sample of police forces from small urban and rural communities. In particular, violent crimes constitute one in four offences reported to the police in First Nations communities, but only one in seven offences in rural communities, and one in ten offences in small urban communities. With respect to assaults, the rates were about four times higher in First Nations communities than in small urban communities or rural communities.

Table 2: **Violent crimes and assaults reported to police in First Nations, small urban and rural communities, 1996**

	First Nations Communities	Small Urban Communities	Rural Communities
Violent Crime as % of total Criminal Code Offences			
Ontario	20.0	11.0	11.0
Quebec	23.0	7.0	8.0
Manitoba	36.0	11.0	20.0
Nova Scotia	26.0	13.0	15.0
Alberta	28.0	12.0	15.0
Average	**26.6**	**10.8**	**13.8**
Assault rates (per 1,000 population)			
Ontario	252	89	77
Quebec	212	37	35
Manitoba	773	105	182
Nova Scotia	472	146	84
Alberta	346	208	98
Average	**411**	**117**	**95**

Source: Kowalski (1996).

Table 3 summarizes Kowalski's results with respect to sexual offences. The data indicate that sexual assaults were two to three times more likely to be reported in First Nations communities than in small urban or rural communities. With respect to other sexual offences, these were approximately four times more likely to occur in First Nations communities than in the comparison communities.

Table 3: **Sexual assaults and other sexual offences reported to police in First Nations, small urban and rural communities, 1996 (rates per 10,000)**

	First Nations Communities	Small Urban Communities	Rural Communities
Sexual Assaults			
Ontario	25.1	9.6	11.2
Quebec	15.7	3.2	4.3
Manitoba	82.9	17.3	22.0
Nova Scotia	39.1	15.2	11.0
Alberta	36.4	30.9	13.6
Average	**39.8**	**15.2**	**12.4**
Other Sexual Offences			
Ontario	11.5	5.6	5.1
Quebec	6.7	1.0	1.5
Manitoba	22.0	1.3	1.4
Nova Scotia	0	1.2	.6
Alberta	0	1.8	1.0
Average	**8.0**	**2.2**	**1.9**

Source: Kowalski (1996).

Other sexual offences mostly involve offences where the victims are children. While sexual assault rates are also higher in the First Nations community, other sexual offences are even more likely to occur relative to the comparison communities. In addition, while the Canada-wide ratio of sexual assaults to other sexual offences has been found to be 7 or 8 to 1, for the First Nations communities in this sample, the ratio was 5 to 1. For the comparison communities, the rates were 7 to 1 for small urban communities, and 6 to 1 for the rural communities. These findings suggest that offences against children make up a larger proportion of sexual offences in First Nations communities.

Other key findings from Kowalski's analysis include the following: (1) the proportion of youth involved in reported violent crimes and sexual offences was similar in First Nations communities and in the comparison communities; (2) women were involved in a higher proportion of reported violent crimes in First Nations communities than in the comparison communities; and (3) there is a wide divergence in reported rates of violence and sexual offences, not only among the First Nations communities included in the study, but in the other communities as well. For example, some communities have twice the reported level of violent offences than others, while sexual offence rates differ by a factor of 4 or 5 or more to 1. These differences may reflect incidence levels of these offences in the community, reporting or enforcement practices, or, in all likelihood, a combination of these factors.

Kowalski's results need to be interpreted with considerable caution. First of all, as previously mentioned, reporting rates often have little to do with the incidence of crime in the community since there is extensive underreporting, particularly of sexual offences. Thus, if members of the First Nations communities in Kowalski's study were even slightly more likely to report these incidents to the police, perhaps because they had a heightened sense of trust or confidence in the ability of their police force to address the issue, this could more than account for the observed differences. In other words, the differences could be due to differences in reporting rather than differences in incidence. Second, very few First Nations communities were examined in Kowalski's study; twenty-four in Quebec and five in Ontario, but only one in each of Manitoba, Nova Scotia and Alberta. Therefore, it is not possible to generalize the findings to other First Nations, Inuit, or Métis communities.

A Further Analysis of First Nations Policing Statistics

A further analysis of First Nations policing statistics was undertaken specifically for this chapter. Through the Canadian Centre for Justice Statistics, Uniform Crime Reporting data for thirty-three First Nations police forces were obtained for each year from 1989 to 1999. As discussed more fully below, not all the forces reported in each of these years. Nonetheless, the data allowed for an examination of some of the issues addressed by Kowalski using more recent data. In addition, having longitudinal data over a period of eleven years allowed for an examination of trends in reporting. This is important since it permitted an assessment of whether or not the problem of sexual offending is becoming more serious in First Nations communities, at least from the perspective of reported incidents. In addition, the analysis allowed a comparison of trends in reporting to First Nations police forces with corresponding trends in reporting to non-Aboriginal police forces throughout Canada.

As mentioned, data for thirty-three First Nations police forces were obtained: one in Nova Scotia, sixteen in Quebec, seven in Ontario, two in Manitoba, three in Alberta, and four in British Columbia. Not every force reported in each of the years we examined. In fact, most of the First Nations forces did not begin reporting until 1996. Specifically, two forces reported in 1989, three reported in each year between 1990 and 1994, seven forces reported in 1995, twenty-four reported in 1996, eighteen reported in 1997, twenty-eight reported in 1998 and thirty-two reported in 1999. Statistics Canada did not release figures if they were too small to be reliable. Thus, data for earlier years is based on the reports of only a few forces, and, even in the later years, data from some forces was omitted. In addition, even in years where a police force reported, some estimates were used because data was missing for part of the year. For this reason, the rates of occurrence, rather than the number of incidents, are the focus of the discussion that follows.

Because of the small populations served by First Nations police forces in this analysis (the average community size was less than 2,400 in 1999), minimal changes in the number of reported incidents make very large differences in the rates per 100,000 population. This helps to explain some of the widely observed differences in the rates between communities, as well as the broad differences in the same community from year to year.

It is also worth recalling that reported incidence does not measure victimization. Moreover, caution is required in making comparisons over time or between communities, since differences could result from varying reporting or enforcement practices. Thus, these results should be regarded as only one more tool for gaining some perspective on the problem of Aboriginal sexual offending.

One more caution is warranted. Solicitor General Canada (2001) has estimated that some 70% of Aboriginal offenders under federal supervision either did not reside in reserve communities prior to their imprisonment, or if they did, they did not commit their offences on reserves. Since it appears that the vast majority of offences committed by Aboriginal people would not have been reported to First Nations police forces, the examination that follows focuses on only one small dimension of a much larger picture.

Table 4 summarizes the number of incidents and rates of sexual assaults and other sexual offences reported to the sample of First Nations police forces. While the rates vary considerably from year to year, in every year, they have been substantially higher than the rate for Canada as a whole (Statistics Canada 2000). It will be recalled that reported rates of sexual assault in Canada have decreased by 20% over the past several years. The rate stood at 78 incidents per 100,000 population in 1999. In contrast, the rate of sexual assault reported to the First Nations police forces in this sample averaged 255 incidents per 100,000 over the past eleven years, about three times the current national rate. In some years, the rate has been considerably higher. In the most recent year, for example, First Nations police in this sample reported sexual offenses at a rate five times the national average. In addition, unlike the Canada-wide rates, there is no clear downward trend in reported incidents to the First Nations police.

With respect to "other sexual offences," which usually involve offences against children, it will be recalled that the Canadian rate has been hovering between 11 and 12 incidents per 100,000 population for the past five years. The rate in the First Nations sample averaged 14 per 100,000 over the eleven-year period, about 20% higher than the 11.4 average rate in Canada over the past five years. However, the average rate of reported incidents to First Nations police forces is low because there were no reported incidents in the early years when there were very few First Nations police forces, and fewer still who were reporting to the Uniform Crime Reporting program. Over the past five years, however, the First Nations rate has averaged 31.4, about three times the Canadian rate.

Table 4: Sexual offences reported to thirty-three First Nations police forces, 1989-99

	Sexual assaults		Other sex offences		Total	
	Number of Incidents	Rate	Number of Incidents	Rate	Number of Incidents	Rate
1989	5	70	0	0	5	70
1990	10	58	0	0	10	58
1991	24	172	0	0	24	172
1992	40	288	0	0	40	288
1993	33	237	0	0	33	237
1994	34	199	0	0	34	199
1995	86	312	4	15	90	327
1996	151	343	25	57	176	400
1997	209	474	14	32	223	506
1998	174	253	15	22	189	275
1999	301	403	23	31	324	434
Average		**255**		**14**		**270**

Source: Customized data set generated by the Canadian Centre for Justice Statistics. Numbers may not add due to rounding.

The trends for reported sexual assaults, other sexual offences for Canada as a whole, and for the First Nations police forces in this sample are summarized in Graph 1. Data for the past five years is presented. The chart indicates much higher reported rates of sexual offences in the First Nations sample. Moreover, unlike the Canadian rates, particularly for sexual assault, there does not appear to be any downward trend in reported sexual incidents in the First Nations sample.

Graph 1: **Sexual offences reported to the police, Canada and First Nations sample, 1995-99**

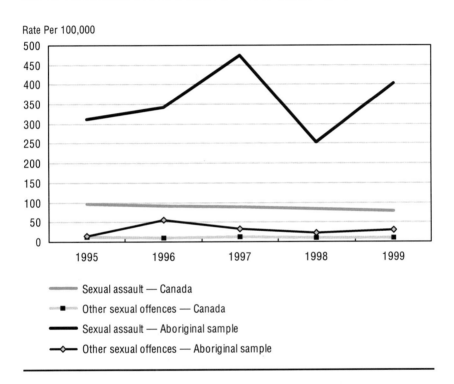

Several other findings from the analysis of data from the First Nations police forces may be mentioned:

- In Canada, sexual assaults outnumber other sexual offences by 7 or 8 to 1. While the rate of other sexual offences in the First Nations sample is higher than the Canadian rate, other sexual offences are a smaller proportion of the sexual offences reported to the police. Over the eleven-year period, the ratio in the First Nations sample was 18 to 1, while in the past five years, the ratio was nearly 12 to 1. There has been speculation (e.g., Kuptana 1991) that sexual offences against Aboriginal children are even less likely to be reported to the police than offences involving other Canadian children. However, these ratios also likely reflect the fact that sexual assaults are much more likely to occur in these Aboriginal communities.

- In Canada, about five adults are charged with a sexual offence for every young offender charged. In the First Nations sample, the proportion is similar at 6 to 1 (Table 5).

- In Canada, 98% of those charged with a sexual offence are male, and 2% are female, although females make up a larger proportion of the young offenders charged. In the First Nations sample, 92.3% of those charged were male. Among young offenders, the ratio of men to women charged was 4.5 to 1 compared to 27 to 1 for Canada as a whole. These findings suggest that the problem of sexual offending may be much more prevalent among Aboriginal women than among non-Aboriginal women (Table 5).

Table 5: **Age and gender of persons charged with sexual offences reported to First Nations police forces**

Persons Charged	Sexual assault		Other sex offences		Total	
	Number	%	Number	%	Number	%
Adult Males	379	81.2	29	67.4	408	80.6
Adult Females	24	5.2	2	4.7	26	5.1
Male Youth	47	10.2	12	27.9	59	11.7
Female Youth	13	2.8	0	0	13	2.6
Total	**463**	**91.5**	**43**	**8.5**	**506**	**100.0**

Source: Customized data set generated by the Canadian Centre for Justice Statistics. Numbers may not add due to rounding.

- In Canada, 8.2% of violent crimes and 1% of all Criminal Code incidents committed by adults and reported to the police are sexual offences. Among the First Nations sample, 7.5% of violent crimes and 1.9% of all Criminal Code incidents are sexual offences.

- In Canada, 97% of sexual assault charges are level 1, the kind that involve the least physical injury to the victim. The remaining 3% are more serious charges. In the First Nations sample, 94% of charges involved a level 1 assault, while 6% involved level 2 or 3 assaults. There were proportionately twice as many serious assaults in the First Nations sample. It is not clear whether this difference reflects more serious offences, different charging practices, or both.

- Among the sexual offences reported to the First Nations police in this sample, 79% were cleared by charge and 31% were cleared otherwise. In Canada, about 50% of charges relating to sexual offences are either stayed or withdrawn. Further research is required to determine if charging and prosecuting patterns for offences dealt with by First Nations police differ from those in Canada.

Aboriginal Sexual Offenders in Correctional Systems

The use of official data from the criminal justice system is an imperfect way to measure the amount and volume of crime in the community. While the limitations are generally well known, it is worth remembering that as few as one in one hundred violent offenders end up being imprisoned, and the number of sexual offenders could be even smaller (Griffiths and Verdun-Jones 1994). Therefore, any data from criminal justice system agencies seriously underestimates the total volume of crime, and it also likely distorts, in a variety of unknown ways, the true nature of the offences that are committed and the characteristics of the offenders and victims involved. Therefore, a good deal of caution is required. Nonetheless, official statistics from correctional agencies confirm what Aboriginal organizations and communities have been saying about the high prevalence of sexual abuse.

The Number of Aboriginal Sex Offenders in the Federal Correctional System

A number of studies carried out by the Correctional Service of Canada over the years shed some light on patterns of Aboriginal incarceration for sexual offending. For example:

- Blanchette (1996) found that Aboriginal sexual offenders were highly overrepresented among inmates in the federal correctional system at the end of 1995. Of those Aboriginal offenders serving over two years in custody, 40% were sex offenders.

- Motiuk and Belcourt (1998) found that Aboriginal inmates made up 13.2% of the population in federal institutions at the end of 1997, but 19% of the sex offenders.

- Johnston (2000) also carried out a survey of federal offenders. In a sample of Aboriginal offenders admitted from the Northern regions of Canada, 36% were sex offenders. Among the Aboriginal sex offenders, 56.3% were Inuit, 14.1% were Metis, 9.4% were Dene, 4.7% were Chippewan, 3.1% were Gwich'in and 12.5%

were from other or mixed Aboriginal ancestries. Over half the Aboriginal sample had a criminal history that included at least one conviction for a sexual offence.

- In their survey, Motiuk and Nafekh (2000) found that Aboriginal offenders in federal institutions were even more disproportionately represented among sex offenders than among inmates. While Aboriginal inmates made up 16.8% of the general population, they were 22.7% of the sex offenders. A more specific breakdown by Aboriginal ancestry was also available. Indians were 11.6% of the institutional population, but 15.7% of sex offenders. Inuit made up 1% of the offender population, but 3.4% of the sex offenders. The Métis, in contrast, were 4.2% of the general population, but 3.6% of the sex offenders. Non-Aboriginal inmates made up 83.2% of the offender population, and 77.3% of the sex offenders.

- Finn et al. (1999) found that 10% of Aboriginal offenders under federal jurisdiction had committed a serious assault, while this was true for only 2% of non-Aboriginal offenders. Whereas 20% of Aboriginal offenders had committed a sexual assault, this was true of only 12% of non-Aboriginal offenders.

- The Aboriginal Issues Branch (2001) of CSC has recently reported that, of Aboriginal people under federal jurisdiction, 71% are Indian, 25% are Métis and 4% are Inuit. While 26% of sexual offenders are Aboriginal, Aboriginal people make up 20% of the overall population. Twenty percent of Aboriginal offenders and 12% of other offenders have committed a sexual offence.

A tabular presentation of some of Motiuk and Nafekh (2000) results clearly shows that the proportion of Aboriginal people under jurisdiction of the federal correctional system has been increasing over the past five years. As Table 6 indicates, Aboriginal sex offenders were 16.5% of all federal sex offenders in 1994, but they made up 20% of sex offenders in 1999, a 20% increase in proportion over the five years. However, the proportion of Aboriginal offenders in the federal system is increasing for all offence types, from 10.5% of all offenders in 1994 to 14.4% in 1999, a 37% increase. Thus, while the number of Aboriginal sex offenders under federal supervision is increasing, it is not increasing as rapidly as one might expect given the general increase in Aboriginal offenders in the federal system.

Another way to examine the data in Table 6 is to focus on the number of sex offenders under federal jurisdiction. The number of sexual offences reported to the police has been declining (Hylton 2002). As might be expected, the number of sex offenders under federal jurisdiction has also been declining for the past four years. In fact, since 1994, there has been a 4.9% decline in the total sex offender population, while the sex offender population in institutions has declined by 10%. Aboriginal sex offenders, however, have made up an increasing proportion of these declining numbers. The result is that, even though the total number of sex offenders has declined, the number of Aboriginal sex offenders has not. Over the past four years, the number of Aboriginal sex offenders has been hovering between 700 and 750.

Table 6: Sexual offenders under federal jurisdiction*1994-99

	Sex offenders				All offenders	
	Non-Aboriginal Number	Aboriginal Number	Aboriginal %	Non-Aboriginal %	Aboriginal %	Non-Aboriginal %
1994	3,748	618	16.5	83.5	10.5	89.5
1995	3,875	639	16.5	83.5	10.9	89.1
1996	4,041	719	17.8	82.2	12.0	88.0
1997	3,914	744	19.0	81.0	13.2	86.8
1998	3,676	732	19.9	80.1	14.0	86.0
1999	3,564	713	20.0	80.0	14.4	85.6

Source: Motiuk and Nafekh (2000).* Studies undertaken by the CSC have determined that the actual number of sex offenders is about 17% higher than the number recorded by CSC's Offender Management System. Therefore, while the proportions would not change, the actual number of sex offenders is likely 17% higher than recorded in this table.

The latest data available about sex offenders under federal jurisdiction has been provided by Sharon Williams, the corporate advisor for sex offender programs at the Correctional Service of Canada.[3] A November 2000 snapshot completed by Williams (Table 7) indicates that there were approximately 778 Aboriginal sex offenders under federal jurisdiction.[4]

The Aboriginal sex offenders in Williams' survey made up just over one-fifth of the sex offenders under federal jurisdiction at that time. The proportion of offenders in institutions was about the same for both Aboriginal and non-Aboriginal populations; for both groups, there were two institutionalized offenders for every offender in the community. It is also noteworthy that two-thirds of Aboriginal sex offenders were under the jurisdiction of CSC's Prairie Region.

Table 7:   Aboriginal and non-Aboriginal sexual Offenders under federal jurisdiction,* November 2000

	Total Offenders	In Institutions	In the Community
Aboriginal			
Atlantic	22	13	9
Quebec	39	30	9
Ontario	101	72	29
Prairie	403	263	140
Pacific	100	70	25
Total	**665**	**448**	**212**
Non-Aboriginal	**2,435**	**1,582**	**858**
Total	**3,100**	**2,030**	**1,070**

* As in the previous table, federal studies have determined that the actual number of sex offenders is about 17% higher than the number recorded by CSC's Offender Management System. Therefore, while the proportions would not change, actual numbers of sex offenders are likely 17% higher than recorded in this table.

Source: Williams (personal correspondence).

A breakdown of more specific Aboriginal origins has been provided by Motiuk and Nafekh (2000). Based on a year-end review of offenders under federal supervision in 1998, the proportions of Indian, Métis and Inuit sex offenders were determined (Table 8).

Aboriginal Sexual Offenders in Provincial and Territorial Correctional Systems

Provincial and territorial correctional systems generally do not have as much information as the federal system about the offenders under their supervision. There are several related reasons for this: (1) many offenders serving time in provincial and territorial correctional facilities are incarcerated for brief periods, thus there is often little point collecting the type of detailed background information that the federal system uses for classification and programming purposes; (2) provincial and territorial jurisdictions, especially the smaller jurisdictions, generally have not developed the type of sophisticated information management systems that are available federally for recording inmate histories and characteristics; and (3) there has been a stronger tradition of research within the federal correctional system that is not paralleled in most provincial and territorial systems—a considerable body of research on federal offenders has been produced by a large in-house research staff, as well as by academics and external consultants.

Table 8: **Aboriginal sex offenders under federal supervision by Aboriginal ancestry, 1998**

	Institutional %	Conditional Release %
Aboriginal		
Indian	15.7	13.2
Metis	3.6	3.9
Inuit	3.4	3.4
Total	22.7	20.4
Non-Aboriginal	77.3	79.6

Source: Motiuk and Nafekh (2000).

While provincial and territorial information is limited, some data is available. The results of a 1996 snapshot reported by the Aboriginal Issues Branch (2001) indicates that 8% of all Aboriginal inmates were incarcerated for sexual assault, compared to 6% for non-Aboriginal offenders. Since the snapshot captured 23,494 provincial and territorial offenders, and 18% of these were Aboriginal (Statistics Canada 1999), it can be estimated that there were approximately 340 Aboriginal sex offenders and approximately 1,150 non-Aboriginal sex offenders in provincial/territorial custody. However, since only 57% of sex offenders receive a sentence of imprisonment, while 43% receive probation or some other disposition, the actual number of Aboriginal offenders under provincial/territorial jurisdiction at any one time is likely closer to 500.

In terms of the experience with Aboriginal sex offenders in specific jurisdictions, the following information was obtained:

- **Manitoba**. On March 13, 2001, a snapshot of Aboriginal people in the custody of the Manitoba correctional system was completed for this review. The snapshot revealed there were 113 Aboriginal people charged or convicted of a sex offence on that day (Coles 2001).[5] Of these, 103 were adults, and 10 were young people. Fifty Aboriginal inmates (44%) were charged, but not convicted, while the remaining 63 had been sentenced for a sex offence. On average, the sentence length for adult Aboriginal sex offenders was 394 days, but there was significant variation in sentence lengths (the standard deviation was 264 days). Although limited information about the characteristics of those charged or sentenced was collected, the available information indicates that these offenders displayed many of the socioeconomic, family and other characteristics of Aboriginal offenders. Few (31%) were in stable marital or common-law relationships, and most (74%) were unemployed prior to their incarceration. For 26% of the offenders, the maximum education attained was elementary school. Substance abuse problems were reported in 18% of cases, while drug abuse problems were reported in 17% of cases.

- **Saskatchewan.** Data regarding sex offender admissions were obtained from Saskatchewan Justice for the four years from 1996 to 1999 (Nasim 2001).[6] The data indicate that during this four-year period, 576 offenders out of 14,514 (4%) who were admitted to provincial correctional centers for Criminal Code violations had been convicted of sex offences. There were 468 admissions for sexual assault and 108 for other sexual offences. Of these offenders, 55% were First Nations, 11% were Metis and 34% were non-Aboriginal. These were approximately the same proportions as for Criminal Code admissions. Whereas one in four non-Aboriginal sex offenders had committed "other" sexual offences, offences which usually involve children, only one in five Aboriginal sex offenders had committed "other" offences. The average sentence for a Criminal Code admission other than sex offences was 230 days, while the average for sexual assault admissions was 916 days. For "other" sexual offences, it was 553 days. Overall, sentence lengths for First Nations, Métis and other offenders appeared to be similar.

- **Nunavut.** Recently, the Nunavut Corrections Planning Committee (1999; Evans et al. 1998) developed a plan for correctional services in Nunavut. In assessing the needs in Nunavut, the plan points out that the NWT and Nunavut have the highest crime rates in Canada, and that an increasing proportion of crimes are violent. While incarceration rates are similar to other parts of Canada, offenders in Nunavut are more likely to be incarcerated if they have committed a violent offence. Over half of the sentenced admissions in Nunavut are for violent offences, and 72% of the correctional centre population in Nunavut has committed a violent offence. This compares with 38% for provincial prison populations in Canada.

  The committee identifies a number of needs of Nunavut inmates that increase the likelihood they will recidivate. These needs relate to substance abuse, previous convictions and imprisonment, criminal associates, unemployment and low educational attainment. Many inmates, according to the plan, have also experienced dysfunctional family life, early exposure to violence and other forms of abuse, Fetal Alcohol Syndrome and Fetal Alcohol Effect, learning disabilities, inability to adapt to school environments, lack of social skills, poverty and despair.

The committee's plan identifies the need to develop a core treatment and rehabilitation program within Nunavut corrections that specifically focuses on sexual offending. The plan points out that, at present, limited programming is provided at the Baffin Correctional Centre. The committee's recommendations call for the development of one or more program modules that would provide culturally relevant relapse prevention programs in conjunction with Northern communities.

Although we did not approach every provincial and territorial jurisdiction, we did approach some others that were unable to provide any statistical information about Aboriginal sexual offending. These included jurisdictions that are known to have high rates of Aboriginal overrepresentation.

These findings suggest that the challenge of providing programs and services for Aboriginal sexual offenders is no less daunting within provincial/ territorial correctional systems than within the federal system. In fact, because many offenders are given community dispositions or short prison sentences, the opportunities available to provincial and territorial correctional systems to effectively deal with Aboriginal sexual offending are quite limited.

Conclusion

All of the available evidence suggests that rates of violence and sexual offending in many Aboriginal communities are substantially higher than corresponding rates for Canada as a whole. While precise figures are not available, it is reasonable to conclude from the available information that overall rates of sexual offending in Aboriginal communities are as much as five times higher than Canadian rates, and perhaps higher.

On any given day in Canada, there are some 1,500 adult and young Aboriginal sexual offenders under supervision of various provincial, territorial and federal correctional authorities. These offenders represent 20%–25% of all sex offenders in the Canadian correctional system. These offenders are the "tip of the iceberg," since only one in one hundred violent offenders is eventually incarcerated and the ratio for sex offenders may be much less.

We do not know how many offences Aboriginal sex offenders commit. However, the use of a very course method for estimating the number yields disturbing figures—some 600,000 sexual offences committed in Canada each year (Hylton 2002). If Aboriginal offenders are responsible for 20%–25% of these offences, as incarceration statistics suggest, Aboriginal sexual offenders may be responsible for some 120,000 to 150,000 offences each year.[7]

Despite the sustained efforts of a few Aboriginal organizations to focus attention on the issue of sexual offending, surprisingly little is known about victimization and offending patterns in Aboriginal communities, about how Aboriginal offenders are dealt with by the criminal justice system, or about Aboriginal community perspectives on the extent of the problems and what should be done about them. Getting a perspective on the enormity and features of Aboriginal sexual offending thus requires a good deal of estimation, extrapolation and outright guesswork. Clearly, the available information does not provide an adequate base upon which to build detailed needs assessments or plans.

Some important research is in the planning stages or is already underway. For example, a second Aboriginal Peoples Survey is being completed by Statistics Canada. In addition, the Social Sciences and Humanities Research Council, and others, have provided support for the completion of an Aboriginal victimization survey. This study, which is being carried out by a group of criminologists at Simon Fraser University, is currently being piloted in British Columbia.

Given widespread sexual offending and victimization in some Aboriginal communities, it is clear that a significant commitment to prevention, recovery and rehabilitation efforts is required. However, a much stronger commitment to adequate research is also needed. Such research is needed not only to help guide the design of these efforts, but also to assess their efficacy.

Endnotes

This paper is based on a more detailed study of Aboriginal sexual offending commissioned by the Aboriginal Healing Foundation. See Hylton (2002).

1. In Canada, sexual offences are classified into two main categories for criminal justice system reporting purposes: sexual assault and other sexual offences. A sexual assault, previously referred to as a rape, involves an adult victim, whereas other sexual offences mostly involve offences against children, including child molestation.

2. Although Canada is a world leader in the relatively new field of sex offender treatment, there are few programs, and little information is available about their effectiveness, particularly for Aboriginal sex offenders. See Hylton (2002).

3. Personal correspondence.

4. The estimate of 778 is derived by applying a 17% correction factor to the number in Table 7. See the note to Table 6 for an explanation.

5. Coles (2001). Personal correspondence from Ron Coles, Manitoba Justice.

6. Nasim (2001). Personal correspondence from Shaukat Nasim, Saskatchewan Justice.

7. Of course, this estimate assumes that Aboriginal and non-Aboriginal offenders are equally likely to be detected and prosecuted. Since this may not be the case, the resulting figures are, at best, "ballpark" estimates.

References

Aboriginal Issues Branch. 2001. *Demographic Overview of Aboriginal People in Canada and Aboriginal Offenders in Federal Corrections*. Ottawa: Correctional Service of Canada.

Blanchette, K. 1996. *Sex Offender Assessment, Treatment and Recidivism: A Literature Review*. Ottawa: Correctional Service of Canada.

Evans, J., Hann, R., and Nuffield, J. 1998. *Crime and Corrections in the NWT*. Yellowknife: Government of the Northwest Territories, Department of Justice.

Finn, A., Trevethan, S., Carriere, G., and Kowalski, M. 1999. "Female Inmates, Aboriginal Inmates, and Inmates Serving Life Sentences: A One Day Snapshot As of 5 October 1996." *Juristat* 19 (5): 1–15.

Griffiths, C.T., and Verdun-Jones, S. 1994. *Canadian Criminal Justice*. 2d ed. Toronto: Harcourt Brace.

Hamilton, A.C., and Sinclair, C.M. 1991. *Report of the Aboriginal Justice Inquiry of Manitoba*. Winnipeg: Aboriginal Justice Inquiry of Manitoba.

Hylton, J.H. 2002. *Aboriginal Sex Offending in Canada*. Ottawa: Aboriginal Healing Foundation.

Indian and Inuit Nurses Association of Canada. 1987. "Consultation on Child Sexual Abuse." Ottawa: Indian and Inuit Nurses Association of Canada, Feb. 11–13, 1987.

_____. 1990. "Child Sexual Abuse in Aboriginal Communities." Annual assembly report for 1990. Ottawa: Indian and Inuit Nurses Association of Canada.

_____. 1991. "Reducing Family Violence in Aboriginal Communities." Proceedings of the annual general meeting. Ottawa: Indian and Inuit Nurses Association of Canada.

Johnston, J. 2000. "Aboriginal Federal Offender Surveys: A Synopsis." *Forum on Corrections Research* (Correctional Service of Canada) 12 (1): 25–27.

Kowalski, M. 1996. *Police Reported First Nations Crime Statistics, 1996*. Ottawa: Canadian Centre for Justice Statistics.

Kuptana, R. 1991. *No More Secrets: Acknowledging the Problem of Child Sexual Abuse in Inuit Communities*. Ottawa: Pauktuutit.

LaPrairie, C. 1996. *Examining Aboriginal Corrections in Canada*. Ottawa: Solicitor General Canada.

LaRocque, E. 1994. *Violence in Aboriginal Communities*. Ottawa: National Clearinghouse on Family Violence.

Motiuk, L., and Belcourt, R.L. 1998. *Homicide, Sex, Robbery and Drug Offenders in Federal Corrections: An End-of-1997 Review*. Ottawa: Correctional Service of Canada.

Motiuk, L., and Nafekh, M. 2000. "Aboriginal Offenders in Federal Corrections: A Profile." *Forum on Correctional Research* (Correctional Service of Canada) 12 (1): 10–15.

Nunavut Corrections Planning Committee. 1999. *Planning for Nunavut Corrections*. Iqaluit: Nunavut Justice.

Pauktuutit. 1989. *A Life Without Violence*. Ottawa: Pauktuutit.

_____. 1991a. *Special Report of Pauktuutit's Family Violence Conference*. Ottawa: Pauktuutit.

_____. 1991b. *Child Sexual Abuse in the North*. Ottawa: Pauktuutit.

_____. 1991c. *No More Secrets: Acknowledging the Problem of Child Sexual Abuse in Inuit Communities*. Ottawa: Pauktuutit.

Royal Commission on Aboriginal Peoples. 1995. *Bridging the Cultural Divide: A Report on Aboriginal People and Criminal Justice*. Ottawa: Royal Commission.

Solicitor General Canada. 2001. *Aboriginal Offenders*. Ottawa: Solicitor General Canada.

Statistics Canada. 1999. "A One-Day Snapshot of Inmates in Canada's Correctional Facilities." *Juristat* 18 (8): 1–15.

_____. 2000. *Crime Statistics in Canada*. Ottawa: Statistics Canada.

Wierzba, J., Bastien, B., and Bastien, E. 1991. "Native Family Violence in Lethbridge." *Native Studies Review* 7 (1): 132–140.

Wood, D., and Griffiths, C. 1999. "Patterns of Aboriginal Crime" in *Crime in Canadian Society*, ed. Silverman et al. 6th ed. Toronto: Harcourt Brace, 222–33.

15

A Cost-Benefit Analysis of Hollow Water First Nation's Community Holistic Healing Process

Ed Buller

Introduction

This chapter is a summary research relating to the costs and benefits of a community healing model in the Hollow Water First Nation (Manitoba). The Community Holistic Circle Healing (CHCH) process in Hollow Water, established in 1985, is arguably the most mature healing process in Canada addressing the needs of sexual assault victims and victimizers.

The study was funded by the Solicitor General of Canada and the Aboriginal Healing Foundation, and undertaken by the Native Counselling Services of Alberta (NCSA). The NCSA research and writing team was lead by Dr. Joe Couture and included Mr. Ted Parker, Ms. Ruth Couture and Ms. Patti Laboucane. The objectives and goals of this research were:

- to recognize the traditional protocols of undertaking research in Aboriginal communities, which included the communities in a participatory process that was satisfactory to workers, community members and their leaders;

- to design and implement a "holistic" research process that was relevant and meaningful;

- to ascertain whether the financial investments made by governments to community healing processes have resulted in any savings to the criminal justice system; and

- to explore the communities' perceptions of other benefits to community healing that extended beyond the justice system.

The relationship between government financial investment in healing processes and potential savings to the criminal justice system is timely. Governments, and the public-at-large, are beginning to question the amount of resources going to Aboriginal communities for what some consider "soft" programs. Aboriginal communities working in the area of healing and wellness have known for some time that the work they do with victims, offenders and their families is not "soft." It is, in fact, very hard in terms of commitment, emotion and results. They know that they are keeping members out of provincial and federal justice, corrections and social service systems. Aboriginal communities know what it costs to have their members go through these systems.

It needs to be recognized that cost-benefit analyses can only portray one part of the whole "benefit" to communities. How does one weigh the intricacies of the healing process, and how does a community define or measure the value-added benefits of these processes? How does one put a dollar value on the mental, emotional, spiritual and physical components of wellness? How can one put a dollar figure on the power of the spiritual resonance that underlies these processes or the core philosophy around which CHCH operates, and to bring healing to offenders and the community? A suitable criteria has not been put into place, nor perhaps can it be, to quantify the threads of value or the parts that comprise the whole.

Research Protocol

The research team recognized that Aboriginal people feel that they have been "researched to death" by governments and academics, and that the time for the examination of problems and issues has passed—it is time for action. Further, many communities have expressed the frustration that researchers have used the information and expertise provided by the communities, have gained status and recognition from their research, but returned nothing to the community for their time, effort and expertise.

Recognizing these frustrations, a participatory research approach was undertaken in both communities that enabled improved research protocols. It incorporated the knowledge and expertise of community workers, community members and researchers—all collaborating in the research process as equals.

> Collaboration, mutual education and acting on results are the three key elements of participatory research. Such research stresses the mutually respectful partnerships between researchers, CHCH, the Band and the community. . . . When people form a group with a common purpose investigate their situation and make decisions. . . . [they] are transformed—losing fear, gaining confidence, self-esteem and direction.[1]

Participatory research maximizes community and lay involvement. It negotiates a "balance" between taking knowledge from the community and returning benefits to the community that is being researched. The partnership is mutually respectful, based on shared responsibilities and the production of results that are satisfactory for all partners.

The notion of "protocol" when doing research in Aboriginal communities took on several different meanings. The first issue of protocol concerned the manner in which research was conducted when it involves sensitive issues, such as sexual abuse. In such a situation, the research must be approached with the utmost caution and consideration. Victims and victimizers needed to feel safe in sharing information with the research team, and the researchers needed to be very concerned with the manner in which data was collected. In addition, to this particular research project, which had a quasi-evaluative function, an additional risk could have been introduced. The community may have felt it was "under the microscope" and that governments could use the research to hinder future healing initiatives in the community.

For this reason, it was decided to approach both communities before the research design was finalized, to seek their approval for the research to take place in the community and to seek their active participation in the design and delivery of the research. This need for protocol formed the basis of the participatory approach the project adopted.

In order to adhere to a participatory research approach, the traditional dimension of protocol in the Aboriginal community—the process of building relationships through the respect of community ritual—needed to be acknowledged and respected. This includes the protocol surrounding the *entrance* into the communities, which allowed the meeting to take place. Second was the protocol surrounding *permission* to undertake research in the communities. Finally, there was the protocol surrounding *relationship* that would not only bind the commitment of both parties to undertake the research, but also commit all participants to create a balance between what would be taken from the community (knowledge), and what would be left in the community (opportunities, information and expertise).

Justice System Costs

The CHCH healing process can be considered a diversion program that enables the victimizer to remain in the community, while participating in an intensive healing process where the victimizers are both accountable to the community and have an opportunity for real and sustainable holistic personal change. For Hollow Water, justice system costs were established by determining a cost for each step that a victimizer would go through. This included all processes from the first reporting of a suspected crime, through the police work, the trial, incarceration and parole, to final release. By far, the most significant cost is incarceration.

Costs were estimated by referring to national publications on such things as sentencing norms for all the offences identified in the victimizer list, and costs of incarceration. Interviews with government and criminal justice officials also took place to verify information concerning the costs of processing individuals through the justice system. Sufficient information was available to determine reliable cost data of what costs would be if the victimizers cared for by CHCH had gone through the Canadian justice system.

When undertaking a cost-benefit analysis of a program or policy initiative, distinction is usually made between the marginal cost and the average (operational) cost. For corrections, the marginal cost would be the cost of adding one additional offender into the system. Average costs, on the other hand, are simply derived from dividing the total costs by the total units of resources used during a given period of time. Average costs, therefore, include fixed costs that are expended with or without the implementation of a new policy or program. From an economic review perspective, fixed costs are less important for this report[2] and the analysis may be subject to criticism for over-estimating any financial benefits to governments.

The difference between marginal and average cost for federal corrections is substantial. For the year 1999–2000, the Correctional Service of Canada reported that the cost per male inmate averaged about $67,686 per year. For female inmates, the average cost was $115,465.[3] On the other hand, the marginal cost of adding one additional inmate into the federal system averaged $13,720 during the same period.[4]

Hollow Water First Nation Community Holistic Circle Healing Process (CHCH)

Background

Hollow Water First Nation is located 150 miles northeast of Winnipeg, Manitoba, and covers 4,010 acres. The band is a signatory to Treaty 5, signed in 1875, and its people speak the Ojibway language. The reserve is home to 457 Aboriginal people, with another 456 living off the reserve, and is accessible by road.

History of CHCH

Up to 1984, Hollow Water was faced with a chronic alcohol and drug abuse problem, violence among men and between men and women, high unemployment and a severe breakdown in traditional cultural values. A number of people began their personal healing journey, and in 1985, a twenty-four person Resource Team was formed. The team included political leaders, service providers from all community agencies, and a strong base of community volunteers. The team not only supported one another, but also began to look at ways to support community development through training and co-ordinated agency efforts.

When the first disclosure of sexual abuse came in 1986, the Resource Team—most of whom had been affected by sexual abuse—knew there was no turning back. It became clear that, as the veil of alcohol was removed, many of the victimizers were holding on to acute anger, hurt and dysfunctional behaviour patterns that were related to sexual abuse or some other violation that had been done to them in the past.[5] The team consulted with a number of groups across North America who were dealing with similar issues and, in 1988, established their own training program based on the Alkali Lake model.

The CHCH model evolved with the dramatic increase in sexual abuse disclosures that followed. It was recognized that a new negotiated relationship was required with all agencies having a stake in addressing sexual assault. Procedures were developed and protocols signed with key stakeholders that defined how disclosures would be dealt with by the police and courts to allow for the community healing process to take place.

The Healing Model

Hollow Water still views CHCH as an evolving process that involves working with victims, victimizers, their families and the community. As Berma Bushie has said:

> the spirit piece is at the very core. It has to be in place to bring people back to balance. The whole field of psychology and psychiatry has developed its own language to determine who has a disorder, and how to get people well. We don't have the same concepts or definitions. Ours is holistic. We don't label people. We understand that the decisions that we make today will affect our people for several generations, and we use a traditional holistic approach to human living problems. We want our people in our community because it's our heart and soul. Without the spiritual, balance will not be achieved, nor healing attained.[6]

CHCH is a thirteen-step process that begins at the time of disclosure and concludes with a Cleansing Ceremony. The thirteen steps[7] have been defined by Hollow Water as follows:

Step 1: Disclosure. Disclosure may come from a victim, a family member, a spouse, a community member who witnesses an abuse, or even the victimizer him or herself. Information regarding the disclosure is passed on to the Assessment Team Co-ordinator who then contacts the RCMP and invites them to an Assessment Team meeting to plan the intervention that will follow.

Step 2: Protecting the Victim/Child. The person(s) from the Assessment Team taking responsibility for assisting the victim must: involve Child and Family Services; identify a safe home and make arrangements for the victim's stay; validate the disclosure; ensure that an ally is available to the victim; ensure training and on-going support to the safe home; and make whatever arrangements are necessary for the victim (e.g., medical assessment, admission to victim's/survivor's group, etc.).

Step 3: Confronting the Victimizer. The confronter must share information gained in the disclosure with the victimizer, ensure that an ally is available, make whatever arrangements are necessary (e.g., psychological assessment, admission to victimizer's group, self-awareness, etc.), and fully explain the process. The victimizer is to be informed that the victim has been removed to a safe home pending a resolution of the situation, and that the matter could be handled by the community—in conjunction with the court system—provided there is no attempt at interference with either the process or the victim. The victimizer must also be informed that it will be necessary to accept full responsibility, undergo a psychological assessment, and that he or she will be contacted within five days as to what the community concludes after completing the assessment.

Step 4: Assisting the Spouse. The person(s) from the Assessment Team taking responsibility for assisting the spouse must share information gained in the disclosure with the spouse, ensure that an ally is available, make whatever arrangements that are necessary (e.g., admission to survivors' group, self-awareness, women's therapy, etc.), and explain what has happened thus far and the process to come.

Step 5: Assisting the Family/ies. The person(s) from the Assessment Team taking responsibility for assisting the family/ies must follow the same steps as presented in Step 4, only on behalf of the family/ies.

Step 6: Meeting of Assessment Team/RCMP/Crown. This meeting will be called by the co-ordinator—as soon as the first five steps of this process have been completed—in order to present all information obtained thus far, decide how to proceed, and review responsibilities of respective meeting participants (who will do what, and when).

Step 7: Victimizer Must Admit and Accept Responsibility. The person(s) from the Assessment Team taking responsibility for assisting the victimizer must inform him or her of the outcome of the investigation, explain that he or she must admit to the offence(s) and accept full responsibility, present the Healing Contract, and ask him or her to choose between the two primary alternatives available (community/legal, legal/community).

Step 8: Preparation of the Victimizer. If the victimizer admits to the allegations and is willing to accept the community alternative, he or she must then be prepared for the next step in the healing process—an appearance before a special gathering of the Resource Group, selected members of his or her family, the victim(s), and selected member of his/her/their family/ies.

Step 9: Preparation of the Victim(s). As with the victimizer, the victim(s) must be prepared for the next step in the healing process—the appearance of the victimizer before him/her/themselves, selected member of his/her/their family/ies, and the Resource Group.

Step 10: Preparation of All the Families. As with the victimizer and victim(s), selected members of the victimizer's family must be prepared for the next step in the healing process—the appearance of the victimizer before themselves, the victim(s), and the Resource Group.

Step 11: The Special Gathering. Once the victimizer, the victim(s), and selected family members have been prepared, the co-ordinator will arrange for the victimizer to come face-to-face with the Resource Group (who represent the healing community), the victim(s), and selected members of the family/ies to answer for his or her misconduct. The Special Gathering has ten steps: (1) the ceremonial opening; (2) the co-ordinator addresses the gathering and explains its purpose; (3) Assessment Team members explain the offence; (4) the co-ordinator asks the victimizer if he/she accepts the charges as true and is willing to participate in the proceedings; (5) the educational process consisting of a "mini-workshop"; (6) the victimizer verbally accepts full responsibility for his or her action; (7) the participants of the gathering speak; (8) the Healing Contract is presented; (9) the victimizer publicly apologizes to the victim, the spouse, and to the group-at-large and agrees to abide by the conditions in the Healing Contract; and (10) the Ceremonial Closure.

Step 12: The Healing Contract Is Implemented. It is the responsibility of the co-ordinator to ensure that the conditions of the Healing Contract are implemented and carried out as intended.

Step 13: The Cleansing Ceremony. This is a ceremony that marks the completion of the Healing Contract, the restoration to balance of the victimizer and a new beginning for all involved.

Government Funding and Operational Costs for CHCH

A review of the CHCH costs for the years under study indicated that a figure of $300,000 as an annual cost would be a representative figure to use when comparing the costs of operating CHCH to the costs that would be incurred by the provincial or federal governments for mainstream services. Staff salaries and benefits account for over 80% of total expenditures and most of the other expenses are directly related to staff activities (such as travel). Of that amount, CHCH receives approximately $125,000 per year from the Department of Justice and $125,000 from the Province of Manitoba.

CHCH also receives considerable benefits from community resources. The Community Resource Pool (CPR)—a core group of volunteers—are trained and assist counsellors in many of their duties. This includes, but is not limited to: driving, suicide watch, participation in circles and accompanying workers for safety. The community also provides support in other ways such as helping visitors who come to Hollow Water to learn and train in this restorative justice program.

The integrated nature of CHCH with the band and the community does not allow the calculation of a precise dollar value for the non-monetary contributions. A conservative estimate of 3,500 volunteer hours, at $10[8] per hour, would indicate that at least $35,000 per year of volunteer time, services and support were provided that would otherwise be paid staff time.

Benefits and Savings to Governments

Over a period of ten years, a total of 107 victimizers participated in the CHCH healing process after having been charged with the following offences:

	Male	Female	Youth	Total
Assault[9]	33	3	5	41
Sexual assault[10]	27	2	8	37
Theft and break and enter	3	0	4	7
Criminal loss of life[11]	1	2	0	3
Other offences[12]	4	0	2	6
Subtotal	**68**	**7**	**19**	**94**
Referred from other reserves	7	0	0	7
Confronted (voluntarily entered treatment)	6	0	0	6
Total	**81**	**7**	**19**	**107**

In the study, the marginal costs for corrections were applied to the victimizer list and a typical cost determined for each offence with two assumptions made:

- that if the victimizers did indeed go to trial, that they would be found guilty and, further, that their sentence would fall within the national averages for that offence; and

- given national trends in Aboriginal corrections, it was assumed that each federal offender would serve 66% of his total sentence in a federal institution.

Of the victimizers sentenced to federal custody, 72 men and 7 women would have served a total of 166.2 years in penitentiaries and a total of 99.7 years in the community under supervision.

The researchers estimated that the total amount that the federal government would have spent on the incarceration and supervision of participants in the CHCH program over the past ten years, had they proceeded through the criminal justice system, would be a minimum of $2,461,318. Most, if not all, of the seventy-two adult male victimizers from Hollow Water would have been placed in Stony Mountain penitentiary, and that number of offenders may have had additional impacts on the operational costs for the institution.

If one were to determine the actual costs, they would vary from individual to individual depending on the specific institution used, treatments, conduct during incarceration and a number of other factors that could not be determined. Further, costs reported in the study did not reflect the additional cost of psychological services and specialized sex offender treatment programs, which are acknowledged to be more costly than standard incarceration costs.

Manitoba would have been responsible for the pre-incarceration costs for all victimizers, including expenditures for the criminal investigation, remand and trial. It was difficult to determine an average total for this expenditure, as it depends greatly on many variables. An individual can spend no time in remand (released on bail or own recognizance), or up to two years in remand awaiting trial. The investigation can take one day or three years. The individual could plead guilty immediately, saving the cost of a trial, or could enter a plea of innocence and have a lengthy trial. Given the above variables, the researchers arrived at an average of $19,500 per client, which was seen as a very conservative estimate.

Of the victimizers sentenced to provincial care, adult men, adult women and young offenders would have served a total of 11.94 years in custody and 21 years in the community.

The total amount that would have been spent by Manitoba over the past ten years for pre-incarceration, incarceration and supervision of the participants was estimated as being $2,631,414.

The second key component of the services provided by CHCH is the work that is done with the victims of the individuals receiving treatment, and the families of both the victims and the victimizer. It is this work that promotes individual, family and community healing and wellness, and is a cornerstone of the restorative justice process in the communities of Hollow Water. The work with those affected by the victimizer's actions provides an opportunity for victimizer accountability, counselling for all people affected by the crime and allows for the community to come to terms with the issue and move forward.

The total of 107 victimizers understates the number of people CHCH deals with and considers their responsibility. For each victimizer, there exists at least one victim and the families of both the victim and the victimizer, who are counselled and supported as a key part of the healing process. Some of the victimizers have been convicted of more than one offence, which also increases the number of people (victims and families) involved. It is estimated that from 400 to 500 people have received support from CHCH, but it is more accurate to say the whole community has benefited.

Due to this unique aspect of the healing process, it was difficult to find another service with which to compare cost value of the service provided. It was, however, appropriate to estimate that at least two counsellor-position-person-years were spent each year providing family and victim services. It was debated whether this service was best aligned with the RCMP (Victim Services) or with family and social services (Child Protection/ Welfare). For the purposes of the study, it was assumed that CHCH was more comparable to the work provided by the provincial government through the Department of Child and Family Services. The work of the CHCH staff was largely counselling, therapeutic and supportive in nature and exceeded that of police-based victim services.

It was estimated that the cost to the government for each position was between $52,000 per year and $60,000 per year, the average being $56,000 per year. If those two counsellors did not exist, and the provincial government was to provide a reasonably similar service for the communities of Hollow Water, it was argued that it would cost Manitoba $56,000 per position, for a total of $112,000 per year. For the ten years of Hollow Water's existence, the estimated total cost to the Manitoba Government would have been approximately $1,120,000.

The final key component to the CHCH program is the work that has been done in community development. This includes presentations, workshops, participating in community recreational events, ceremonies and other activities. CHCH members are active in the community and dedicated to strengthening the circle within the community. Again, finding a manner of comparing the cost of participating in the community restoration is very difficult. Some of this work is done through the volunteer efforts of staff, over and above the work that they do with victims, families and victimizers.

As previously mentioned, CHCH has received approximately $120,000 per year from each of the federal and provincial governments, as well as other contributions, to create an average of $300,000 each fiscal year. Through interviews with CHCH staff, and a review of program documents, it is estimated that 60% of staff time is spent on victimizer treatment, 30% is spent with the victims or families and 10% is spent providing services that are oriented towards community development. Using these percentages, a comparison could be drawn between the cost of providing the CHCH services with the cost of providing services by federal and provincial government departments.

Estimated Cost Comparisons

	CHCH $	Provincial costs $	Federal costs $	Total costs to governments $
Victimizer services (60%) X 10 years	1,800,000	2,631,414	2,461,318	4,863,346
Victim and family services (30%)	900,000	1,120,000		1,120,000
Community development services (10%)	300,000			
Total	**3,000,000**	**3,751,414**	**2,461,318**	**6,212,732**

The above table indicates that the benefit of the CHCH process is very significant. CHCH has been operating for about ten years with government funding, during which time the governments of Canada and Manitoba have contributed a combined total of $240,000 per annum or $2,400,000 over the period under study. There have been some additional—relatively minor—grants by governments, but these did not materially affect the overall totals. The financial benefit to both governments (the total government expenditure less the CHCH expenditure) has been, at minimum, $3,812,732 over the past ten years.

The total saving to Manitoba was estimated to be approximately $2,551,414, or an average saving of about $255,140 per year, when their contribution to Hollow Water is deducted from the overall provincial costs. Likewise, the savings to the federal government would be, at minimum, $1,261,317, or an average saving of $126,132 per year.

To put it another way, for each dollar Manitoba spends on CHCH, it would otherwise have to spend approximately $3 for policing, court, institutional, probation and victims' services. For each dollar the federal government spends on CHCH, it would otherwise have to spend a minimum of $2 for institutional and parole services.

There are additional considerations that need to be noted. For example, the CHCH process works toward wellness and these costs do not include costs that would otherwise be borne by governments to support the broader community development processes that are undertaken by CHCH.

These estimates do not take into consideration the costs associated with victimizers reoffending and victims requiring additional assistance as a result. Research indicates that the recidivism rate for sex offenders is approximately 13%, and for any form of recidivism, the figure rises to approximately 36%. Given that CHCH has had only two clients reoffend during the past ten years (approximately 2% recidivism rate), one can conclude that the total amount saved by the government of Manitoba and the federal government is understated.

Value-Added Benefits to Hollow Water

The research pointed to a number of other developments in Hollow Water that the communities see as benefits arising from the community healing process, and the community development work that has taken place over the past decade. CHCH has established a leadership position in Manitoba and in Canada in terms of alternative justice. They are accountable and responsible for their unmatched low rate of recidivism, and are a model for other communities to follow.

The following are other benefits to Hollow Water, as a direct or indirect result of CHCH:

- PEER, Headstart, and day care programs are in operation.

- Children are happier, feel safer, and are more confident.

- Parents are seen to be more involved with raising children.

- Approximately fifty children from other First Nations are in foster care in Hollow Water.

- Hollow Water is expanding its healing process to address young offender needs.

- No gang-related activities are reported in Hollow Water.

- Youth are remaining in school longer and remaining in the community.

- Number of Grade 12 graduates consistently average between 10–12 per year. Average Grade 12 class size is between 12–15 students.

- Slight decrease in dropout rate.

- Growing number of dropouts are returning to complete high school.

- Fewer Hollow Water residents are out-migrating and more are returning.

- Residents from other First Nations are moving to Hollow Water—a good place to live.

- Housing and full-time employment (major issues) are being addressed strategically.

- Alcohol abuse has almost stopped in the older population and the community is addressing drug abuse among youth.

- Overall health of individuals fares well against the average Manitoban.

- Community awareness has been heightened about proper nutrition.

- Life expectancy has risen from 63 to 70 years.

- No Residential School litigation to date.

Conclusion

The research has shown that community healing processes have the real potential to use traditional values, culture and spiritual practices to improve treatment for offenders, their victims, families and the community. The research also points to the value to governments for the funds invested in community healing processes. The research completed in Hollow Water included a number of observations from noted individuals that exemplify the potential of healing processes that could evolve in Canada over the coming years.

Regarding the Hollow Water experience, the Canadian psychologist and internationally recognized authority on sex offender treatment, William Marshall, concluded that:

> [t]he real advantage of the Hollow Water program is that it is holistic in the sense of integrating treatment of the offender and the victim, their families, and the whole community. . . . [T]he tradition of non-Aboriginal responses to sexual abuse is to separate treatment for offenders and victims, and to largely neglect reintegration with the community. . . . [P]erhaps for a change nonAboriginal people can learn from Aboriginal approaches rather than our traditional strategy of attempting to foist our ways on other people. . . .

If we have learned anything from the errors of our past, it ought to be that Aboriginal peoples should have control over their own destiny and over their own problems. Indeed, we should have the good sense to learn from Aboriginal ways. Certainly their way of dealing with offenders of all types could teach us as much as we are likely to teach them.[13]

Geral Blanchard, a noted psychologist, also underscores the Hollow Water attitude and approach by referring to its method as "revolutionary." He states:

While our psychologically defined culture may find psychopathy in a violent sex criminal and sentence that individual to life in prison, or even to death, Aboriginal healers believe such serious "disorders" are symptomatic of a serious rift in one's relationship to his/her fellow band members.[14]

Dr. Joe Couture, a respected psychologist and Elder, adds:

The story of Hollow Water is a community who is struggling to take back the power to help their people; they are doing this through cooperation, sharing of self and reverence for life. Using their knowledge of sacred teachings, they have found a manner of being that successfully realigns the individual inside the family, which is inside the community, which is a part of the universe/cosmos.[15]

One staunch proponent of CHCH, The Honorable Associate Justice Murray Sinclair, speaks to the contributions made by Community Holistic Circle Healing in ways that marks the millennium of their achievements. In Justice Sinclair's words, Hollow Water plays a very important leadership role in establishing principles and benchmarks that solidify the relationship between justice and Aboriginal communities:

[CHCH] has certainly enhanced the relationship between the community and the Justice system, and in particular, the Provincial court which is the main contact with the justice system, in addition to its relationship with the RCMP and probation services and the Crown attorney's office. The relationship historically has not been good and all the reports point to the deteriorating relationship that was the hallmark of Aboriginal and court contacts in the recent past, and since 1991. But in Hollow Water, it's different. The relationship has grown stronger. The court has recognized the excellent work of the Circle of Healing program and has recognized as well, the commitment of the people of Hollow Water toward resolving crime and addressing it in the way that's not only appropriate to their cultural needs, but is also in keeping with the principles that the justice system itself is now adopting and adapting to.[16]

Endnotes

The material in this paper is primarily taken from the Solicitor General of Canada's "A Cost-Benefit Analysis of Hollow Water's Community Holistic Circle Healing Process" (Aboriginal Peoples Collection APC 20 CA, 2001). The report is available through the Solicitor General and on the Solicitor General of Canada's website at: sgc.gc.ca.

1. S.E. Smith, D.G. William, and N.A. Johnson, *Nurtured by Knowledge: Learning to Do Participatory Action-Research* (New York: Apex Press, 1997).

2. A. Leung, *Understanding Social Costs of Crime Trough Costing Analysis* (draft report for the Department of Justice, 2000).

3. Solicitor General Canada, *Corrections and Conditional Release Statistical Overview*, November 2000.

4. Statistics Canada, *Juristat* 21 (5), 2001.

5. B. Bushie, "Community Holistic Circle Healing—A Community Approach." Building Partnerships for Restorative Practices Conference Report (1999), 60.

6. Solicitor General Canada, "A Cost-Benefit of Hollow Water's Community Healing Process," 25.

7. These steps are in constant review to reflect the evolution of the process, and should thus be considered a draft. For a detailed description of the thirteen steps, see the original report at www.sgc.gc.ca.

8. The figure of $10 per hour was derived through researching other agencies/funding sources that recognize volunteer work as "in kind" fund raising. For example, the Alberta Provincial government (through the Wild Rose Foundation) recognizes volunteer hours as "matched funding," at $10 per volunteer hour.

9. The assault category includes a variety of similar criminal charges such as common assault, family violence, assault with a weapon and aggravated assault.

10. The sexual assault category groups together charges such as incest, gross indecency, sexual touching, sexual interference and sexual exploitation.

11. The loss of life category includes one conviction of second-degree murder, one of manslaughter and one of failure to provide the necessities of life.

12. The other offences category includes three offenders who passed away after their convictions, but before treatment was completed by CHCH.

13. Solicitor General Canada, "The Four Circles of Hollow Water" (Aboriginal Peoples Collection APC 15 CA, 1997), 88. This report is available on the Solicitor General of Canada's website at: www.sgc.gc.ca.

14. G. Blanchard, *Aboriginal Canadian Innovations in the Treatment of Sexual Violence* (1997), 2. Available at: www.sexhelp.com/aboriginal.cfm.

15. As written by Dr. J. Couture, Principal Researcher, in "A Cost-Benefit of Hollow Water's Community Healing Process," 22.

16. Justice Murray Sinclair's full commentary may be found in "A Cost-Benefit of Hollow Water's Community Healing Process," 22–23.

Notes on Contributors

Karen Abbott

Karen Abbott is a member of the Wet'suwet'En Nation from northwestern British Columbia. She was appointed Associate Judge of the Colville Tribal Court in Nespelem, Washington State, on July 15, 2002. She works in the area of criminal, civil and family law and is a lawyer with the Law Society of B.C. Karen attended law school at the University of Toronto and recently finished her Masters of Laws in Alternative Dispute Resolution through York University in Toronto. Her area of focus is indigenous dispute resolution as it applies to indigenous women.

Dan Beavon

Daniel Beavon is the director of the Research and Analysis Directorate, Indian and Northern Affairs Canada. He has worked in policy research for twenty years and has dozens of publications to his credit. He manages an Aboriginal research program on a variety of issues, increasing the amount and quality of strategic information available to the policy process. Much of his work involves complex horizontal and sensitive issues requiring partnerships with other federal departments, academics and First Nations organizations.

Ed Buller

Ed Buller is a Plains Cree from Saskatchewan and is currently the Director of Aboriginal Corrections Policy with the Solicitor General of Canada. He has worked for a number of years with the Hollow Water First Nation and other Aboriginal communities that are exploring traditional community healing approaches as a way to address the needs of victims, victimizers and their families in those communities.

Jesse L. Cale

Jesse L. Cale is a Ph.D. candidate in the School of Criminology at Simon Fraser University. His research areas include anti-state terrorism, restorative justice, Aboriginal victimization and young offenders. Jesse is currently the project manager on several research projects focussing on serious and violent young offenders, Aboriginal mental health, Aboriginal shelter access, housing discrimination, and Aboriginal victimization and service access. In addition to co-authoring several manuscripts, Jesse has presented his research in numerous national and international academic and professional conferences.

Michael J. Chandler

Michael J. Chandler, Ph.D., is a distinguished CIHR/MSFHR professor in Developmental Psychology at the University of British Columbia in Vancouver, Canada. His research centres on the study of young people's social-cognitive development, especially as such age-related changes bear on matters of interest to developmental psychopathologists and health professionals. Most recently his work has come to focus on cross-cultural comparisons of epistemic and identity development as these unfold differently in Canada's Aboriginal and culturally mainstream youth.

Cynthia Chataway

Cynthia Chataway is an associate professor at York University and research director of the project on Understanding the Strengths of Indigenous Communities (USIC), which involves seven communities across Canada that were nominated by Native people as relatively strong. In addition to this type of participatory action research, Dr. Chataway works in the field of conflict resolution, particularly focussing upon protracted social conflicts between societies and groups.

Stewart Clatworthy

Stewart Clatworthy, of Four Directions Project Consultants, has provided socioeconomic research, information systems development and program evaluation services for the past twenty-five years. Since 1980, he has been active in Aboriginal research and has completed numerous studies on Aboriginal demography and migration, housing and employment conditions, population, membership and school enrolment projections. Through this research, he has gained a national reputation as a leading scholar of Canadian Aboriginal socioeconomic and demographic matters.

Dr. Irwin M. Cohen

Dr. Irwin M. Cohen is a professor in the Department of Criminology at the University College of the Fraser Valley. Irwin's research interests include young offenders, juvenile justice, Aboriginal victimization and resource access, state torture and terrorism. He has co-authored several manuscripts on state torture, terrorism, juvenile justice, young offenders, restorative justice and mentally disordered offenders. Irwin is currently the project director and/or co-principal investigator on several research projects. In addition, Irwin is a member of the Institute of Mental Health, Law, and Policy at Simon Fraser University.

Wendy Cornet

Wendy Cornet (née Moss) is a resident of Ottawa and heads a local consulting firm, Cornet Consulting & Mediation Inc. She received her L.LB. in 1983 at the University of British Columbia. Wendy has worked for several national and regional Aboriginal peoples organizations since 1976, and for the government on issues relating to the *Indian Act*, northern and Inuit issues, land rights, self-government, human rights, and constitutional and international indigenous issues.

Dr. Raymond R. Corrado

Dr. Raymond R. Corrado is a full professor in the School of Criminology and the Department of Psychology at Simon Fraser University. Dr. Corrado has co-authored four books and published many articles and book chapters on juvenile justice, young offenders, terrorism, mental health and Aboriginal victimization. Currently, Dr. Corrado is working on a number of research projects involving Aboriginal issues. He has also been working on a NATO sponsored project, with leading experts in many NATO countries, regarding the development of a needs/risk assessment instrument for children, youth and adolescents.

Catherine Curtis

Catherine Curtis is a research affiliate of the Harvard Project on American Indian Economic Development and a policy scholar of the Native Nations Institute at the University of Arizona. She has also worked as a policy analyst for the Canadian government. Her research interests include self-government capacity building and community economic development.

Dominique Fleury

Depuis 2000, Dominique Fleury occupe un poste d'analyste de recherche dans la division des Études sur la sécurité du revenu et le marché du travail de la Direction générale de la recherche appliquée, Développement des ressources humaines Canada. Elle concentre ses activités de recherche empirique sur les thèmes de la pauvreté et de l'exclusion sociale. Plus précisément, elle s'intéresse au cinq groupes ayant été identifiés à haut risque d'exclusion sociale au Canada soit, les parents seuls, les immigrants récents, les Autochtones, les personnes avec limitations au travail et les personnes seules de 45 à 64 ans. Dominique est diplômée de deuxième cycle en sciences économiques de l'Université du Québec à Montréal depuis 2001.

Éric Guimond

Éric Guimond est démographe avec expérience en recherche et en développement, présentement à l'emploi du ministère des Affaires Indiennes et du Nord Canada, direction de la recherche et de l'analyse. Éric détient une formation multidisciplinaire en démographie, en santé communautaire, en éducation physique et en études autochtones. Il a œuvré en recherche et en enseignement dans le milieu universitaire. Éric est en voie de compléter ses études doctorales à l'Université de Montréal sur la mobilité ethnique des groupes autochtones du Canada.

Jeremy Hull

Jeremy Hull is a consultant in Winnipeg with twenty-five years of experience in research on educational, social and Aboriginal issues. He has worked for a variety of clients including federal and provincial governments, the Royal Commission on Aboriginal Peoples, individual First Nations, Aboriginal associations, private companies and others. Recently he has completed several studies for Indian and Northern Affairs Canada on Aboriginal post-secondary education, Aboriginal single mothers and the Inuit.

Dr. John H. Hylton

John Hylton is president and CEO of the Council for Health Research in Canada, an Ottawa-based national non-profit organization that advances health research in Canada on behalf of leading national health charities and non-profit health research institutes. He has previously served as a health administrator, university educator, senior public servant and consultant specializing in health, justice, Aboriginal and social policy issues. His previous publications include over a hundred books, articles and research reports on a wide variety of public policy issues. Hylton is a graduate of St. Francis Xavier University, Carleton University and the University of California at Berkeley.

Richard Jock

Richard Jock is a member of the Mohawks of Akwesasne. He has held numerous positions in the health field, working for both First Nations organizations and the federal government. Currently executive director of the

National Aboriginal Health Organization (NAHO), Mr. Jock's previous positions include: Director General for Program Policy, Transfer Secretariat and Planning within Health Canada, Director of Health and Social Services for Mohawk Council of Akwesasne; Ontario Regional Director for Health Canada; Director of the First Nations Health Commission at the AFN; and Director of the National Native Alcohol and Drug Abuse Program.

Miriam Jorgensen

Miriam Jorgensen is the research director of the Harvard Project on American Indian Economic Development and associate director of Research at the Native Nations Institute at the University of Arizona. During the past dozen years, she has worked primarily on issues of governance and economic development in Indian Country in the U.S. and Canada, and written about a variety of related public policy topics (including welfare reform, Native constitutional reform, and tribal policing and justice systems).

Ali Kouaouci

Dr. Ali Kouaouci est chargé de cours et chercheur au département de démographie de l'Université de Montréal depuis 1997. Auparavant, il dirigea l'Institut des Sciences Sociales de Blida en Algérie, puis la Division Recherches et Évaluation de l' International Planned Parenthood Federation (IPPF), région du Monde Arabe.

Christopher E. Lalonde

Christopher E. Lalonde is an assistant professor in Life Span Development in the Department of Psychology at the University of Victoria in Victoria, Canada. His research interests include social-cognitive development in childhood and adolescence, and the influence of culture on identity development and determinants of health within Aboriginal youth.

Laurel Lemchuk-Favel

Laurel Lemchuk-Favel is a health policy consultant specializing in Aboriginal issues. She began her career in microbiology research—spending fifteen years at the University of British Columbia, University of Regina and University of Ottawa—and then moving on to the field of Aboriginal health. The consulting group, FAV COM, which she and her partner established in 1993, provides Aboriginal policy and communications services primarily to national Aboriginal organizations and the federal government.

Allison B. Lendor

Allison B. Lendor was raised in Toronto and currently resides in Ottawa. She is a sole practitioner practicing primarily in the area of family law. She received her B.A. in 1989 (York) and her L.LB in 1997 (Ottawa). Allison was called to the Ontario bar in 1999.

Janet Longclaws

Ms. Longclaws is the co-ordinator for the Manitoba First Nations and Inuit Regional Health Survey at the Centre for Aboriginal Health Research. She has served as an elected trustee and tribal councillor at Long Plain First Nation, and is presently the chair for the Long Plain First Nation's Dakota Ojibway Child & Family Services Committee. Ms. Longclaws has a background in counselling and has extensive experience in working with sexual abuse, incest and residential school survivors, and working with offenders.

Javier Mignone

Javier Mignone, Ph.D., is a research associate with the Centre for Aboriginal Health Research (CAHR) at the University of Manitoba and assistant professor at the same university. His research interests centre on the area of social determinants of health. Among his involvement in various projects within the CAHR, he has led a study on the conceptual development of social capital in First Nations communities and the validation of an instrument for its measurement.

John-Patrick Moore

John-Patrick Moore is a research officer at the Correctional Service of Canada's Research Branch. He is currently working in the area of Aboriginal offenders and community corrections. Mr. Moore has conducted a number of studies profiling Aboriginal offenders, examining the institutional and community needs of various Aboriginal offender populations, and is currently involved in an evaluation of an Inuit sex offender treatment program. Mr. Moore holds a master's degree in criminology and a bachelor's degree in psychology from the University of Ottawa. He also has prior experience as a private and public sector contractor in the Ottawa-Gatineau region.

Dr. Cameron Mustard

Dr. Mustard is president and scientific director of the Institute for Work and Health. He is also a professor in the Department of Public Health Sciences, Faculty of Medicine, University of Toronto, associate director of the

Population Health Program of the Canadian Institute for Advanced Research and an institute advisory board member of the CIHR's Institute of Aboriginal Peoples' Health. A specialist in the area of population health, Dr. Mustard is the recipient of numerous competitive awards and grants.

Dr. John O'Neil

Dr. O'Neil is a professor and director of the Centre for Aboriginal Health Research and head of the Department of Community Health Sciences in the Faculty of Medicine at the University of Manitoba. He also chairs the Advisory Board of the Institute for Aboriginal People's Health at the Canadian Institutes for Health Research and is a CIHR Senior Investigator. Dr. O'Neil has published over seventy-five papers and several monographs on a variety of Aboriginal health issues.

Norbert Robitaille

Doctorat en démographie, Université de Paris 1976 Professeur au Département de démographie de l'Université de Montréal depuis 1973. M. Robitaille s'intéresse aux populations autochtones du Canada depuis plus de 20 ans. Il a publié sur les Inuit du Nunavik en 1988: *"La fécondité des Inuit du Nouveau-Québec depuis 1931: passage d'une fécondité naturelle à une fécondité contrôlée"* avec Robert Choinière dans la revue *Population,* et en 1994 en collaboration avec Eric Guimond *"La situation démographique des groupes autochtones du Québec". Recherches sociographiques* 35, 3, 433-454. Il travaille actuellement l'analyse de la reproduction des groupes autochtones du Canada à partir des données du Recensement du Canada.

Shelley Trevethan

Shelley Trevethan is director of the Community and Aboriginal Research Division of Correctional Service of Canada. She has a B.A. (Honours) in criminology from Carleton University, a Masters of Arts in developmental psychology from the University of British Columbia, and pursued doctoral studies in psychology at the University of British Columbia. Shelley's research interests include Aboriginal offenders, women offenders, restorative justice, halfway houses, victimization, family violence, youth justice and recidivism. She has authored articles and made presentations on a variety of research projects in these areas.

Jerry White

Professor Jerry White, Ph.D., is chair of the Sociology Department and a Pleva Award recipient for excellence at the University of Western Ontario. He is currently co-director of the First Nations Cohesion Project at Western, a member of the Centre for Health and Well-being at Western, and the former vice chair of the Health Professions Regulatory Council of Ontario. He is a leading member of several research teams across Canada and, through this work, has published nine books and dozens of scholarly articles on a range of topics. His latest book, *Aboriginal Conditions: The Research Foundations of Public Policy*, co-authored with Paul Maxim and Dan Beavon, was released in September 2003 by the University of British Columbia Press.

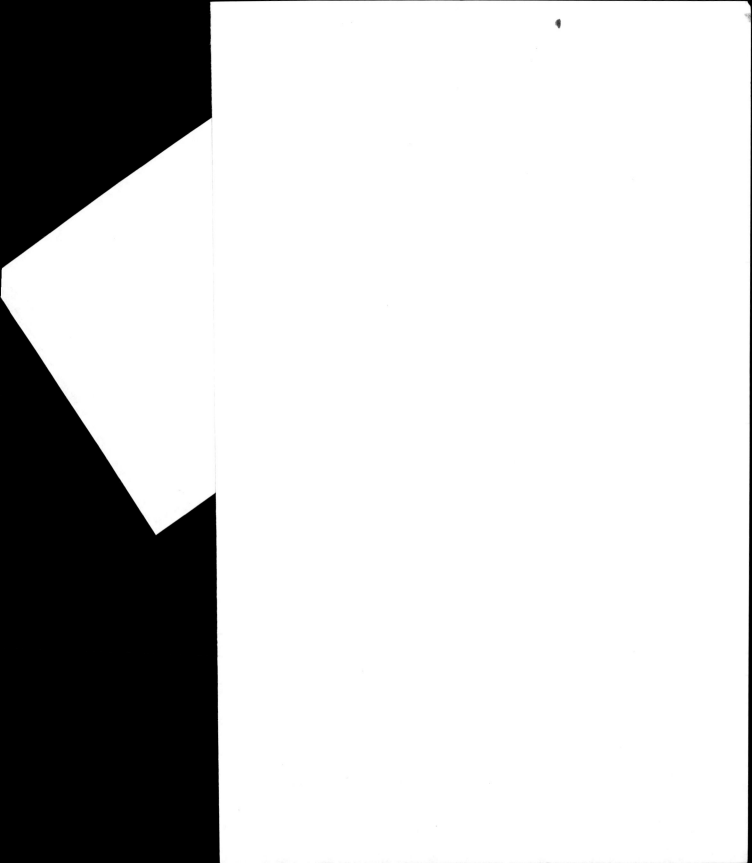

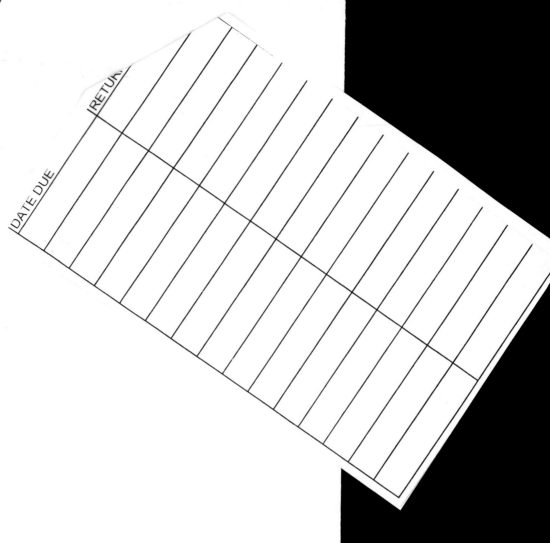

DATE DUE | RETUR...

MARQUIS

Marquis Book Printing Inc.

Québec, Canada
2008